The Parental Alienation Syndrome and the Differentiation Between Fabricated and Genuine Child Sex Abuse

The Parental Alienation Syndrome and the Differentiation Between Fabricated and Genuine Child Sex Abuse

RICHARD A. GARDNER, M.D.

Clinical Professor of Child Psychiatry
Columbia University
College of Physicians and Surgeons

Creative Therapeutics
155 County Road, Cresskill, New Jersey 07626-0317

PRINTED IN THE UNITED STATES OF AMERICA

10 9 8 7 6 5 4 3 2 1

Library of Congress Cataloging-in-Publication Data

Gardner, Richard A.
  The parental alienation syndrome and the differentiation between
fabricated and genuine child sex abuse.

  Bibliography: p.
  Includes indexes.
  1. Child molesting. 2. Truthfulness and falsehood.
3. Parent and child. 4. Custody of children. I. Title.
[DNLM: 1. Child Abuse, Sexual—legislation. 2. Child
Abuse, Sexual—psychology. 3. Divorce. 4. Lie
Detection. 5. Parent–Child Relations. WA 320 G228p]
RC560.C46G37   1987   616.85'83   87-27455
ISBN 0-933812-17-5

I dedicate this book to

The children of divorce from whose ordeals and grief
I have learned much that is contained herein.
My hope is that this book will play some role in the
prevention and alleviation of such sorrows in others.

Other Books by Richard A. Gardner

The Boys and Girls Book About Divorce
Therapeutic Communication with Children: The Mutual Storytelling
    Technique
Dr. Gardner's Stories About the Real World, Volume I
Dr. Gardner's Stories About the Real World, Volume II
Dr. Gardner's Fairy Tales for Today's Children
Understanding Children: A Parents Guide to Child Rearing
MBD: The Family Book About Minimal Brain Dysfunction
Psychotherapeutic Approaches to the Resistant Child
Psychotherapy with Children of Divorce
Dr. Gardner's Modern Fairy Tales
The Parents Book About Divorce
The Boys and Girls Book About One-Parent Families
The Objective Diagnosis of Minimal Brain Dysfunction
Dorothy and the Lizard of Oz
Dr. Gardner's Fables for Our Times
The Boys and Girls Book About Stepfamilies
Family Evaluation in Child Custody Litigation
Separation Anxiety Disorder: Psychodynamics and Psychotherapy
Child Custody Litigation: A Guide for Parents and Mental Health
    Professionals
The Psychotherapeutic Techniques of Richard A. Gardner
Hyperactivity, The So-Called Attention-Deficit Disorder, and The
    Group of MBD Syndromes
Psychotherapy with Adolescents
Psychotherapy of Psychogenic Learning Diabilities

Contents

Acknowledgments

I am deeply indebted to my son, Andrew K. Gardner, President of MEDCAL, an educational computer software company, for his invaluable and creative contributions to the *Sex Abuse Legitimacy Scale (SAL Scale)*. I am indebted as well to my daughter, Nancy T. Gardner, Esq., for her valuable comments on the chapter on the history of the adversary system. Accordingly, my children have not only served to enhance the value of this book, but have provided their father with a sense of pride that is enormous. Additional valuable suggestions on the *SAL Scale* were provided by Charles A. Opsahl, Ph.D., Assistant Professor of Psychology, Department of Psychiatry, Yale University Medical School, and Roni Tower, Ph.D. I am grateful to Rev. Michael Slusser,

Associate Professor of Theology, Duquesne University, for his review of the material relating to the Catholic Church.

Once again, I want to express my deep gratitude for the contributions of my secretaries Linda Gould, Carol Gibbon, and Donna La Tourette. They have dedicated themselves fully to the typing of the manuscript in its various renditions. I am indeed fortunate to have such committed assistants. I am grateful to Muriel Jorgensen for her astute editing of the manuscript. I am also grateful to Mr. Robert Tebbenhoff of Lind Graphics in Woodcliff Lake, New Jersey, for his valuable contributions to the production of this book, from manuscript to final volume.

My greatest debt, however, is to the children of divorce who have taught me much over many years about the kinds of grief they can suffer. From their parents, as well, I have learned many things that are contained herein. Attorneys have also taught me a great deal about the adversary system, both its weaknesses and strengths (unfortunately, more of the former than the latter). My hope is that what I have learned from these sources will be put to good use in this book and will contribute to the prevention and alleviation of the sorrows of divorce ordeals in others.

INTRODUCTION

During the last 10 to 15 years, we have witnessed a burgeoning of child custody disputes unparalleled in history. Its increase has primarily been the result of two recent developments in the realm of child custody litigation, namely, the replacement of the tender years presumption with the best interests of the child presumption and the increasing popularity of the joint custodial concept. In association with this burgeoning of litigation, we have witnessed a dramatic increase in the frequency of a disorder rarely seen previously, a disorder that I refer to as the *parental alienation syndrome*. In this disorder we see not only programming ("brainwashing") of the child by one parent to denigrate the other parent, but self-created contributions by the child in support of the preferred parent's campaign of denigration against the nonpreferred parent. In the context of this disorder we have more recently been seeing a rash of fabricated sex-abuse allegations, which may serve as an effective weapon in these disputes. Also during the last few years we have become increasingly appreciative of how ubiquitous is bona fide sexual abuse of children. It is difficult to determine whether there has been an actual increase in child sex abuse or whether it is more frequently brought to the attention of authorities involved in dealing with such abuse.

These new developments have created significant problems for those who work with sexually abused children, especially with regard to the issue of differentiating between children who have been genuinely abused (a common phenomenon) and those who fabricate abuse (not uncommon in the context of child custody litigation). Obviously making this differentiation is extremely important. Not to do so may result in many innocent parties being prosecuted and many perpetrators going free. During the last few years many lives have literally been ruined because of false accusations of sex abuse. And the recent recognition that fabrication is becoming increasingly common has made prosecution of bona fide offenders extremely difficult. Pervading all these developments, and infusing itself significantly into them, has been the utilization of the adversary system as a method of settling child custody disputes as well as prosecuting alleged sex-abuse perpetrators.

In this volume I first trace the historical development of the adversary system, the method most commonly used today to investigate and deal with such disputes. I then trace the historical development in western society of parental preference for child custody (mother versus father) following marital dissolution. Appreciation of these historical sequences help put the reader in a better position to understand and put in proper perspective the problems with which we are dealing today.

I then describe in detail the etiology, manifestations, pathogenesis, and psychodynamics of the parental alienation syndrome, especially as they relate to adversary proceedings and child custody litigation. Next, I describe the mechanisms by which fabricated allegations of sex abuse emerge from the parental alienation syndrome. Particular emphasis is then given to a series of criteria examiners can utilize to differentiate between fabricated and bona fide sex-abuse allegations. Emphasis is placed on the importance of the examiner's having full access to all concerned parties: the allegedly abused child, the accuser, and the alleged perpetrator. Specific details are provided regarding interviewing techniques—so important to master if one is to assess properly these children and make the important differentiation between bona fide and fabricated sex-abuse allegations.

Next, I describe the *Sex Abuse Legitimacy Scale* (SAL Scale), an instrument I have designed to objectify the aforementioned differentiating criteria. It is my hope that other examiners will find it as useful as I have. However, the cutoff points delineating the ranges for the two classes of sex abuse must presently be viewed as tentative, considering the newness of the scale. My hope is that with further experience—by myself and other examiners—the cutoff points will become more valid (either at their present levels or different levels, if warranted).

Over the years I have read numerous *in camera* transcripts of judges interviewing patients with parental alienation syndrome and have recognized that many judges have been "taken in" by these children and have accepted at face value their ostensible hatred of the denigrated parent. Unfortunately, such receptivity has resulted in what I consider to have been many injudicious rulings regarding child custody. In addition, I have also read with dismay judicial naiveté when interviewing children who are alleging sex abuse. Accordingly, I have devoted a section of this book to providing judges with guidelines and specific questions that should enable them to interview more astutely children in both of these categories, whether it be in chambers or on the stand. Obviously, the more skilled the judge is when interviewing these children, the more judicious will be his or her conclusions, and the greater the likelihood that a proper decision will be made regarding custodial placement and/or whether the child has been sexually abused.

In the final chapter I present guidelines for changes that could contribute significantly to the prevention of the parental alienation syndrome and the fabricated sex abuse allegations that often emerge from it. I then discuss what I consider to be basic weaknesses in the adversary system, especially when it is utilized to resolve child custody disputes. Next, I provide recommendations for mental health professionals and emphasize the importance of their serving as impartial examiners, rather than as advocates, in child custody disputes. I also emphasize the use of mediation as a first step toward resolving such disputes. Specific guidelines are given for both mental health professionals and legal professionals who are involved in dealing with parental alienation syndrome children and their parents. The implementation of these guidelines could reduce significantly the incidence of the parental alienation syndrome and the fabricated allegations of sex abuse that commonly derive from it. Accordingly, the final chapter (and, in a sense, this book) is basically a proposed contribution to the field of preventive psychiatry.

ONE

A BRIEF REVIEW OF THE HISTORICAL DEVELOPMENT OF THE ADVERSARY SYSTEM

INTRODUCTION

Throughout this chapter, when I use the term *adversary system,* I am referring to a legal procedure that prevails in the United States, England, and its former colonies. It is a system based on the principle that the best way of learning the "truth," when two parties have diametrically opposed positions, is for each to present his or her case before an impartial decision maker(s) (a judge and/or a jury). Each side is permitted to withhold (within certain guidelines and procedures) facts that might compromise its position and to present those that support it. The theory is that these opposing presentations provide the impartial evaluators the best opportunity for ascertaining the truth. In the adversary system, this method of data (evidence) collection is used primarily as a method of dispute resolution. The fact finder

1

(whether it be a judge or jury) serves primarily in a neutral position. Although it originated in criminal proceedings, where the dispute is between a prosecutor and an accused person, it is also used in civil proceedings as well, where the dispute is between a plaintiff and a defendant.

When I use the term *European* legal system I am not including the English legal procedure (from which the American is more directly derived) but the European *continental* procedure, which is generally referred to as the *inquisitorial* system. In this system the judge is less neutral and more active in the cross-examination process than the judge in the adversary system. It has been used more extensively for criminal than for civil proceedings. Later in this chapter I will discuss these two systems in greater detail. The adversary system is also the predominant one in countries that were formerly English colonies. Furthermore, countries on the European continent have utilized varying degrees of adversarial procedures within the inquisitorial structure. For example, Spain, Italy, and France utilize systems that are direct derivatives of the inquisitorial procedures from the 15th century, whereas in Germany, the inquisitorial system is fused with a number of traditional adversarial procedures. And the Soviet system, although modeled after the inquisitorial system, has been modified by Marxist principles and restrictions on certain freedoms taken for granted in the West.

It is not my purpose to present here a detailed history of the adversary system. Not only do I not consider myself knowledgeable enough to do this, but it goes beyond the purposes of this book. Rather, I will outline the system's development, with particular emphasis on issues that are relevant to modern-day practices in divorce law and especially custody litigation. My main purpose here will be to demonstrate that we are still using techniques that have their origins in the ritualistic practices of primitive tribes, ancient societies, and the "Dark Ages" (literally) and that these techniques are used in only a small fraction of present societies, namely England (and its former colonies) and the United States. As I trace the historical development of the adversary system, I will point out how some of these early practices have served as the basis for many of our present-day procedures in divorce and custody litigation.

In the preparation of this material, I first sought references from attorneys, friends, and colleagues—many of whom I hold in high regard. I was surprised how little they knew about the historical development of the system, and I was even more surprised to learn that it is rarely taught as a formal course (or even part of a course) in the majority of law schools in the United States. Law students are presented with the adversary system as *the* system for resolving various kinds of disputes. Most are not even told about alternative methods of dispute resolution traditionally used in many other societies. Many, at the time of graduation, automatically assume that the adversary system is the best and the most efficient. And many maintain this unquestioned allegiance to the system until the end of their professional careers.

The material on the history of the adversary system presented in this chapter was obtained primarily from the comprehensive articles by M. Neef and S. Nagel (1974), S. Landsman (1983), and G.J. Alexander (1984). In addition, some material was obtained from the sections on the legal profession and the law of evidence in the *Encyclopedia Britannica* (1982). These thorough and extensive articles provide numerous references to the primary source material from which this chapter has been derived. I would strongly recommend these articles to those readers who wish more detailed information on this subject. In addition to these sources, I present information that has become part of my general knowledge and experience, the sources of which are no longer known to me. The reader will soon note that my comments on the adversary system are quite critical. This is the result, I believe, of the fact that my experiences with it have primarily been in its utilization in divorce/custody proceedings. I recognize that its utilization in other kinds of cases may be less psychologically damaging to the clients. Accordingly, the reader does well to keep this in mind when reading this book and to recognize that the reforms I will recommend at the end relate primarily to its utilization in custody/visitation disputes. I suspect, however, that its utilization in other areas may also be psychologically traumatic and that the criticisms I present here may very well be applicable to these areas of utilization as well.

PRIMITIVE SOCIETIES

Our knowledge of the kinds of dispute-settling mechanisms utilized by primitive societies is largely speculative. There are, however, some general principles subscribed to by those who have investigated this area. One cannot put a particular date on this phase. What is described here is a *developmental theory* that ascribes a sequence of procedures utilized for dispute resolution. The sequence began at different times in different places, and there are some societies today still operating in accordance with these primitive principles.

In the earliest primitive societies, wherein the whole society lived in a small cluster in which everyone knew one another, the general method for dispute resolution was through compromise. The purpose was to reach a solution that would enable the individuals to live as harmoniously as possible with one another after the settlement of the dispute. Such groups avoided any system that might result in residual animosity between the disputants. This was especially important because the extended families of the disputants might harbor residual animosity toward one another, which could be even more detrimental to the survival of the small group. Accordingly, compromise techniques were utilized rather than the winner-take-all principle that the modern adversary system employs. Although many judges attempt to get the disputants to compromise, if they are unsuccessful and the dispute goes to trial there is often a winner-take-all victory for the party that prevails. Present-day compromise analogies are labor management disputes and disputes between businessmen and customers, wherein both parties recognize that, following the dispute, they may still have to have a relationship with one another. It is only when communities become larger and individuals are able to remove themselves entirely from one another that a more adversarial and permanently divisive arrangement comes to prevail.

Another method of primitive dispute resolution that could insure cohesiveness was one in which leaders imposed punishments in accordance with speculations regarding what ghosts, dead ancestors, and other spirits considered to be justifiable punishments. In this way, the punishers were not viewed as being personally responsible for implementing the punishment, but were merely considered to be the vehicles through which these higher powers operated. As a result, the system still allowed for a certain amount of cooperation between the accusers and the accused, between the punishers and the punished. The system was also a reflection of the ignorance of tribal leaders. By ascribing wisdom to spirits and other unseen powers, tribal leaders compensated for their own lack of understanding of the complex and even unknown issues that were involved.

As societies became larger and more complex, the likelihood increased that the disputants would not subsequently have to live with one another. Under these circumstances, other methods of dispute resolution evolved. However, the aforementioned method by which supernatural powers were brought into play served in later phases as well. Invoking these unseen powers served to protect the accusers and the punishers from the acrimony of the guilty party and thereby allowed for ongoing cooperation between the parties.

I believe it was unfortunate that more complex and recent societies developed systems that did not take into proper consideration the factor of ongoing cooperation between the disputants. Had they done so, we might not have gone so far afield regarding our methods of dispute resolution; we might have maintained the systems of compromise first utilized by the earliest societies. In a sense, these most primitive methods were the most advanced in that they were the methods most likely to insure resolutions that promised ongoing conciliation.

In many Asian societies the mediation/conciliation notion is very much present to this day. In Japan, for example, people who are unable to resolve their disputes themselves generally take them to mutually respected elders who attempt to resolve the dispute privately. People who are unable to resolve their disputes by themselves or with the help of elders are generally viewed as socially atypical and may be stigmatized. The fear of such social stigma deters them from carrying the dispute further. When, however, a situation does warrant intervention by third parties, they may resort to neighborhood dispute-resolution centers. It is rare that individuals must go further and use attorneys to resolve their disputes. This is one of the reasons why there is now only one attorney for every 10,000 people in Japan; in the United States there is one attorney for every 850 people.

In recent years we have witnessed evidence of increasing appreciation of conciliatory procedures in the United States. Alternative methods of dispute resolution are now being taught in some law schools, and divorce mediation has also gained some limited popularity recently (O.J. Coogler, 1978; J. Folberg and A. Taylor, 1984).

GREEK SOCIETY

The ancient Greeks, as the first step toward the resolution of a dispute, submitted the conflict to an arbitrator. This was the earliest form of dispute resolution used by the ancient Greeks. The arbitrator was often paid a small fee and his goal was to try to reconcile the parties. One could not go to court before one had gone through the arbitration process. As is the case with the inquisitorial system, all the information from both the disputants and the witnesses was submitted to the court in written form before the trial began. This information was sealed in a special box and opened when the court was ready to hear the case. These documents were read by a panel who decided the case on the basis of this written material. It is of note here that at that point in Greek history the disputants did not confront one another. Residua of this absence of confrontation is to be found in the inquisitorial system used in the Middle Ages. And it may be that some residua of this is present in our present-day adversary system, where there is still some restriction on the disputants confronting one another, although they are certainly in the courtroom together.

As the Greek society became more complex, the disputants were permitted to be represented by orators or rhetors (people who used rhetoric). It was in this setting that there developed the practice of dramatic presentations, a practice that probably has its counterpart in modern-day courtroom lawyers, especially those who pride themselves on their oratorical skills. When used in moderation, this residuum of the Greek system is probably of benefit to the client; however, when the dramatizations reach the point of bombast, then the courtroom becomes the stage for melodrama, hyperbole, and even a circus-like atmosphere.

It is important for the reader to note that I am referring here only to free men of ancient Greece, not to slaves. Slaves could not hope to get redress in court or bring suit against another person unless they could find a citizen to represent them. On occasion, however, a slave could be a witness. The assumption was generally made that slaves lied. Accordingly, their testimony was often accompanied by torture in order to extract the "truth." This practice discouraged masters from allowing their slaves to testify because they might be worthless as workers following their testimony. (It would seem to me that if it were indeed true that all slaves automatically lied, then a more judicious and humane way of dealing with their testimony would be to assume that the *opposite* of what they said was true. This would save both the tortured and the torturer much time and trouble.) Sometimes an ordeal (see below) was utilized when the judges were unable to arrive at a decision.

Juries were used in the Greek courts, but they voted secretly (as they do today in the United States). Following the jury's decision, the accused and the accuser together were permitted to suggest to the court a reasonable punishment, suggestions which were given serious consideration. This practice is often seen in courtrooms today when both sides are given the opportunity for input to the judge before sentencing.

Among the ancient Greeks, trial by ordeal was commonly used as a method of ascertaining whether or not a party was guilty or innocent of a crime. It generally involved subjecting the accused to a wide variety of pains and tortures. Guilt or innocence was established on the basis of the accused's reactions to the ordeal. Ordeal by water was especially popular among the ancient Greeks. The system operated in a world that was viewed as anthropomorphized, i.e., inanimate objects were considered to contain spirits, have wills, thoughts, and feelings. The Greeks assumed that if the accused were to float in the river, then it indicated that the river found the accused objectionable and did not wish to embrace him or her. If the accused sank, this indicated that the individual was innocent and good and that the river thereby wanted to embrace him or her. Attempts were usually made to pull to safety the sinking innocent. In contrast, the person who floated would be punished for the crime, often by being put to death.

Ordeal by fire was also common among the ancient Greeks. The accused might prove innocent by walking on fire, swallowing fire, or passing through flames unharmed. The use of boiling liquids and hot irons were also used to determine guilt or innocence, based on the extent of the injuries sustained after exposure. Other ordeals involved the use of snakes, swords, and poisons. Girls whose virginity was questioned were compelled to descend into a cavern in which a poisonous snake had been placed. If they were bitten by the snake, it indicated that they were no longer virgins. Among the ancient Greeks, male nonvirgins were not considered to have committed a crime. This attitude toward male nonvirginity persists in many societies to this day, and there are many societies today that basically do not deal with *female* nonvirgins any differently than the ancient Greeks did.

ROMAN SOCIETY

In *early* Rome a priest was generally considered crucial when dealing with legal matters. Priests were considered to be the ones most knowledgeable about how to deal with the problems of finding out which of the disputants was telling the truth. The priests kept their laws and techniques in personal secret books. Gradually, however, lawyers did evolve, replacing the priests. They advised their clients and pleaded for them in court. The parties rarely engaged in direct confrontation with each other in the courtroom. As was true in Greek society, slaves as a matter of course were tortured on the witness stand. Juries were used, but only in cases involving senators and equites (horse-mounted warriors with status half-way between senators and common men). Either the defendant or the plaintiff could object to the selection of certain jurors at his trial (a practice still in operation today).

Like the Greeks, the Roman lawyers enjoyed their orations. Sometimes a client would have many lawyers representing him, each of whom would provide elaborate speeches to the magistrate and jury. Histrionics were accepted and even considered desirable. It was not uncommon to display the wounds of a client and bring injured children before the court. Lawyers were in oversupply and they often competed with one another to obtain clients. They were allowed to hawk their wares in the streets and often hired "clappers" to applaud their orations in the courtroom. They hoped thereby to enhance their reputations and obtain more clients. Although the judge and jury might decide that a defendant was guilty, it was the accuser's responsibility to impose the punishment, and sometimes he did not have the means to do so.

In the early fourth century A.D. a new development took place in Roman law. Whereas previously trials were open and public, they now became secret. This was rationalized by the argument that members of the judicial hierarchy were beyond criticism, were dedicated to work honestly and efficiently, and could be trusted to make judicious decisions. They also rationalized secret judicial decisions as necessary for the stability of the empire. Accordingly, prior to the downfall of the empire, the Romans abandoned a very complex and sophisticated courtroom system for a somewhat totalitarian one. It regressed thereby from a more democratic and egalitarian legal system to one that infringed much more on the freedom of individuals. However, certain aspects of the Roman system persisted and can be found in the legal profession today, e.g., lawyers representing their clients, juries and jury selection, and lawyers advertising.

TRIAL BY ORDEAL

Trial by ordeal was one of the three commonly used methods of trial used in the Middle Ages. Reference was made to it in my discussion of ancient Greek society. However, in the Middle Ages it became much more commonly used. Trial by ordeal is based on the belief that God will intervene and by a miraculous sign indicate whether the litigant undergoing the ordeal was in the right. It has appeared in many countries and at different times. Ordeal by fire is an ancient tradition. The accused might establish innocence by walking on fire, swallowing fire, or passing through the flames unharmed. In many societies the ordeal was only used after the judge or jury found itself unable to arrive at a decision. Trial by ordeal was especially popular during the Middle Ages in Europe and England. A priest usually administered an oath before the ordeal, and quite frequently the ordeal was conducted on Church grounds. Of the three forms of trial used in the Middle Ages (trial by battle and trial by wager being the others), trial by ordeal was the most likely to be under church auspices. In England common forms of ordeal required the litigant to carry a red-hot iron bar a certain distance or place an arm in boiling water for a prescribed period. If the litigant's burns did not fester after a prescribed period (usually three days), he or she was considered to be in the right. A typical example of trial by ordeal was to place the litigant's arm in a seething cauldron. Afterward, it was carefully enveloped in cloth, sealed with the signet of the judge, and three days later was unwrapped. The guilt or innocence of the party was ascertained by the condition of the hand or arm. The theory was that the guilty individual's arm would be infected or seriously scarred and the innocent person would remain unhurt.

Immersion in deep water was another common form of ordeal. The person was considered to be in the right if he or she sank rather than floated. Ordeal was used for women who were charged with witchcraft. In the Middle Ages (and subsequently) women charged with witchcraft were often assumed to have had sexual intercourse with Satan. In the course of such sexual relations, part of his spirit was considered to have entered into and invested them. Their human attributes were considered to be altered by his spirit, which, because it is lighter than air, lightens the body. The woman charged with witchcraft was dropped into a river with her hands and feet tied. If she sank she was considered innocent, because the presumption was made that the devil had not invested her. If she floated she was considered guilty and punished, sometimes by being burned to death. The Salem Witchcraft water-dunking ordeal is an example of the utilization of trial by ordeal in America.

Trial by ordeal is basically a statement of mankind's feelings of impotency and appreciation of ignorance regarding dispute resolution and the determination of whether or not an alleged perpetrator did indeed commit a crime. In trial by ordeal the assistance of supernatural powers is brought into play. There is a certain grandiosity in trial by ordeal in that it is based on the assumption that the deity, the Great Judge, is paying attention to the particular ordeal and manipulating the events in the service of helping the good or the innocent survive the ordeal.

Trial by ordeal was generally an earlier phenomenon

than trial by battle (to be discussed below). In trial by ordeal the individual is helpless in playing a role in his or her fate, and it is left entirely in the hands of higher powers. In trial by combat, which generally came later, some power was placed in the hands of the combatants in the decision regarding guilt and/or innocence.

Trial by ordeal in English society was traditionally for the lower classes, whereas trial by combat was for the upper classes. This was especially the case because trial by combat required the ownership or utilization of horses and often involved disputes concerning land ownership (which poor people, obviously, did not have). Trial by ordeal was declared unacceptable in England and on the Continent in 1215 by the Fourth Lateran Council (to be discussed below). Once the Church removed priest participation, the practice quickly fell into disuse. However, residua of the method, I believe, exists today in adversary proceedings. Many attorneys, by design, will subject witnesses to ordeals of exhausting and painstaking interrogation. The individual is brought to the point where he or she may not even realize what is being said. Such tactics could also be viewed as a method of extracting a confession by subjecting the individual to such an ordeal. Here, verbal whips are used as the method of torture.

TRIAL BY COMBAT (TRIAL BY BATTLE)

Trial by combat (or trial by battle) was a common form of trial utilized in the Middle Ages, especially on the Continent. In trial by battle the disputants or their representatives (sometimes referred to as *champions*) engaged in physical combat until one side yielded or was subdued. The party who prevailed was considered to be telling the truth. The defeated party could admit defeat by speaking the word "Craven" (*Middle English, cravant:* overthrown, coward) or by stopping the battle when it was obvious that that party was defeated. Or the battle continued until one party no longer had the capacity to go on or was slain. In certain serious criminal matters, it was understood from the outset that the fight would continue until one party was indeed killed. It was overseen by judicial officers, and the combat began only after each of the combatants had taken a solemn oath that his cause was just. Each party would invoke the judgment of God and declare that he did not use sorcery or enchantment. A fundamental assumption of trial by combat is the notion that being right is expected to be productive of the just result. This is related to the belief that justice will prevail and that God will see to it that good will win out over evil.

In this form of trial, as in trial by wager (to be discussed below) and trial by ordeal, divine intervention was considered to be the important determinant as to who would prevail. There was no presentation of evidence. The individual was often permitted to be represented by a substitute, called a champion. Accordingly, trial by combat has also been called trial by champion. Because women and children were considered unable to fend for themselves, they were almost routinely provided with champions. Professional champions were available to fight for anyone who paid them. The battle would begin when the challenger threw down a glove and the person who accepted the challenge picked it up. Sometimes the weapons used were not designed to be lethal; rather they were made of wood, bone, or a horn. In criminal cases, however, the loser was hanged or mutilated. In civil cases the loser would cry "Craven," which meant that he had perjured himself, was a liar, and was guilty. He then paid a fine and came to be known as a liar. On occasion the two combatants would continue to fight until nightfall ("before the stars appeared"), at which point the battle would be discontinued and the person who appeared to be prevailing was considered the innocent party. This practice protected people from being killed. Sometimes champions were individuals who had proven themselves successful in previous trials by battle. Trial by battle clearly favored the rich, who either had better martial skills or could afford to hire those with such skills. Trial by battle was common throughout most of northern Europe in the early Middle Ages and was introduced into England from France after the Norman Conquest in 1066. It was never a very popular or influential form of adjudication in England.

In one form of trial by combat the accuser might have been a public prosecutor. He would then battle the accused, the defendant. Accordingly, the accuser was not only a prosecutor, but in many cases also served as the executioner. This was especially the case when champions were not used. Although champions were probably used earliest for women or children because women and children were less capable of "fighting their own battles" and thereby less capable of proving their innocence, champions later came to be used by men as well. The use of champions came after the realization that it didn't seem reasonable that the taller, stronger, and more powerful defendants would almost invariably be innocent.

An interesting tradition evolved in trial by battle. In criminal proceedings between an accuser and an accused, the men themselves would fight. However, if the dispute was about ownership of land, then the battle was fought by champions who represented the disputants. This was done because, if the participants themselves fought and both died in battle, there would be no owner for the land in dispute.

It was not until 1819 that trial by combat was abolished in England, but it had fallen into disrepute long before that time. The last recorded trial by champion took place in England in 1571. Many critics of the adversary system (including the author) claim that the adversary system is a direct extension of trial by battle. Those who defend the system claim that this is not the case, for the following reasons: 1) trial by battle was basically outlawed in England by the 13th century, 2) there is no evidence for its use beyond the 16th century, and 3) adversarial proceedings in their present form did not emerge until about the 18th century. However, the tradition in trial by battle of the litigants being represented by another party has its equivalent in the adversary system. I believe that we have not moved as far from trial by combat as many proponents of the adversary system profess. In many cases it is still very much a "bloody battle." Peoples' lives have literally been destroyed by the system. Many have been drained completely of all financial resources. Many have suffered irreparable psychological damage over the course of protracted litigation. The practice of ending the battle at sunset, and making a decision then, is in a sense more humane than the system today where litigation can go on for years.

TRIAL BY WAGER

Wager of law and ordeal were more common in England than trial by battle. Wager of law required each of the litigants to take an oath that his claims were true and to produce other persons, usually referred to as *compurgators*, to support the litigant's oath by making their own oaths. It was also called *trial by compurgation*. It was basically a "character test" in which the oath taker established his or her case by demonstrating good standing in the community. The compurgators were not asked to provide testimony about the facts of the case, but only served to guarantee that the oath taker was an honest person. The more compurgators who would swear on behalf of a litigant, the greater the chances of acquittal.

In trial by wager the person took an oath. Such an oath involved invoking supernatural powers, who were allegedly listening to the oath, operating at the time of the trial, and would intervene on behalf of the person who was innocent or right. There was an appeal here to a supernatural power, with the implication that if one was not telling the truth, God would somehow punish the individual. The participants did not expect that God would rule immediately; instead the perjurer would be punished at some future date. Such oaths were taken seriously by primitive peoples. They were also taken seriously by people in the Middle Ages, who genuinely believed that if they lied, there might be some punishment in the hereafter.

Residua of trial by wager exist today. The oath that we take in court with hand on the Bible is a derivative of this system, as is the use in court of character witnesses. There is little reason to believe that the vast majority of people who take such oaths today under the European/American system take them seriously and can be relied upon not to perjure themselves from the fear that they will be punished by God. They might fear punishment by the court for perjury, but not punishment by a supernatural power. Perjuring oneself before a court of law is routine nowadays and most often promulgated by the attorneys (the champions). Recent examples of this are the Watergate hearings and the more recent Iran-contra congressional hearings. On the basis of my own experiences with divorce/custody litigation, I would say that 80 to 90 percent of all the clients I have seen will lie in court without any hesitation or guilt. Although attorneys profess publicly that it is unethical for them to encourage their clients to perjure themselves, this is routinely done. One method is to foster lies of omission. Because there may be some readers who are not familiar with the difference between lies of omission and lies of commission, I will define here this important distinction. A lie of omission is simply a kind of deceit in which an individual knowingly omits data in the service of misleading the listener. In a lie of commission the individual adds fabrications toward the same goal, namely, that of misleading the listener. Lies of commission are not permitted by the adversary system, but lies of omission are not only permitted but actively encouraged. As I see it, a lie of omission is no less a lie than a lie of commission; it is a form of deceit. A man who does not tell a woman with whom he is amorously involved that he has a sexually transmitted disease is lying by omission. A woman who does not tell her husband that he is not the biological father of the child she is bearing is also lying by omission. Obviously, the consequences of such silences may be grave. Although the system will not uniformly condone all such egregious examples of lies of omission, its principle of sanctioning such withholding of vital data often produces similar grievous results. But clients and their attorneys often go further and actively support lies of commission as well. Even character witnesses are generally not uncomfortable perjuring themselves. Accordingly, the residua of trial by wager are primarily ritualistic. They exist in the oath taken on the Bible and in the character witnesses. And, like most rituals, their original purposes have long since passed into oblivion.

In recent years, some states have changed their courtroom procedure and no longer require a witness to take an oath on the Bible and/or may omit the word "God" from the oath taken before testifying. In some European countries witnesses are allowed to object to taking an oath and are permitted to substitute a solemn affirmation. In Denmark, oaths in legal procedures have been abolished. In the Soviet Union, consistent with the antireligious position of the government, oaths or solemn affirmations are prohibited in the courtroom.

FOURTH LATERAN COUNCIL — 1215

The three methods of trial used in the Middle Ages were not mutually exclusive and often coexisted in the same area. Often the accused could choose the method of trial. All three methods were based on the premise of Divine intervention. Direct Heavenly intercession was postulated for ordeal and battle, and eternal damnation was supposed to enforce trial by wager. The emphasis was on the judgment of God rather than on the judgment of man. Very little use of evidence was considered necessary, nor were fact-finding procedures considered important. Because of the heavy reliance on Divine intervention, there was little concern with the appellate process. Active participation by both the accused and the accuser was central to the three medieval methods, as it is to the adversary system. Such participation is not central to the inquisitorial system (to be discussed below).

In the year 1215, the Fourth Lateran Council prohibited Church participation in trial by ordeal. The Lateran Councils were ecumenical councils held in the pope's palace in Rome (the Lateran Palace) between 1123 and 1517. The 1215 edict against trial by ordeal ended the practice, because priestly participation had been one of its fundamental components. At the same time, both ecclesiastical and secular critics began a series of sustained attacks on trial by wager and trial by battle, but these were not prohibited. These systems of determining guilt or innocence did, however, become far less frequently utilized. As a result, a partial vacuum was created that permitted the development of alternative systems for ascertaining whether or not an accused did indeed commit a crime. On the Continent the inquisitorial system emerged as the predominant system, as is the situation today. In England, however, other systems evolved, culminating in the adversary system, which took its present form in the 18th and 19th centuries. I will first discuss briefly the inquisitorial system and then discuss in greater detail the evolution of the adversary system, first in England and then in the United States.

THE INQUISITORIAL SYSTEM

As mentioned, in 1215 the Fourth Lateran Council banned Church participation in ordeals. In addition, wager of law and trial by battle were also on the wane. On the Continent the inquisitorial system evolved. This procedure was the product of combining certain aspects of the laws of ancient Rome (Roman law) with judicial principles developed in European ecclesiastical circles (canonical law). By the 16th century this amalgam of Roman and canonical approaches was dominant throughout continental Europe. A central element in this approach was active inquiry by the judge in order to uncover the truth. He wielded great power, so much so that it became prudent to limit his authority by means of strict evidentiary requirements. Generally, the judge could only convict a criminal defendant under two circumstances: 1) when two eye witnesses were produced who observed the crime or 2) when the defendent confessed. Circumstantial evidence was generally not considered sufficient to warrant conviction. However, under these same laws, judges were authorized to use torture to extract the necessary confessions. Torture came to be viewed as an excellent and reliable method of finding out "the truth." Thus, torture became a tool of judicial inquiry and was used to generate the evidence upon which the defendant would be condemned.

At this point I will discuss some of the reasons why the inquisitorial system developed on the Continent and why the adversary system evolved in England. In 1215, the same year that the Fourth Lateran Council convened, the English barons forced King John to sign the Magna Carta, which guaranteed certain rights and liberties to Englishmen (men, not women; nobility, not lower classes). Certain rights of individuals (upper class) were thereby established, and a precedent was set for the democracy that ultimately evolved in England. In contrast, on the Continent, derivatives of Roman law still prevailed—especially the notion of the centralized authority of the state. Another factor that contributed to the expansion of the inquisitorial method on the Continent was the Catholic Church's fear of the spread of anti-Catholic movements.

One of the earliest and most powerful of the anti-Church groups was the Albigenses (a name derived from the city of Albi in southern France), who spread anti-Church doctrines throughout Europe (especially southern Europe) in the 11th and 12th centuries. They posed such a threat to the Church that a special crusade, the Albigensian Crusade (1208–1213) was organized in the attempt to exterminate them. In addition, the earliest papal inquisition, the medieval Inquisition, was set up to bring to trial and execute these and related groups of heretics. These proved successful in obliterating almost completely the Albigensians and related movements.

However, in the late 15th century the Spanish Inquisition was established in Spain to extinguish Jews and Muslims, who were then considered to be a threat to the Church. And in the 16th century the Roman Inquisition was set up, this time to stem the rising tide of Protestantism. The methods utilized by the medieval and Spanish Inquisitions were much more brutal and sadistic than those used by the later Roman Inquisition. The methods described below were more typical of the two earlier inquisitions than the third. All three, however, served in part, as models for the secular inquisitorial systems that developed on the Continent.

The Church did not consider the relatively primitive

judicial systems operative at that time to be sufficient to handle the widening threat of the anti-Catholic movements. The key word here is *heresy*, and the inquisitions were constantly searching for heretics who were brought before them. Heretics were rounded up, persecuted, and tried for their heresy. There was little concern for evidence and veracity of witnesses. Accused individuals did not know the names of the witnesses against them, lest retaliation be possible. Witnesses in support of the accused were not permitted to appear. There was no confrontation (cross-examination) of witnesses. Death by fire was made the official punishment for heretics, and they were usually burned at the stake. If they warranted special clemency, they were sentenced to life imprisonment. However, because life imprisonment was a much more expensive proposition, it was rarely utilized. Torture was used to elicit confessions. The Church and the State worked together, with the Church authorizing the torture and the State being the arm of enforcement. The inquisitors could excommunicate and label as heretic any civil magistrate who refused to inflict the punishment the inquisitors prescribed. The methods of torture commonly used to elicit confessions included the rack, thumbscrew, and flogging. There was an extremely high rate of conviction; acquittal was rare. Archbishops traveled throughout the Continent and would force people to denounce one another. Those who refused risked being considered heretics themselves. Often the cases were judged without the names of the accused or witnesses. The inquisitions were not universally embraced. It was not utilized in Scandinavian countries, nor did it take root in England. This is partly related to the fact that these countries were geographically isolated from the Continent. Also, the Albigenses and related sects did not spread as far north as Scandinavia or across into England. Thus, there was little need for the utilization of the medieval Inquisition in these areas. In addition, as mentioned, a parallel system of adjudication was developing in England, one based more on individual rights.

Whereas the adversary system is based on the premise that truth will emerge as an outgrowth of a clash between adversaries, the inquisitorial system is based on the assumption that truth is most likely to emerge as a result of an inquiry by neutral persons, such as judges. The judge in the inquisitorial system is a fact finder, but a very active fact finder. It is he who controls the mechanisms of inquiry. In the American and English adversarial system, the lawyers collect and present the facts and the judge is a more neutral hearer of the facts, although he does have some power of inquiry.

In the European system, both sides generally provide all pertinent information to the court and to one another prior to the onset of the proceedings. In the adversary system, each side tries to keep "aces up its sleeve" in order to catch the other side off guard and limit opportunity for response. In the adversary system, the attorneys call in the witnesses. In the European system, the judge calls in the witnesses and interviews them in the presence of the attorneys and the clients. Whereas in the adversary system the witnesses are generally selected because they are likely to support a particular side's position, in the European system the witnesses are more neutral and are generally called in by the judge.

In the inquisitorial system the judge is an active fact finder. The European trial is more an investigation rather than a battle of two opposing sides. The judge collects all the information before the trial and is given information by both attorneys. Witnesses are not interviewed by the attorneys for either side before the trial begins. Rather, they are interviewed by the judge. They do not belong to either side; rather, they belong to the judge. The witnesses testify in an uninterrupted narrative. The judge is the one who questions the witness. After the judge interrogates the witness, the lawyers can do so but not in the restrictive type of cross-examination type of inquiry used in the United States and England.

As a person who has appeared as a court-appointed expert on many occasions, I am sympathetic to the inquisitorial system's practice of giving witnesses (expert and nonexpert) free rein to present their testimony. The argument given by proponents of the adversary system that such restriction ultimately balances out and that all the facts are ultimately presented to the judge is a myth. I have never been involved in a case where this has proven to be true. What usually happens is that only a fraction of opposing arguments are presented to the court. But even those that are brought forth are usually presented at some other date, long after the judge (no matter how brilliant and no matter his or her memory) has forgotten the initial points.

THE DEVELOPMENT OF THE ADVERSARY SYSTEM FROM THE 13TH TO THE 17TH CENTURIES

The foundations of our present-day adversary system in England and the United States were laid down primarily between the 13th and the 17th centuries. As mentioned, the Fourth Lateran Council created a partial vacuum with regard to methods of dispute resolution and determination of guilt or innocence. On the Continent conditions prevailed that led to the development of the inquisitorial system. In England, for reasons already stated, the climate was one in which the adversary system gradually evolved. Four institutions developed that served as foundations for the system: juries, witnesses, judges, and lawyers. I will discuss each of these separately and then describe how they coalesced into the adversary system, first in England and then in the United States. Of course, discussing them separately is somewhat artificial in that each influenced the others.

Juries

The Normans probably brought the jury system to England at the time of the Norman Conquest in 1066. The jury has served many different functions over the years. In the 11th century juries served to inform the court of cases it should try because jurors, as friends and neighbors of the parties involved in the litigation, were more likely to know what was going on in the community. The early jurors, however, were not really peers of the litigants because they were generally freeholders (landowners and titled individuals). They were free men, and they were often higher on the social ladder than those on trial.

Originally jurors were not the neutral fact finders they are today, listening to others present the facts; rather, they were actively involved in collecting evidence. Traditionally, they were individuals who lived in the same community as the litigants and were thereby more likely to have information about the events to be dealt with at the trial. In fact, not to have such knowledge was considered reason for disqualification. In addition, there was often a time gap between the assignment of the jury members and the beginning of the trial, during which time the jurors were expected to collect facts relevant to the dispute. They were empowered to make investigations, to ask questions, and to acquaint themselves with the details of the case. Accordingly, Divine guidance was replaced by collection of pertinent data. Jurors could be punished if the judge decided that their decision was the "wrong" one. This check on the jury system enhanced dedication and honesty and was probably a factor in its survival. The growth of the jury system as a method of fact finding reduced and obviated the utilization of torture, another method of fact finding. The jury, then, was the adversary system's method of fact finding, in contrast to torture, which was the inquisitorial system's method of obtaining information.

From the 13th to 15th centuries, the practice evolved that the litigants could challenge the jurors; if the jurors were found to be biased, they could be removed. From the 15th century onward, jurors generally became less involved in out-of-court investigations and began to rely upon facts presented in court as the basis for their decision. The use of a considerable volume of evidence had the effect of shifting the function of the jury from active inquiry to passive review and analysis. Juries also evolved from being the king's representatives to being independent entities, unconnected with the objectives and infuences of the government. It was not until 1705 in civil cases and 1826 in criminal cases that jurors could be drawn from places other than the immediate locality in which the dispute arose. This was done to reduce the likelihood that jurors would enter the courtroom with preliminary, and possibly prejudicial, information. Our present-day grand jury is similar in its function to the earlier juries (prior to 1705); it is primarily an inquisitorial body that seeks evidence in order to determine whether a trial should be held.

In the late 1300s and early 1400s contact between the litigants and the jurors after the submission of a case were significantly curtailed to reduce the possibility of prejudice and influence. Separation of the litigants from the jury is a central element in the adversary process and is one of the ways in which the jury system laid the foundation for the development of the adversary system.

By the 18th century the jury was not only viewed as a neutral and passive fact-finding group but as a check on judicial despotism. The Constitution of the United States, fashioned in the 1780s, specifically incorporated the right to jury trial as a check on other institutions of government, not only the judiciary but those who chose the judges and wrote the laws. The juries served as monitors of the laws by having the power to control the judges empowered to implement them.

Witnesses

Up through the 15th century the testimony of witnesses was held in low esteem. In fact, witnesses were not generally used in English trials until about 1500. Voluntary testimony was viewed with suspicion, and witnesses could not be compelled to testify against their will. However, in the 16th century the presentation of testimonial evidence grew dramatically. The information provided by witnesses came to replace private juror inquiry as the basis for decisions in criminal cases. Prior to 1555 witnesses were not compelled to testify, but after 1565 witnesses were compelled to do so. This change entrenched more deeply the role of the jury as a passive fact-finding group, and the witnesses became primary sources of information for the court. Attention shifted away from the juror's private knowledge, toward witnesses' testimony as a primary source of evidence.

In the mid-1500s, we see the beginnings of the development of rules governing the presentation of evidence, especially by witnesses. During that period rules were developed that prohibited the use of data from untrustworthy informants, such as proven perjurers. In addition, wives were not permitted to testify against their husbands. Other rules that came into being were the *best evidence rule* (the court must only consider evidence that has high credibility and must deem as inadmissible evidence of low credibility), the *opinion rule* (the court has the power to give priority to the opinions of experts over those who have no expertise in a particular area), and the *hearsay rule* (the court has the power to give priority to testimony based on direct observations of the witness as opposed to information transmitted indirectly and/or via second and third parties). The opinion rule defined the kinds of testimony lay people could provide and the kinds experts could provide—with strict definitions for each. It was not until the 18th and 19th centuries, however, that the rules of evidence became more formalized and stringent.

Judges

During the 12th and 13th centuries the offender was generally forced to pay the family or his victim compensation for causing the victim's death or injury. However, it gradually evolved that the state became viewed as the wronged party, because offenses were viewed as breaches of the "king's peace." Judges then became viewed as representatives of the king. By the 13th century English law and procedure had become sufficiently technical to warrant the designation of full-time judges. Before 1300 judges were civil servants, often appointed by the king. After 1300 judges were appointed *only* from among the ranks of the serjeants (sic), a small group that constituted the elite of the bar.

The aforementioned changes notwithstanding, judicial procedures between 1300 and 1700 were not truly adversarial. In the typical trial of the 1500s and 1600s, the judge served as an active inquisitor, whereas the jury was passive. The judge would directly question the defendant and the witnesses. Following these inquiries there was a kind of freewheeling discussion among the witnesses, defendant, and judge. When the judge was satisfied that he had heard enough, he would summarize the case to the jury, charge them to decide it, and they were generally not allowed to eat or drink until a decision had been rendered. Lawyers were not involved in the judicial process to an active degree. The defendant was not usually represented by counsel and was often prohibited from having legal representation. The defendant was not allowed to call witnesses, conduct any real cross-examination, or develop an affirmative case. The judge wielded great power over the jury and was free to urge a verdict upon the jury. Up until 1670 jurors who refused to follow the judge's directions could be jailed or fined. There was no appellate procedure by which the litigants could secure review of the decision. These procedures did, however, have certain germs of the adversarial system: they were orally contentious, were decided upon by the evidence of witnesses, and were judged by a neutral and passive jury. However, the emphasis was not upon adversarial presentation of evidence. The judge was a very active participant, the protection against misleading prejudicial evidence was minimal, and appellate review was not available. The focus was not so much on accurate data collection and evidence, but on the development of legal principles of procedure.

In the latter part of the 17th century, judges became less active fact finders and took a more passive role in the courtroom. They devoted themselves more to serving as an umpire. Judges today in the English and American adversarial system are neutral. Their duties are to interpret the laws by which the contestants are operating and to enforce the rules of procedure during the trial. They do, however, have great power in that they can manipulate the court procedures in a manner prejudicial to the party he or she believes to have the better case.

In the United States, since the beginning of the 19th century, further developments insured that judges would remain neutral and passive fact finders. They were required to adopt a neutral political stance, could not run for office, and were discouraged from supporting political candidates.

They were also required to adhere strictly to rules of evidence and were limited as to the kinds of remarks that they could make in the course of a trial.

In the 19th century the appellate courts developed. They were designed to be the guardians of the adversary system, insuring that judges complied with the rules of evidence and procedure. If not, the appellate courts could reverse a decision in order to insure compliance with the new principles. In addition, appelate courts could reverse what they considered to be the trial court's misinterpretation or misapplication of the law.

Lawyers

About the beginning of the 14th century, requirements were established regulating the education and conduct of those who would be allowed to argue cases in the king's courts. In time, the advocates formed special organizations, called Inns of Court, for training members of the bar. In the 15th and 16th centuries, as the jury's investigative role diminished and juries became more passive, the responsibilities of the advocates increased. Lawyers undertook the job of supplying the jury with the evidence upon which the decisions would be based. By 1600 lawyers had established for themselves their special status as masters of the evidence-gathering process.

It was around 1577 that an important change occurred that became central to the development of our present-day adversary system. It was at this time that the concept of the attorney-client privilege came into being. It granted lawyers special exemption from the obligation to provide evidence that had been provided by clients, if divulgence of such evidence might compromise the client's position. Lawyers then developed a special status of immunity from certain courtroom obligations. I consider this to be a mixed blessing.

On the one hand, it increased the likelihood that the client would be honest to the attorney in a manner similar to the confidential relationship that patients have with their doctors. On the other hand, it gave sanction to lies of omission, a practice that reflects a basic weakness in the system that has produced grief for many over the centuries.

During the 15th through 17th centuries lawyers were generally less concerned with gathering accurate evidence than they were with narrowly defining various legal principles. The lawyers involved themselves in endless nitpicking about formal legal rules and procedure. They wasted incredible amounts of time arguing fine points of law rather than the substance of their cases.

Codes governing lawyers' behavior are basically products of the 18th and 19th centuries. One of the central ethical conflicts was this: On the one hand, attorneys were expected to be officers of the court and speak the truth. On the other hand, they were expected to be loyal advocates on behalf of their clients. This problem has been resolved, primarily, by allowing attorneys to withhold from the court any information that might compromise their client's position. This is basically a lie of omission. It is justified on the grounds that the adversary is also permitted to engage in lying by omission. At the same time, both sides are encouraged to present before the court those arguments that support their clients' positions. Presumably, such evidence will also include what each side has attempted to withhold. The assumption, then, is that all the data and evidence will ultimately be brought before the court. In practice, this assumption is rarely realized because of the complexity of the process and the fact that very few can afford the indulgence of a trial in which all pertinent evidence is brought before the court. Furthermore, lies of commission are frequent. If one sanctions lies of omission, one cannot be surprised if lies of commission soon follow. The result of all of this, I believe, is that attorneys are trained in law school to be liars. In Chapter Seven I will discuss in detail further views of mine on the lawyer's role in adversary proceedings, especially with regard to their participation in bringing about stress and psychopathology in their clients.

THE DEVELOPMENT OF THE
PRESENT-DAY ADVERSARY SYSTEM
IN ENGLAND

The development of the adversary system, which prides itself on giving the accused and the accuser the opportunity to confront one another directly in an open courtroom, was retarded significantly in 1487 by Parliament, when it established the judicial proceedings that came to be known as the Star Chamber proceedings. The Star Chamber proceedings were established at the instigation of King Henry VII in order to curb the power of feudal nobles. The council met in the royal palace of Westminster in a room decorated with stars on the ceiling, thus the name *Star Chamber*. Initially, Parliament defined the Star Chamber's jurisdiction over riots, unlawful assembly, and other events beyond the power of ordinary courts to control. Subsequently it widened its jurisdiction to include any other issues with which its judges or the king wished to deal. Juries were not used, the meetings were often secret, rumor was accepted as evidence, and torture was often utilized to obtain testimony. Rising sentiment resulted in Parliament abolishing the Star Chamber in 1641. On the one hand, the Star Chamber's dictatorial and repressive habits played a role in suppressing the development of the adversary system. On the other hand, when the Star Chamber was finally discontinued, memory of its repressive tactics encouraged reforms that resulted in the guarantees of openness central to adversary proceedings.

The present-day adversary system dates its origins to the mid-17th century, the time of the abolishment of the Star Chamber. By the end of the 18th century the adversary system, as we know it today, was established both in the United States and England. It was during this 150-year period that both judge and jury came to conform closely to the ideals of neutrality and passivity. By 1700 decisions could be reversed and a new trial ordered if the judge believed that evidence was insufficient to warrant a verdict. By 1756 the retrial mechanism was effectively extended to all cases. After 1705, in civil cases, there was an abolishment of the requirement that juries be drawn from the exact neighborhood in which the case arose. This reduced the likelihood that jurors would have any private information to rely on when making their decisions.

In the 19th century we see the development of cross-examination. The lawyer's obligation to provide zealous representation and loyalty to his or her client's cause was the product of the 18th and 19th centuries. However, lawyers were restricted from harassing or intimidating an opponent. As proceedings became more adversarial, however, conflicting ethical demands were exerted upon lawyers. On the one hand, attorneys were expected to be officers of the court and to seek the truth; on the other hand, they were expected to be keen advocates on behalf of their clients. In the mid-19th century the emphasis shifted to zeal and loyalty (denials notwithstanding), and this is the present state of affairs. In the 19th century we see the development of courts set up for the sole purpose of deciding appeals. They reviewed trial records and determined whether errors warranting reversal had occurred. They did not conduct open hearings with clients or witnesses.

Over the last 300 years, three sets of rules have evolved that are generally considered crucial for the successful utilization of the adversary system. First, there are the *rules of procedure*, which are designed to produce in an orderly fashion a climactic confrontation between the parties in the trial. The *rules of evidence* protect the integrity of the evidence. They prohibit the use of evidence that is likely to be unreliable and might bring about misleading information to the judge and jury. These rules also prohibit the use of evidence that poses a threat of unfair prejudice against one of the parties. Last, there are certain *ethical rules* designed to serve as guidelines and controls for the attorneys. They require, for the clients' protection, the counsels zealously protecting the clients' interests at all times. They require the attorney to be loyal to the client. Because of the danger that attorneys will become excessively swept up in the battle, they are not permitted to harass or intimidate an opponent. Courts of appeal insure that litigants and judges will comply with these mandated procedures.

THE ADVERSARY SYSTEM
IN THE UNITED STATES

In the early days of colonization the legal systems were very much like those of primitive societies, because there were few individuals in any particular setting and the need for compromise was very great. Because of the separation of the various colonies and their colonization by different countries, there was little uniformity in their legal procedures. However, arbitration was commonly used. Many of the emerging middle class who came to America had been abused by the aristocratic government in England. Because many colonists came to America with a feeling of antagonism toward the status quo and the entrenched establishment, there was resistance against the incorporation of English law into the colonies. The colonists were intent on preventing the formation of another aristocracy. This reluctance predictably became even more pronounced at the time of the American Revolution. The American system of government is based heavily on the concepts of self-reliance and individualism. Accordingly, there was great distrust of a central authority, and the judiciary was the target of such distrust. Any move toward centralization was resisted, and individuals were viewed as capable of defending themselves in courts. However, in time the English adversary system came to be viewed favorably because the judge, as umpire, exerted far less authority than the magistrates under Continental law. The adversary system, then, came to be viewed as the best protection of the middle class against the aristocracy. It was viewed as an excellent protection against judges becoming arms of the state. The framers of the Constitution, then, included such revisions as due process, the right to a trial by jury, habeas corpus, the right to counsel, the right to bail, and the privilege against self-incrimination. It would be an error to conclude that the founding fathers were particularly interested in the protection of the lower classes of society; they were interested in protecting the middle class's commercial and entrepreneurial interests.

During the pre-revolutionary period judges and juries became increasingly independent of political and governmental influence. This was one of the cornerstones of the American Constitution. The founding fathers were adamant in their belief that trial by jury was a central protection for the freedom of individuals. But juries had to be established that were independent of government control (while still complying with the law). Prior to the 1800s, judges were likely to have been political partisans who openly advertised their opinions in court. After Thomas Jefferson was elected, his supporters removed a number of incompetent or partisan Federalist judges from office. Supreme Court Chief Justice John Marshall became the standard by which the propriety of judicial behavior came to be measured. He was the first of the truly impartial chief justices. Since the early 1800s, judicial conduct was controlled by applying strict rules of evidence and by placing exacting limits on the types of remarks that could be made at the close of a case.

The adversary system has flourished in the United States, so much so that it is reasonable to say that there is no other country in the world in which it has enjoyed such widespread utilization. It is also reasonable to say that the United States, at this time, is the most litigious country on earth. J.K. Lieberman (1981) devotes significant sections of his book to a description of the reasons why litigation has burgeoned so much in the United States. He states that the further one goes back in history, the more individuals have considered themselves to be at the mercy of nature and the less likely they were to view calamities that befell them to be related to indignities they suffered at the hands of other human beings. As man gained more control over the environment, other individuals came to be blamed more frequently for the traumas and catastrophes that inevitably befell humans. If one views botulism, for example, to be God-sent, then one cannot blame fellow human beings for one's suffering. However, if one considers the disease to be caused by food contamination, which was the result of negligence on the part of those who packaged the food, then the blame is easily traced back to some human agent. In such situations the sufferer is likely to want to gain retribution, or at least to prevent the recurrence of the event. Because the United States has been one of the countries at the forefront of modern scientific advances and its associated environmental control, this shift of blame from God to mankind has been particularly evident here, especially in the last century.

Another factor that has contributed to the litigiousness of the American people relates to the fact that we are a "melting pot." In the countries from which our immigrants came, there was generally a greater degree of homogeneity among the population than exists in the United States. Accordingly, there was general unanimity with regard to what customs and traditions should be adhered to. In the United States, however, we have a potpourri of traditions that are often in conflict with one another. Thus there has been a greater need to utilize higher powers to enforce uniformity of behavior. In a democratic country, the imposition of rules by a dictator, monarch, aristocrat, or group of oligarchs is not considered to be a viable source of such regulation. Rather, the rule of law, equally applied to all, has been the guiding principle for bringing about compliance with social standards.

With an ever-enlarging body of laws, there has been an ever-growing number of methods for challenging and altering the legal structure. This is an intrinsic concomitant to the growth of a democratic system governed by laws. Accordingly, since the earliest days of our government, litigation has been ubiquitous. Although the democratic countries of Europe have also witnessed a significant growth in the body of their laws, there has been an important difference with regard to the growth of litigation. Specifically, in the past only those highest on the social hierarchy enjoyed the protection of the laws, and it was only they who were significantly involved in litigation. In America, however, every person, no matter how low on the social scale, has the right to the protection of the law and can litigate. Although poorer people were (and still are) less likely to enjoy the services of the most skilled attorneys, the route to litigation was (and is) very much available to them—a situation that did not prevail in Europe where the litigation potential was enjoyed primarily by the aristocracy.

Another factor that has contributed to the litigiousness of Americans is our individualism, which lessens the likelihood that people will submit to more community types of dispute settlement. Our spirit of individualism has gone so far that people are increasingly representing themselves in court and refusing the assistance and guidance of attorneys. Part of this practice relates to the expense of engaging professional counselors, but part relates to a system that allows individuals to represent themselves pro se. Although there is some general recognition that one is likely to do better in litigation when one is represented by an attorney, the court systems provide ready vehicles for pro se representation.

Since World War II, litigation has expanded in other ways in the United States. Whereas in the past it was generally considered unethical for attorneys to solicit litigants (this is generally referred to as *ambulance chasing*), this is no longer the case. At the time of this writing there is approximately one lawyer for every 850 people in the United States. Obviously, competition is keen, and under these circumstances it is not surprising that soliciting litigants has become an acceptable practice. For example, a well-known American litigator recently instituted a suit against the Union Carbide Company for the death of thousands of Indians in Bhopal as the result of a leakage of lethal chemical gases from one of its plants there. He is asking for 15 billion dollars. If successful, he can conceivably retain as his fee one-third of this amount. Although it is not clear from newspaper accounts whether this lawyer solicited clients in India, with incentives such as this, it is no surprise that other attorneys quickly found their way to India to sign up clients in the streets, hospitals, and their homes. Of course, personal monetary gain is denied as the primary motivating factor for these gentlemen; rather, they self-righteously proclaim that innocents must be protected from the negligence of giant corporations and that they are thereby serving in justice's cause.

At one time in the United States there was an adage, "You can't fight City Hall." This is no longer the case. One cannot only sue City Hall; one can sue local governments, states, civic officials, and even the federal government. People who are only tangentially and remotely involved in a case may be sued. People can be liable for acts undertaken by others. For example, the National Broadcasting Company (NBC) was recently sued by a girl's family because her rape followed a film depicting a similar assault from which they claim the assailant obtained his ideas. Law suits may be initiated on mere suspicion, the extent of the injury may remain unknown, and the plaintiff's lawyer may hope that a discovery procedure may force the defendant to prove the case against him- or herself. Recently, I saw a magazine cartoon depicting a man watching a salesman giving his pitch on television. The caption: "Having trouble with your next-door neighbor? Sue; it's less trouble than you may think." A court may impose a liability on an entire industry because the wrongdoer could not be identified. In such a setting it is no surprise that litigation is ubiquitous and that most of the best law schools are flooded with applicants.

The adversary courtroom battle is often viewed as a sport similar to that of a traditional sporting event. Each side has its attorney(s), client(s), and witness(es). The court's rules of procedure, evidence, and lawyer ethics have their analogies in the rules of the various sports. People cheer for their side, especially if brought to public attention. Attorneys get swept up in their clients' battles, and the name of the game is to win. The game or sport theory becomes even more apparent when a trial is brought to public attention and gets significant coverage in the public media. The litigants, however, may not view the adversary trial as a game; rather, they might justifiably view themselves as the pawns in the game.

One could argue that the adversary system is indeed a blessing and that it is a manifestation of the most powerful and effective way that individuals in a democratic society can protect themselves from indignities, whether they be inflicted by other individuals or by the government. If a government is oppressive, then should we not have a means of fighting back? If someone breaks a contract, should we not have the means of enforcing commitment?

One cannot deny that individuals should have a means of fighting back, and it may very well be the case that the adversary system provides us with the best method for protecting ourselves. However, it is not well designed to deal with situations in which there was no intrinsic opposition at the outset. When the doctor's intent is to help and he errs, should one make him or her an adversary? Should two parents who have differences regarding who is the better parent utilize the adversary system to make this decision? In our conflictual society we create conflicts when there may initially not have been any. Courts working within this system are not permitted to decide disputes that are not brought to them by genuinely adverse parties. A controversy *must* be created—even if there was none before—if the courts are to consider hearing the case. For example, courts decide whether or not to remove life-sustaining machinery from terminally ill comatose patients. Adversaries are created in order to function within the structure of the adversary system. The courts thereby manufacture an adversarial situation out of one that is not intrinisically adversarial for the purposes of fitting individuals into the Procrustean bed of the adversary courtroom proceeding.

As mentioned, the adversary system is based on the assumption that the truth can best be discovered if each side strives as hard as it can to bring to the court's attention the evidence favorable to its own side. It is based on the assumption that the fairest decision can be obtained when the two parties argue in open court according to carefully prescribed rules and procedures. They face each other as adversaries in a kind of constrained battle procedure. Criticism of this method of dispute resolution dates back to ancient times:

> Both Plato and Aristotle condemned the method. They considered the advocate as one who was paid to make the better cause appear the worse, or endeavor by sophisticated tricks of argument to establish as true what any man of common sense could see was false. The feeling against advocacy in the criminal law was so strong that, at least in the case of the more serious kinds of crime, a right to representation by a trained advocate was nowhere generally recognized until the 18th century A.D. (Encyclopedia Britannica, 1982).

In this chapter I have provided a brief survey of the adversary system's development, with particular focus on what I consider to be its weaknesses. In the next chapter I will focus more specifically on the utilization of the system as a method of dealing with divorce and custody disputes.

TWO

BRIEF REVIEW OF WESTERN SOCIETY'S CHANGING ATTITUDES REGARDING PARENTAL PREFERENCE IN CUSTODY DISPUTES

ANCIENT TIMES TO WORLD WAR II

A brief review of the criteria used in Western society to determine custody will enable the reader to place in better perspective our present situation regarding custody determination. Again, I will not simply present historical data, but will present my opinions regarding the significance of the various developments.

In the days of the Roman Empire, fathers were automatically given custody of their children at the time of divorce. (Divorce was quite common, incidentally, when the empire was at its peak.) Mothers had no education or reasonably marketable skills, and so were not considered as fit as fathers to care for their children alone. Fathers had such power that they could, at their whim, sell their children into slavery and, after proper release from councils convened for

43

the purpose, literally kill their children. The power of fathers to kill their children extended up to the 14th century, but the power to sell children into servitude was retained for another 100–200 years (A.P. Derdeyn, 1976). Serfs on feudal manors were often children who were sold into slavery. However, divorce was extremely uncommon because there was no easily available route to it, either via secular or ecclesiastical channels. People like King Henry VIII could defy papal authority and provide themselves with a divorce, but lesser souls had to "hang in there" and remain married until the end of their days.

In the 17th and 18th centuries we see the introduction of the notion that custody involved not only *rights* but *responsibilities* as well. If the father (still the automatic custodial parent) showed evidence that he was not capable of or interested in assuming parental responsibilities, then the state considered its right to assume the role of the parent in order to protect the children. This concept became known as the *doctrine of parens patriae* (*Latin*: parenting by the state). In England this concept was incorporated in 1839 in *Talfourd's Act*, in which the court was given power to determine custody of children under the age of seven. The state then, operating through the courts, would assign the child to the parent who could provide better protection. In some cases this would be the mother. However, such designation was rare because divorce was rare.

In 1817, in a well-publicized case, Percy Shelley, the poet, lost custody of his children because of his "atheism" and "immorality" (specifically, marital infidelity). It is reasonable to assume that it was not the adultery alone that caused him to lose his children: If that were the case, there would have been few fathers retaining custody. It is reasonable to assume also that it was not the atheism alone that caused him to lose his children, in that there were many atheists in England at that time who were not losing custody.

It was probably the *combination* of adultery *and* atheism (if one can imagine such a terrible combination coexisting in a *single* human being) that "did him in." In addition, it is reasonable to assume that there were many other adulterous atheists in England who were still retaining custody, but that Shelley, as a well-known figure, probably served well as an example to other would-be adulterous atheists to mind their manners and mend their ways.

But Shelley's was an isolated case. It was not until the middle of the 19th century that we see the first indications of what came subsequently to be called (in the 20th century) the *tender years presumption.* The courts began to work under the presumption that there were certain psychological benefits that the child could gain from its mother that were not to be so readily obtained from its father. The notion of wresting a suckling infant from its mother's breast came to be viewed as somehow injudicious and "wrong." Accordingly, mothers began to be given custody of their infant children. But when the children reached the age of three or four (the age at which breast-feeding was usually discontinued in the 19th century), they were considered to have gained all that they needed from their mothers, and they were transferred to their fathers, their "rightful and just" parents.

We also see in the mid-19th century the increasing utilization by the courts of the concept of *parent culpability* when considering custody disputes. Specifically, before granting custody the court not only considered which parent would provide the child with better treatment but also made the assumption that the parent who obeyed marriage vows was more likely to provide the child with a proper upbringing. Although this might initially appear to have been an advance, the main vow that was under consideration by the courts was the vow not to commit adultery. Furthermore, it was most often the adulterous mother who was deprived of custody, rather than the adulterous father. Punitive attitudes toward adulterous mothers were certainly prevalent until the 1950s and 1960s. It has only been since the 1960s that adultery (adultery by mothers or fathers) has not been given serious weight in determining parental capacity. The courts generally appreciate that private sexual activities, which do not directly affect the children, are not likely to have any significant and/or immediate effect on parenting capacity. However, parents who expose their children to sexual activity are generally considered to be demonstrating a parental deficiency.

In the late 19th century we see the birth of the Women's Liberation movement. Women began to wrest entrance into educational institutions and gained training in various skills (to a very limited degree, however, in the 19th century). By the end of the 19th century, little headway was made regarding custody of children. This was primarily related to the notion (supported by the courts) that to give a mother custody of the children while requiring the father to contribute significantly, if not entirely, to their financial support was unjust to the father. And the courts ultimately reflect prevailing notions of what is just and unjust. What we accept today as perfectly reasonable was beyond the comprehension of the 19th-century father. Until this change in attitude came about, mothers could not reasonably hope to gain custody. The only women who could hope for custody were those who had the wherewithal to support their children independently.

The change in attitude came about by what was possibly an unanticipated route—the Child Labor laws, passed in the early part of this century. Prior to the 20th century, children were an important economic asset. Before the appearance of the Child Labor laws, children as young as five or six years of age worked in such places as factories and mines and contributed to the family's support. In agricultural communities they were used as farm hands as well. Fathers,therefore, had the power to keep—and were very desirous of keeping—these important economic assets. With the passage of the Child Labor laws, children became less of a financial asset and more of a liability. These laws made fathers more receptive to giving up their children to their ex-wives and were an important factor in the 20th-century shift in attitude. Fathers no longer rallied around the flag of "injustice" when asked to support children in the homes of their ex-wives (Ramos, 1979).

In the 1920s the states gradually changed their laws, and custody was no longer automatically given to fathers. Rather, in many states the sex of the parent was not to be considered a factor in determining parental preference. Only criteria related to parental capacity—regardless of sex—were to be utilized. This change was incorporated in England in 1925 in the *Guardianship of Infants Act*, in which mothers and fathers were considered to be equal regarding the right to have custody of their children. During the next 50 years these statutes were generally interpreted in favor of mothers. A father had to prove a mother grossly unfit (e.g., an alcoholic, drug addict, or sexual "pervert") before he could even hope to gain custody. The notion that mothers were intrinsically preferable to fathers as child rearers came to be known as the *tender years presumption*. To the best of my knowledge this term was introduced by Justice Benjamin Cardozo in 1925. For the reader who is not appreciative of the significance of the word *presumption* as used in the law, the term generally refers to the principle that the judge, when making a decision regarding custody, must *presume* that the mother is the preferable parent. Under this presumption, the only way a father can get custody is if he is able to provide compelling evidence that the mother is unfit to bring up the children. It is the father, then, who had an uphill fight in custody disputes, not the mother. From the mid-1920s to the mid-1940s, i.e., until the end of World War

II, the divorce rate was relatively low. Accordingly, custody litigation was not too common. Since World War II, however, there has been a progessive increase in the divorce rate as well as a burgeoning of divorce litigation, especially custody litigation. Accordingly, after World War II we entered into what (at least from many lawyers' points of view) could be called the "Golden Age" of divorce and custody litigation. At no point in the history of the legal profession has there been a greater opportunity to earn "gold" from divorcing litigants than the mid-to-late 20th century.

WORLD WAR II TO THE 1960s

From the post-war period until the mid-1960s, the adversary system was the main one utilized in divorce cases. This was consistent with the concept that the kinds of indignities complained of in divorce conflicts were minor crimes called *torts* (*Latin:* wrongs). Because they were viewed as crimes, divorce conflicts were justifiably considered in the context of adversary proceedings. Divorce laws in most states were predicated on concepts of guilt and innocence, i.e., within the context of punishment and restitution. The divorce was granted only when the complainant or petitioner proved that he or she had been wronged or injured by the defendant or respondent. In most states the acceptable grounds for divorce were very narrowly defined and, depending upon the state, included such behavior as mental cruelty, adultery, abandonment, habitual drunkenness, nonsupport, and drug addiction. The law would punish the offending party by granting the divorce to the successful complainant. During this period, as was true at other times in history, adultery was one of the more common grounds for suing for divorce. But one had to have proof if one was to use this complaint successfully in the divorce litigation. Accordingly, it was common for people to bring in as evidence photographs taken in motel rooms. Sometimes these were bona fide, in that the spouse was actually involved in such an extramarital escapade. On occasion, however, a prostitute was used to provide the "photographic evidence" when there had been no actual infidelity.

If the court found that both the husband and the wife were guilty of marital wrongs, a divorce could not be granted. If *both* parties, for instance, had involved themselves in adulterous behavior, they could not get a divorce. Therefore, in such situations, the parties often agreed to alter the truth in a way that would result in their obtaining a divorce. Frequently one party would agree to be the adultress or the adulterer, or agree to be considered the one who had inflicted mental cruelty on the other. "Witnesses" were brought in (usually friends who were willing to lie in court) to testify in support of the various allegations, and everyone agreed to go through the theatrical performance. Even the judge knew that the play was necessary to perform if he or she was to have grounds to grant the divorce. All appreciated the cooperation of the witnesses, and there was practically no danger of their being prosecuted for their perjury. Although such proceedings rarely made headlines in the newspapers, the records were available for public scrutiny and distribution. The knowledge of this possibility became an additional burden to the person who, because of the greater desire for the divorce, was willing to be considered guilty while allowing the spouse to be considered innocent. In addition, there were possible untoward psychological sequelae resulting from the acceptance of the blame, and this could contribute to residual psychological problems following the divorce.

People involved in custody litigation are fighting. They are fighting for their most treasured possessions—their children. The stakes are extremely high. Litigation over money, property, and other matters associated with the divorce produce strong feelings of resentment and anger. However, they are less likely to result in reactions of rage and fury than are conflicts over the children. Children are the extensions of ourselves, our hopes for the future, and thereby closely tied up with our own identities. Fighting for them is almost like fighting for ourselves. The two may become indistinguishable, and the fight becomes a "fight for life."

The adversary system, which professes to help parents resolve their differences, is likely to intensify the hostilities that it claims it is designed to reduce. It provides the litigants with ammunition that they may not have realized they possessed. It contributes to an ever-increasing vicious cycle of vengeance—so much so that the litigation may bring about greater psychological damage than the pains and grief of the marriage that originally brought about the divorce. Although some attorneys appreciate well the terrible psychological trauma that may result from protracted adversary proceedings, other attorneys do not. For the latter, the name of the game is to win. They believe their reputations rest on their capacity to win, and they fear that if they appear to be moderate and conciliatory, they will lose clients. Lawyers recognize that the more protracted the litigation, the more money they are going to earn. In addition, they may lose perspective once they are swept up in the battle, so intent are they on winning. L. Nizer, in his book *My Life in Court* (1968), states: "All litigations evoke intense feelings of animosity, revenge and retribution. Some of them may be fought ruthlessly. But none of them, even in their most aggravated form, can equal the sheer, unadultered venom of a matrimonial contest." I would add to this the following: Of all the forms of marital litigation, the most vicious and venomous by far is custody litigation! The stakes are higher than in any other form of courtroom conflict in that the parents' most treasured possessions—the children—are at stake. Conflicts over money and property pale in comparison to the ruthlessness with which parents will fight over the children.

P.S. Weiss (1975) states the problem well:

> It is possible for lawyers to negotiate too hard. In pursuit of the best possible agreement for their clients, some lawyers seem to worsen the post-marital relationship of their clients and the clients' spouses. They may, for example, actively discourage a client from talking with his or her spouse for fear that the client will inadvertently weaken his or her negotiating position, or will in thoughtless generosity make concessions without obtaining anything in return. Or they may take positions more extreme than their client desires in order eventually to achieve an advantageous compromise, but by so doing anger the client's spouse and further alienate the spouse from the client. Some separated individuals reported that until negotiations were at an end, their relationship with their spouse became progressively worse.

S. Gettelman and J. Markowitz (1974) provide a good example of the problem:

> For many divorcing couples, their biggest headaches begin after they retain their respective attorneys. Recently we talked with the ex-wife of a famous and wealthy stage actor. It had taken her three years to obtain a divorce in California, which is one of the more progressive states! In her words, "Once the lawyers smelled money, they acted in cahoots to bleed us and draw out the proceedings." Although their separation had started out amicably, they grew to loathe each other; she believed that both his lawyers and her own successfully manipulated her and her husband into feeling victimized by each other.

C. Sopkin (1974) describes in dramatic terms how sordid and sadistic such litigation can be. He focuses particularly on the role of attorneys in intensifying and prolonging such conflicts. In his article "The Roughest Divorce Lawyers in Town" (although the "town" referred to by Sopkin is New York, the legal techniques described are ubiquitous and by no means confined to that city), he describes a brand of attorney often referred to in the field as a "bomber." Sopkin quotes one such bomber (Raoul Lionel Felder, a New York City divorce attorney) as saying: "If it comes to a fight, it is the lawyer's function using all ethical, legal and moral means to bring his adversary to his knees as fast as possible. Naturally, within this framework the lawyer must go for the soft spots." The kinds of antics that such lawyers utilize and promulgate are indeed hair-raising. One husband is advised to hire a gigolo to seduce his wife into a setting while a band of private detectives are engaged to serve as witnesses. Another husband is advised to get his English-born wife deported because she is not yet a citizen.

Elsewhere Sopkin states:

> Getting a lawyer out of his office is expensive, but to crank up a bomber, pump him full of righteous indignation and ship him down to the matrimonial courts can be terribly expensive—running from 15-, 20-, or 25-thousand dollars-....Bombers are in business to accommodate hate....But the incontrovertible fact remains that if there is big-time money at stake, or serious custody questions at stake, or you want to leave your husband/wife with nothing but a little scorched earth, get a bomber.

Although Sopkin's examples are not typical, they are not rare either. In litigation, winning is the name of the game. The lawyer with the reputation for being a "softie" is not going to have many clients. Although more humane and less pugilistic attorneys certainly exist, even their "fighting instincts" often come to the fore when they are caught up in adversary proceedings. Although the more sensitive may even then not be willing to stoop to the levels of the bombers, they still are likely to utilize a variety of deceptive maneuvers to win for their clients.

One attorney, H. A. Glieberman, in his book *Confessions of a Divorce Lawyer* (1975) states:

> I made sure that each client I handled—whatever else he or she thought about me—came away feeling two things. One, I was thorough as hell. Two, I was out to win. Frankly the second was easy. I love to argue and win....
>
> If a divorce was what someone wanted then my client and I became a team, did everything in our power, not just to win but to win big....
>
> There's only one rule on divorce settlements: If you represent the wife, get as much as possible. If you represent the husband, give away as little as possible....
>
> Now, as I walk through the outer door of my office heading for the courtroom, I know that I'm walking to a case where there will be no compromises, no conciliations, no good feelings to balance the bad. This will be an all-out confrontation, a real tooth and nail fight. I'll love it....
>
> Now finally we're here. And it's a real circus. The other side has two accountants, a tax lawyer, three expert witnesses and a defendant; our side has one accountant, a comptroller, no tax lawyer because I've become an expert at that, and seven expert witnesses.

The criticisms of the adversary system as applied to divorce and custody proceedings come not only from mental health professionals, but from some lawyers and judges as well. A judge, L.G. Forer (1975), criticizes the legal profession's own Code of Professional Responsibility—a criticism that is most relevant to divorce and custody litigation:

> A lawyer is licensed by the government and is under a sworn duty to uphold and defend the law and the Constitution of the United States. Despite the license and the oath, the role of the lawyer is by definition and by law amoral....He must press the position of his client even though it is contrary

to the public good, popular opinion and widely accepted standards of behavior. Canon 7 of the Code of Professional Responsibility promulgated by the American Bar Association declares in part, "The duty of the lawyer, both to his client and to the legal system, is to represent his client zealously within the bounds of the law." In other words, the skilled judgment of the lawyer that his client's case is spurious or without merit is irrelevant. The lawyer must, therefore, be a Hessian, a mercenary, available for hire to do the bidding of whoever pays him....If the client wishes to sue or contest a claim, the lawyer must either zealously pursue his client's interest or withdraw from the case. If Lawyer A withdraws, Lawyer B will accept the case and the fee.

Another judge, B.C. Lindsley (1980), is critical of the utilization of the adversary system in custody disputes. He states:

The adversary process, historically effective in resolving disputes between litigants over contracts, torts, business matters, and criminal charges, where objective evidentiary facts have probative signifiance, is not suited to the resolution of most relations problems. In family disputes, the evidence that we would find most meaningful is more likely to consist of subtle, subjective human relations factors best identified and discerned by psychologists and behaviorists who do not approach the inquiry as antagonists. When you add the concept of "fault" as the necessary basis for deciding questions relating to the family, I think it is fair to say that no other process is more likely to rip husband, wife, father, mother, and child apart so thoroughly and bitterly.

A highly respected judge who has concerned himself deeply with mental health issues, D.L. Bazelon (1974), holds that the adversary system is not necessarily detrimental to clients. Its ultimate aim, he states, is to gain knowledge and resolve differences. It attempts to resolve differences through the opposition of opposing positions. Its ultimate aim is resolution, and the cross-examination process is one of the important ways in which information is gained. I am in agreement with Bazelon regarding the methods and aims of the adversary system. I am not, however, in agreement with his statement regarding the risk of detriment to clients. His statement that the adversary system is "not necessarily" detrimental implies little risk for the development of psychopathology. My experience has been that in divorce, and especially custody cases, the risk for the development of psychopathology is extremely high. Elsewhere (1986a) I have described in detail a wide variety of psychopathological reactions to protracted divorce and/or custody litigation. Bazelon's position is idealistic in that he does not make reference to the sly tricks, duplicity, courtroom antics, and devious maneuvers that lawyers will often utilize in order to win. He makes no mention of attorney's attempts to unreasonably discredit the experts, cast aspersions on their characters, and try to make them look silly or stupid.

Although Judge Bazelon's view is that of the majority of jurists today, there are dissenters among the judiciary. One of the most outspoken critics of the use of the adversary system in solving custody disputes is Judge B.C. Lindsley, who states (1976):

> The adversary process, historically effective in resolving disputes between litigants where evidentiary facts have probative significance, is not properly suited to the resolution of most family relations problems....Where there are children and the parties cannot or will not recognize the impact of the disintegration of the marriage upon the children, where they fail to perceive their primary responsibilities as parents—i.e., custody and visitation—we make it possible for parents to carry out that struggle by the old, adversary, fault-finding, condemnation approach....This kind of battle is destructive to

the welfare, best interests, and emotional health of their children.

S.J. Berger, a Cleveland attorney, has made what may be the most compelling statement about adversarial proceedings in divorce/custody litigation (1985):

> In all that is decent...in all that is just, the framers of our Constitution could never have intended that the "enjoyment of life" meant that if divorce came, it was to be attended by throwing the two unfortunates and their children into a judicial arena, with lawyers as their seconds, and have them tear and verbally slash at each other in a trial by emotional conflict that may go on in perpetuity. We have been humane enough to outlaw cockfights, dogfights, and bullfights; and yet, we do nothing about the barbarism of divorce fighting, and trying to find ways to end it. We concern ourselves with cruelty to animals, and rightfully so, but we are unconcerned about the forced and intentionally perpetrated cruelty inflicted upon the emotionally distressed involved in divorce. We abhor police beating confessions out of alleged criminals, and yet we cheer and encourage lawyers to emotionally beat up and abuse two innocent people and their children, because their marriage has floundered. Somewhere along the line, our sense of values, decency, humanism and justice went off the track.

I fully appreciate that many attorneys begin their involvement with divorcing litigants by attempting to calm them down and bring about some compromises in their demands. However, when such efforts fail, many get swept up in the conflict and join their clients in trying to win the battle and punish the spouse. (Taking the children away is one predictable way of implementing such punishment.) The training of lawyers primes them for such encounters. Therapists, because of their orientation toward understanding and reducing hostility, are less likely to rise so quickly to a patient's cry for battle and lust for vengeance. Accordingly, lawyers are often criticized for inflaming their clients, adding to their hostility, and thereby worsening divorcing spouses' difficulties. A common retort to this criticism is: "We're only doing what our clients ask us to do." Such lawyers claim that they are just the innocent tools of their clients and that their obligation is to respond to their clients' wishes, even though such advocacy may be detrimental to the client, the spouse, and the children.

I believe that this response is a rationalization. I believe that lawyers have greater freedom to disengage themselves from a client's destructive behavior than they profess. I believe that financial considerations often contribute to their going along with the client. (I fully recognize that there are physicians, as well, who recommend unnecessary medical treatment. For both professions the practice is unconscionable.) There are attorneys who discourage their clients from litigating in court with the professed reason that it may be psychologically damaging. This may only be a coverup. In actuality they appreciate that they may reduce their income per hour if they go to court—because only the wealthiest clients can afford the formidable expense of protracted courtroom litigation. To the wealthy client, the latter consideration does not often serve as a deterrent for the lawyer, and the psychological considerations are then often ignored.

There are many couples who, at the time of the separation, make a serious attempt to avoid psychologically debilitating litigation. Having observed the deterioration of friends and relatives who have undergone prolonged litigation, they genuinely want to make every attempt to avoid such unnecessary and traumatic sequelae to their own divorce. Unfortunately, many such well-meaning couples, in spite of every attempt to avoid such a catastrophe, gradually descend into the same kind of psychologically devastating experience. An important contributing element to such unfortunate disintegration relates to the anger and rage engendered by their having involved themselves in protracted adversary proceedings. The system fosters sadism. The aim of simply *winning* often degenerates into one in which each side is bent on depleting the other of funds, producing psychological deterioration, or even destroying the other party. The result, however, is most often a Pyrrhic victory in which both sides lose, even though one may ostensibly be the winner.

Venting anger tends to feed on itself. The notion that anger merely needs to be dissipated, and then the individual is free from it, is probably an oversimplification. The fact that some expression of anger is necessary and that its release can produce some feeling of catharsis is certainly the case. However, it appears that another phenomenon may also be operative, especially when anger is great. Here the expression of anger does not result in its dissipation but rather in its intensification. When a person starts to "roll" with anger, more anger may be generated. It appears to have an existence of its own. An extreme example of this is the murderer who stabs the victim to death with a knife thrust into the heart. Although the victim is now dead, the murderer continues to stab the dead body repeatedly. Obviously, there is no further useful purpose for such anger release. In less dramatic ways individuals, once angry, tend to perpetuate the process. And protracted divorce litigation is an excellent demonstration of this phenomenon. The fight intensifies and rolls on for months and even years, having a life of its own, almost independent from the original issues that began the litigation in the first place.

A common result of parents being swept up in such litigation is that they blind themselves to the stupidity of what they are doing. A father, for example, may be so blinded by his rage that he fails to appreciate that he is giving far more money to his attorney (and possibly his wife's, in that he may be paying her lawyer as well) than he would have given to his wife had he agreed to her original request at the outset. The depletion of funds to his wife not only compromises her psychological stability but that of his children as well. The more psychologically and/or financially debilitated she is, the more impaired will be the children's upbringing. One mother, who lived in a large house with the children, made every attempt to increase her husband's bills as much as possible. She turned on the heating system to maximum capacity and, simultaneously, turned on every air conditioning unit in the house. Both systems would operate simultaneously, sometimes up to 24 hours a day. Every electrical outlet was used to maximum capacity at the same time, to the point where the house was blazing with light for days and weeks, especially on vacations. All this was done with the knowledge and support of her lawyer! Every form of destructive act known to mankind has been perpetrated by one parent upon the other in the course of custody litigation—and even murder is not unknown (I myself had such a case recently).

1960s TO THE MID-1970s

In the 1960s we began to witness greater appreciation by state legislatures of the fact that the traditional grounds for divorce are not simply wrongs perpetrated by one party against the other, but that both parties have usually contributed to the marital breakdown. In addition, the kinds of behavior complained of by the petitioner came to be viewed less as crimes and more as personality differences, aberrations, and/or psychopathology.

With such realization came the appreciation that adversary proceedings were not well suited to deal with such conflicts. Accordingly, an ever-growing number of states have changed their laws regarding the grounds for divorce and the ways in which people can dissolve their marriages. These recent statutes are generally referred to as *no-fault divorce laws*. They provide much more liberal criteria for the granting of a divorce. For example, if both parties agree to the divorce, their living apart for a prescribed period may be all that is necessary. (And the period may be shorter if no children are involved.) One does not have the problem of designating a guilty and an innocent party. Some states will grant a divorce on the basis of "incompatibility." The term may not be defined any further, and it may be quite easy for the couple to demonstrate that they are incompatible. The latest phase of such liberalization enables some individuals to divorce entirely without legal assistance. In California, a state that has often been at the forefront of such liberalization, a couple can now obtain a divorce via mail and the payment of a small fee, if they have no children and there is no conflict over property.

The passage of no-fault divorce laws has been, without question, a significant step forward. By removing it from adversary proceedings, a divorce is more readily, less traumatically, and usually less expensively obtained. However, many no-fault divorce laws require the agreement of *both* parties to satisfy the recent liberal criteria. Divorce can rarely be obtained unilaterally. If one party does not agree, then adversary proceedings are necessary if the person desiring the divorce is to have any hope of getting it. In addition, the new laws have not altered the necessity of resorting to adversary proceedings when there is conflict over such issues as visitation, support, alimony, and custody. Although no-fault divorce laws have reduced considerably the frequency of courtroom conflicts over divorce, litigation over custody is not only very much with us, but for reasons to be described soon, is on the increase. And the adversary system—a system designed to determine whether an accused individual has committed a criminal act—is being used to determine which of two parents would serve better as custodian for their children.

MID-1970s TO THE PRESENT

In the mid-1970s we began to see a male "backlash" to the tender years presumption. Maternal preference is "sexist" complained many fathers. The notion that a woman is automatically a preferable parent, they claimed, is as much a sexist concept as the idea that a man should automatically be considered the preferable parent. The courts were asked to look again at the laws with which they were working and to apply more closely what was stated therein. In many states the old statutes, passed in the mid-1920s, were applicable and were interpreted more strictly along "sex-blind" lines. In most states, however, new statutes were passed that clearly stated that the sex of a parent should not be a consideration when courts were asked to settle custody disputes. The tender years presumption was replaced with the *best interests of the child presumption.* And the assumption was made that children's interests would be best served if the courts were "sex blind" in their ruling of custody disputes. (In Chapter Seven I will discuss in detail my views on the judiciousness of the concept that sex-blind custody decisions necessarily serve the best interests of the child.)

Suddenly, fathers who had previously thought that they had no chance of gaining custody found out that they had. But love of the children and concern for their welfare was not the only motive for fathers who were now beginning to fight for custody. Less noble motives such as vengeance, guilt assuagement, and competition were now allowed expression and possibly even realization. Since the mid-1970s, then, children have become "open territory" in child custody conflicts. The frequency of such litigation is burgeoning, and there is no evidence for a decline in the near future. New interpretations (or, strictly speaking, reexamination) of the original statutes have increased the complexity of such litigation as well. As A.P. Derdeyn (1978) points out, courts now have to work much harder. Traditional formulas all fell along what would now be considered sexist lines. Using such formulas made the judge's work easier. The child automatically went either to the father or the mother, depending on the particular period in history. Now a detailed inquiry into each parent's parental assets and liabilities is necessary before anything approaching a judicious decision can be made.

During the half-century (the mid-1920s to the mid-1970s) when the tender years presumption prevailed, fathers recognized that they had little chance of gaining custody of their children following separation and divorce. During that period a father might say to his lawyer, "Look, she's making inordinate financial demands. They're crazy. Let's do this. Let's go for custody of the children and then, at the final negotiations, we'll give up our demand for custody if she'll come down on her financial requests." The lawyer might then ask the father whether his wife was a prostitute, drug addict, chronic alcoholic, was sexually promiscuous in front of the children, had been committed to an insane asylum, etc. If the answer to these questions were all negative, then the lawyer would inform the client that there was absolutely no chance that he could gain custody. However, under the best interests of the child presumption, such a father need not prove that his wife exhibits profound impairments in parenting capacity. Presumably, he comes before the court as an equal to his wife and presumably has as much a chance as she for gaining custody. Presumably the courts are operating on the principle that the sex of a parent shall not be a consideration when ruling in such disputes. I have repeated and emphasized the word *presumably* here because, in fact, courts have not rejected the tender years presumption so quickly. Many so-called old-fashioned judges still hold that a mother is intrinsically superior to the father when it comes to raising children. (Later in this book I will comment on this idea.) We see then, when we look back over the span of history, that there was only a 25-year period—from the mid-1920s to the mid-1970s—when mothers were viewed to be the preferable custodial parent following divorce. Prior to that time fathers were generally considered to be the preferable parent, and since then mothers and fathers have been considered to be equally capable, at least in the eyes of the law.

In the late 1970s and early 1980s we see the development of another phenomenon that has markedly affected judicial procedures regarding custody determinations. This has been the increasing popularity of the joint custody concept. The idea that one parent should be designated the sole custodial parent and the other the visitor came to be viewed as inegalitarian in that the visiting parent could not but feel inferior regarding his or her status as a parent contributing to the child-rearing process. The basic theory of the joint custody concept is that every attempt should be made to approximate as closely as possible the kind of situation that prevailed in the marital home, a situation in which both parents contributed to the child's upbringing. The concept has become so popular that in some states the judge must order a joint custodial arrangement unless there are compelling reasons to consider another custodial plan. Ideally, in order for the joint custodial concept to work, both parents must be able to communicate and cooperate well with each other and to be equally capable of assuming child-rearing responsibilities. Furthermore, their living situation must be one in which they can both participate in bringing the children to and from school. Central to the concept is that there is no specific schedule. Rather, the determination as to where the children will be at any particular point is decided by criteria relevant to the needs and obligations of the parent and, to a lesser degree, the desires of the children.

The main drawback of granting joint custody so frequently and automatically is that it may do many children more harm than good. For example, it increases the chances that they will be used as weapons or spies in parental conflicts. Because no restraints are placed on noncooperating parents, such use of the children is likely. Children then become used like ropes in a tug of war. They are in a no-man's land in which they are "up for grabs" by either parent. Obviously, in such situations the children may suffer formidable psychological damage. Certainly the sole custodial arrangement cannot protect children entirely from being so used, but it does reduce the opportunities for parents to involve their children in such manipulations. Furthermore, automatic awarding of joint custody seldom takes into consideration the logistics of school attendance. Therefore, it can cause problems in the educational realm as well. Parents now litigate for joint custody. I believe that if one litigates for joint custody one is not a candidate for the arrangement. A meaningful joint custodial arrangement requires the parents to be able to cooperate and communicate well with one another, especially with regard to caring for their children. Parents who resort to litigating for custody have proven themselves incapable of cooperating with one another and, in most cases, are not communicating well either.

Strong proponents of the joint custodial concept hold that it circumvents the loss of self-esteem suffered by the parent who is designated the visitor and makes him or her (usually him) feel like a second-class citizen when compared to the parent who is designated to have primary or sole custody. I believe that the attempt to enhance self-esteem by giving an individual a different label is psychologically naive.

Self-esteem is far too complex an issue to be affected significantly by this relatively minor factor. Yet there are individuals who will litigate for joint custody because they believe that such designation will thereby enhance their feelings of self-worth. Although I am basically in sympathy with the joint custodial concept I believe that its injudicious utilization has contributed to the burgeoning of divorce litigation that we have witnessed since the concept came into vogue.

Joint custody decisions enable judges to avoid a complex and difficult fact-finding task by offering a seemingly benevolent resolution. It certainly is easier for a judge to award joint custody than to deliberate about all the mind-boggling issues involved in a custody conflict. And judges who circumvent such challenges often justify their actions by considering themselves advanced and modern thinkers, in tune with the sexual egalitarianism of today's society. It is for these reasons that many family lawyers and psychiatrists are beginning to view joint custody as a judicial "cop-out."

And this is where we stand today in the late 1980s. At no time in the history of Western civilization has there been more litgation over custody and, unfortunately, the adversary system—a system designed to determine whether an accused party has committed a criminal act—is the method most commonly used to determine which is the preferable parent. In most cases, the people primarily involved in making such decisions—judges and attorneys—have little, if any, training in child development and psychology. Yet it is they who have traditionally been left with the decision as to who is the better parent for custodial purposes, working within the context of a system that may be one of the poorest yet devised to help investigate and deal with such disputes. Many forms of psychopathology result from the utilization of this system as a method for resolving divorce and/or custody conflicts. I have described these in greater detail elsewhere (1986a). In the next chapter I will focus on the parental alienation syndrome, one of the most common forms of psychiatric disorder that results from the attempt to deal with divorce/custody disputes within the adversary system.

THREE

THE PARENTAL ALIENATION SYNDROME

INTRODUCTION

Prior to the early 1980s I certainly saw children whom I considered to have been brainwashed by one parent against the other. However, since that period I have seen, with ever increasing frequency, a disorder that I rarely saw previously. This disorder arose primarily in children who had been involved in protracted custody litigation. It is now so common that I see manifestations of it in about 90 percent of children who have been involved in custody conflicts. Because of its increasing frequency and the fact that a typical picture is observed – different from simple brainwashing – I believe a special designation is warranted. Accordingly, I have termed this disorder the *parental alienation syndrome.*

I have introduced this term to refer to a disturbance in which children are preoccupied with deprecation and criticism of a parent—denigration that is unjustified and/or exaggerated. The notion that such children are merely "brainwashed" is narrow. The term *brainwashing* implies that one parent is systematically and consciously programming the child to denigrate the other. The concept of the parental alienation syndrome includes the brainwashing component, but is much more inclusive. It includes not only conscious but subconscious and unconscious factors within the programming parent that contribute to the child's alienation from the other. Furthermore (and this is extremely important), it includes factors that arise within the child—independent of the parental contributions—that play a role in the development of the syndrome. In addition, situational factors may contribute, i.e., factors that exist in the family and the environment that may play a role in bringing about the disorder.

There are two important reasons for the recent dramatic increase in the prevalence of this syndrome. The first relates to the fact that since the mid-to-late 1970s, courts have generally taken the position that the tender years presumption (that mothers are intrinsically superior to fathers as parents) is sexist and that custodial determinations should be made on criteria relating directly to parenting capacity, independent of a parent's sex. This concept became known as the *best interests of the child presumption*. In the late 1970s and early 1980s the joint custodial arrangement became increasingly popular. The notion that one parent be designated the *sole* custodian and the other the *visitor* was considered inegalitarian; joint custody promised a more equal division of time with the children and decision-making powers. Both of these developments have had the effect of making children's custodial designations far more unpredictable and precarious. As a result, parents are more frequently brainwashing their children in order to insure "victory" in custody litigation. And the children themselves have joined forces with the preferred parent in order to preserve what they consider to be the most stable arrangement, without appreciation of the fact that in some cases primary custody by the denigrated parent might be in their best interests.

As will be discussed in greater detail in Chapter Seven, the aforementioned two changes have placed women at a disadvantage in custody disputes. Under the tender years presumption, mothers were secure in the knowledge that fathers had to prove compellingly significant deficiencies in their wives' parenting capacity before they could even hope to wrest custody of the children. Under the best interests of the child presumption, especially when the sex-blind doctrine was used in its implementation, mothers' positions became less secure. And, with the subsequent popularization of the joint custodial concept, their positions became even more precarious. Accordingly, mothers have been more likely than fathers to attempt to alienate their children against fathers in order to strengthen their positions in custody conflicts. And, for reasons to be elaborated upon in Chapter Seven, children have been supporting their mothers much more than their fathers, providing thereby their own contributions to the parental alienation syndrome.

Because of this clinical phenomenon, namely, that mothers are more likely than fathers to be the alienators ("brainwashers"), I will, for simplicity of presentation, refer more frequently to the mother as the preferred or "loved" parent and the father as the rejected or the "hated" parent. I place the words *loved* and *hated* in quotes because there is still much love for the so-called hated parent and much hostility toward the allegedly loved one. This does not preclude my observation that on occasion (probably in around 10 percent of cases) it is the father who is the preferred parent and the mother the despised one. It would be an error for the reader to conclude that the designation of the mother as the preferred parent and the father as the hated represents some sexist bias on my part. Rather, it is merely a reflection of my own observation as well as others who work in the field. It also would be an error for the reader to conclude that my belief that mothers, more often than fathers, as the active contributors to the brainwashing components necessarily implies condemnation of these women. Actually, as I will discuss in detail in Chapter Seven, I am in sympathy with mothers here and believe that they have been "short-changed" by the aforementioned recent developments.

In this chapter I will first describe the most common manifestations of the parental alienation syndrome. I will then describe the factors that I consider to be operative in bringing about the disorder. I will divide such contributing factors into four categories: 1) brainwashing (conscious programming), 2) subconscious and unconscious programming, 3) the child's contributions, and 4) situational factors. In Chapter Seven I will discuss approaches to the prevention and treatment of this disorder.

THE MANIFESTATIONS OF THE PARENTAL ALIENATION SYNDROME

Typically the child is obsessed with "hatred" of a parent. (The word *hatred* is placed in quotes because, as will be discussed, there are still many tender and loving feelings felt toward the allegedly despised parent that are not permitted expression.) These children speak of the hated parent with every vilification and profanity in their vocabulary—without embarrassment or guilt. The denigration of the parent often has the quality of a litany. After only minimal prompting by a lawyer, judge, probation officer, mental health profession-al, or other person involved in the litigation, the record will be turned on and a command performance provided. Not only is there a rehearsed quality to the speech, but one often hears phraseology that is not usually used by the child. Many expressions are identical to those used by the "loved" parent. (Again, the word *loved* is placed in quotations because hostility toward that parent may similarly be unexpressed.) Typical examples: "He harrasses us." "He sexually molested me." "His new girlfriend is a whore."

Even years after they have taken place, the child may justify the alienation with memories of minor altercations experienced in the relationship with the hated parent. These are usually trivial and are experiences that most children quickly forget, e.g., "He always used to speak very loud when he told me to brush my teeth." "He used to tell me to get his things a lot." "She used to say to me 'Don't interrupt.'" "He used to make a lot of noise when he chewed at the table." When these children are asked to give more compelling reasons for the hatred, they are unable to provide them. Frequently, the loved parent will agree with the child that these professed reasons justify the ongoing animosity.

The professions of hatred are most intense when the children and the loved parent are in the presence of the alienated one. However, when the child is alone with the allegedly hated parent, he or she may exhibit anything from hatred, to neutrality, to expressions of affection. When these children are with the hated parent, they may let their guard down and start to enjoy themselves. Then, almost as if they have realized that they are doing something "wrong," they will suddenly stiffen up and resume their expressions of withdrawal and animosity. Another maneuver commonly seen in this situation is the child's professing affection to one parent and asking that parent to swear that he or she will not reveal to the other parent the professions of love. And the same statement is made to the other parent. In this way these children "cover their tracks" and thereby avoid the disclosure of their schemes. Such children may find family interviews with therapists extremely anxiety provoking because of the fear that their manipulations and maneuvers will be divulged. The loved parent's proximity plays an important role in what the child will say to the hated one. The closer the loved parent, when the child is with the hated one, the greater the likelihood the hated parent will be denigrated. When seen alone, the child is likely to modify the litany in accordance with which parent is in the waiting room. Judges, lawyers, and mental health professionals who interview such children should recognize this important phenomenon.

The hatred of the parent often extends to include that parent's complete extended family. Cousins, aunts, uncles, and grandparents, with whom the child previously may have had loving relationships, are now viewed as similarly obnoxious. Grandparents, who previously had a loving and tender relationship with the child, who welled up with joy and pride over their relationship with the child, now find themselves suddenly and inexplicably rejected. The child has no guilt over such rejection nor does the loved parent. Greeting cards are not reciprocated. Presents sent to the home are refused, remain unopened, or even destroyed (generally in the presence of the loved parent). When the hated parent's relatives call on the telephone, the child will respond with angry vilifications or quickly hang up on the caller (These responses are more likely to occur if the loved parent is within hearing distance of the conversation.) With regard to the hatred of the relatives, the child is even less capable of providing justifications for the animosity. The rage of these children is so great that they become completely oblivious to the privations they are causing themselves. Again, the loved parent is typically unconcerned with the untoward psychological effects on the child of this rejection of relatives who previously provided important psychological gratifications.

In family conferences, in which the children are seen

together with both the loved and hated parent, the children reflexly take the position of the loved parent—sometimes even before the hated parent has had the opportunity to present his or her side of the argument. Even the loved parent may not present his or her argument as forcefully as the supporting child. These children may even refuse to accept evidence that is obvious proof of the hated parent's position. For example, one boy's mother claimed that her husband was giving her absolutely no money at all. When the father showed the boy cancelled checks, signed by him and endorsed by the mother, the boy claimed that they were "forged." One girl claimed, after the death of her paternal grandfather from cancer, that it was her mother who had murdered him. Even after the father denied that the mother had murdered his father, the child still persisted with the accusation. Commonly these children will accept as 100 percent valid the allegations of the loved parent against the hated one. One boy's mother claimed that her husband had beaten her on numerous occasions. The child presented this as one of the reasons why he hated his father. The father denied that he had ever laid a finger on the mother; in contrast, he claimed that the mother on a number of occasions had struck him. When I asked the child if he had ever *seen* his father hit his mother, he claimed that he had not, but he claimed that he believed his mother and insisted that she would never lie to him. In this situation, as a result of an exhaustive evaluation, I concluded that the father's rendition was far more likely to have been valid.

Another symptom of the parental alienation syndrome is complete lack of ambivalence. All human relationships are ambivalent, and parent-child relationships are no exception. The concept of "mixed feelings" has no place in these children's scheme of things. The hated parent is "all bad" and the loved parent is "all good." Most children (normals as well as those with a wide variety of psychiatric problems), when asked to list both good and bad things about each parent, will generally be able to do so. When children with parental alienation syndrome are asked to provide the same lists, both good and bad things about each parent, they will typically recite a long list of criticisms of the hated parent, but will not be able to think of one positive or redeeming personality trait. In contrast, they will provide only positive qualities for the preferred parent and claim to be unable to think of even one trait they dislike. The hated parent may have been deeply dedicated to the child's upbringing, and a strong bond may have been created over many years. The hated parent may produce photos that demonstrate clearly a joyful and deep relationship in which there was significant affection, tenderness, and mutual pleasure. But the memory of all these experiences appears to have been obliterated. When these children are shown photos of enjoyable events with the hated parent, they usually rationalize the experiences as having been forgotten, nonexistent, or feigned: "I really hated being with him then; I just smiled in the picture because he made me. He said he'd hit me if I didn't smile." "She used to beat me to make me go to the zoo with her." This element of complete lack of ambivalence is a typical manifestation of the parental alienation syndrome and should make one dubious about the depth of the professed animosity.

The child may exhibit a guiltless disregard for the feelings of the hated parent. There will be a complete absence of gratitude for gifts, support payments, and other manifestations of the hated parent's continued involvement and affection. Often these children will want to be certain the alienated parent continues to provide support payments, but at the same time adamantly refuse to visit. Commonly they will say that they *never* want to see the hated parent again, or not until their late teens or early twenties. To such a child I might say: "So you want your father to continue paying for all your food, clothing, rent, and education—even private high school and college—and yet you still don't want to see him at all, ever again. Is that right?" Such a child might respond: "That's right. He doesn't deserve to see me. He's mean and paying all that money is a good punishment for him."

Those who have never seen such children may consider this description a caricature. Those who have seen them will recognize the description immediately, although some children may not manifest all the symptoms. The parental alienation syndrome is becoming increasingly common, and there is good reason to predict that it will become even more common in the immediate future if custody conflicts become even more prevalent and if the recommendations presented in Chapter Seven are not implemented.

FACTORS THAT CONTRIBUTE TO THE DEVELOPMENT OF THE PARENTAL ALIENATION SYNDROME

As mentioned, the parental alienation syndrome should not be viewed simply as due to *brainwashing*—the act of systematic programming of the child by one parent against the other, in a consciously planned endeavor. This is only one of four factors, each of which I will discuss separately.

Brainwashing

The brainwashing factor may be present to varying degrees. In some cases it may be minimal or even absent, and the disturbance results from one or more of the other contributing factors. More often, however, it is one of the predominant factors. I confine the word brainwashing to *conscious* acts of programming the child against the other parent. Most often the brainwashing is overt and obvious to the sensitive and astute examiner. The loved parent embarks upon an unrelenting campaign of denigration that may last for years. A mother, for example, whose divorce was the result of marital problems that contributed to her husband's seeking the affection of another woman, may continually vilify the father to her children with such terms as "adulterer," "philanderer," and "abandoner." Similarly, she may refer to the father's new woman friend as a "slut," "whore," and "home breaker." No attention is given to the problems in the marriage, especially this mother's problem(s), that may have contributed to the new involvement.

At times the criticisms may even be delusional, but the child is brought to believe entirely the validity of the accusations. The child may thereby come to view the hated parent as the incarnation of all the evil that has ever existed on earth. A father, for example, may develop the delusion that his wife has been unfaithful to him and may even divorce her without any specific evidence for an affair. Innocent conversations with strange men are viewed as "proof" of her infidelity, and the children may come to view their mother as an adulteress. Often the infrequency of visits or lack of contact with the hated parent facilitates the child's accepting completely the loved parent's criticisms. There is little or no opportunity to correct the distortions by actual experiences.

A common form of criticism of the father is to complain about how little money he is giving. I am not referring here to situations in which the divorce has brought about a certain amount of predictable privation. The healthy mother in such a situation recognizes that she and the children will not enjoy the same financial flexibility that they had prior to the separation. I am referring here to the use of the financial restrictions in the service of deprecating the father. A mother may complain so much about her financial restrictions that she will lead the children to believe that they may actually go without food, clothing, shelter, and that they may very well freeze and/or starve to death. I have seen cases in which extremely wealthy women utilized this maneuver, women who have been left with so much money that they will be comfortable for the rest of their lives. They may be spending thousands of dollars on extravagances, and yet the children may come to believe that because of their fathers' stinginess they are constantly on the verge of starvation.

There are mothers who, when talking to the children about their husbands having left the home, will make such statements as, "Your father's abandoned us." In most cases the father has left the mother and has not lost any affection for the children. Lumping the children together with herself (by using the word "us" rather than "me") promulgates the notion that they too have been rejected. In this way the mother contributed to the children's view of the father as reprehensible. The father in such situations may attempt (often unsuccessfully) to reassure the children that he has left the mother and not them, that he no longer loves the mother, but he still loves them.

Another way of brainwashing is to exaggerate a parent's minor psychological problems. The parent who may have drunk a little extra alcohol on occasion will gradually become spoken of as "an alcoholic." And the parent who may have experimented occasionally with drugs comes to be viewed as "a drug addict." Even though the accusing parent may have joined with the former spouse in such experimentation with drugs, the vilified parent is given the epithet. The deprecated parent might then be described in quite "colorful" terms: "He was dead drunk that night and he was literally out cold on the floor. We had to drag him to the car and dump him in the back seat." "The man was so stoned that he didn't have the faintest idea where he was and what he was doing." Often denial by the accused parent proves futile, especially if the accuser can provide concrete evidence such as a pipe used to smoke marijuana or a collection of bottles of liquor (which may be no more than the average person has in one's home anyway).

There are parents who are quite creative in their brainwashing maneuvers. A father calls the home to speak to his son. The mother answers the telephone and happens to be in the son's room at the time. The father simply asks if he can speak with his son. The mother (with the boy right next to her) says nothing. Again, the father asks to speak with his son. More silence (during which the son is unable to hear his father's pleas for a response). Finally, the mother responds: "I'm glad he can't hear what you're saying right now" or "If he heard what you just said, I'm sure he would never speak with you again." When the father finally speaks with the boy and explains that he had said absolutely nothing that was critical, the boy may be incredulous. The result is that the father becomes very fearful of calling his son, lest he again be trapped in this way. A related maneuver is for the mother to say to the calling father (again when the boy is within earshot of the mother and the father has made an innocuous statement): "That's *your* opinion. In *my* opinion he's a *very fine* boy." The implication here is that the father has made some scathing criticism and that the mother is defending the child.

Another mother greets her husband at the front door while their daughter is upstairs awaiting her father's visitation. Although the conversation is calm and unemotional, the mother suddenly dashes to the corner of the room, buries her head in her arms, and while cowering in the corner screams out, "No, no, no. Don't hit me again." The girl comes running into the living room, and although she did not actually observe her father hit her mother, she believes her mother's claim that her father had just pulled himself back from beating her when he heard the girl coming down the stairs.

Selected use of pictures can also be used in the brainwashing process. There is hardly a child who hasn't at some time or other refused to be in a family picture. There is hardly a family who hasn't had the experience of cajoling the child to join them in the photograph. In many families a picture of the crying child will be taken, with a fond memory of the situation, the child's crying notwithstanding. Such a picture may be used by a brainwashing parent to convince the child that the other parent caused the child's grief and tears. The parent who is collecting evidence for litigation may be very quick to take pictures that could be interpreted as proof of the other parent's hostility toward the child. The healthy parent will argue with a child, scream once in a while, and make threatening gestures. If these can be caught on the camera they are considered to be good evidence for the parent's sadistic behavior toward the child.

Sarcasm is another way of getting across the message that the father is an undesirable character. A mother might say, "Isn't that wonderful, he's taking you to a ballgame." Although the words themselves are innocent enough, and might very well apply in a benevolent or noncharged situation, the sarcastic tonal quality says just the opposite. It implies: "After all these years he's finally gotten around to taking you to a ballgame" or "He really considers himself a big sport for parting with the few bucks he's spending to take you to a ballgame." Another mother says, in a singsong way, "Well, here he is again, your good ol' Daddy-O." Another says to her daughter, "So, the knight-in-shining-armor took his damsel to the movies." These comments are powerful forms of deprecation. If a therapist were to attempt to point out to such a mother how undermining these comments are, she might respond that she was "only kidding" and he or she might be accused of not having a good sense of humor.

A common maneuver used by these mothers is to instruct their children to tell their father that they are not at home when he calls. Or, they will tell them to give excuses like "She's in the bathroom" or "She's in the shower." These children are not only being taught to be deceitful, but they are being used as accomplices in the war between the parents. Of pertinence here is the message that the father is not an individual who is worthy of being treated with honesty and respect. Furthermore, there is the implication that he has objectionable qualities that warrant his being lied to and rejected. One mother told her children not to reveal the name and location of the day camp they were attending, and the children dutifully submitted to their mother's demand. When questioned in family session as to why she gave her children these instructions, she could only come up with a series of weak rationalizations: "He'll go to the camp and make trouble," "He'll embarrass them when he visits," and "I just get the feeling that it's not good for them for their father to know where they're going to camp." I knew the husband well enough to know that there was absolutely no justification for these concerns. Clearly, this mother was using the children as accomplices in her war and they were submitting.

Subtle and Often Unconscious Parental Programming

The aforementioned attempts to denigrate a parent are conscious and deliberate. The brainwashing parent is well aware of what he or she is doing. There are, however, other ways of programming children that can be equally if not more effective, but which do not involve the parents actually recognizing what is going on. In this way the parent can profess innocence of brainwashing propensities. The motivations and mechanisms here are either unconscious (completely unavailable to conscious awareness) or subconscious (not easily available to conscious awareness).

There are many ways in which a parent may subtly and

often unconciously contribute to the alienation. A parent may profess to be a strong subscriber to the common advice: "Never criticize the other parent to the child." A mother may use this advice with comments such as: "There are things I could say about your father that would make your hair stand on end, but I'm not the kind of a person who criticizes a parent to his children." Such a comment engenders far more fear, distrust, and even hatred than would the presentation of an actual list of the father's alleged defects. A mother who insists that a father park his car at a specific distance from the home and honk the horn, rather than ring the doorbell, is implicitly saying to the child: "The person in that car is a dangerous and/or undesirable individual, someone whom I would not want to ring the doorbell of my house, let alone enter—even to say hello." The parent who expresses neutrality regarding visitation ("I respect her decision regarding whether or not she wishes to visit with her mother") is essentially communicating criticism of the noncustodial parent. The healthy parent appreciates how vital is the children's ongoing involvement with the noncustodial parent and encourages visitation, even when the child is "not in the mood." The healthy parent does not accept inconsequential and frivolous reasons for not visiting. Under the guise of neutrality, such a parent can engender and foster alienation. The "neutrality" essentially communicates to the child the message that the noncustodial parent cannot provide enough affection, attention, and other desirable input to make a missed visitation a loss of any consequence. Such a parent fails to appreciate the fact that neutrality is as much a position in a conflict as overt support of either side.

Related to the neutrality maneuver is the parent who repeatedly insists that *the child* be the one to make the decision regarding visitation. Such a parent hammers away at the child with this principle. The child generally knows that the parent basically does not want the visitation, and so the child then professes the strong opinion that he or she does not wish to visit. Such a mother might say, after the child refuses: "I respect your strength in standing up for your rights." I once saw a mother in this category who went further and said, "If you don't want to visit with him, you can count on my full support. If we have to go to court to defend you we'll do it. I'm not going to let him push you around. You have your right to say no, and you can count on me to defend you." In extreme cases I have seen mothers who will actually hire an attorney to "protect" the child from this so-called coercing father who is insisting on visitation. Such mothers will give their children the impression that they would go to the Supreme Court if necessary in order to support them in "their" decision not to visit. And the more vociferous and determined the mothers become, the more adamant the children become in their refusal—refusal based not on the genuine desire not to see the father, but refusal based on the fear of not complying with their mothers' wish that they not visit. The mother and children then build together a stone wall of resistance against the father's overtures for involvement with the children.

One separated father calls, the mother answers, exchanges a few amenities, and then calls the child to the phone. Another father calls, the mother says absolutely nothing, and in an angry tone says to the child: "It's your father!" The implication is that the person on the other end of the phone is not even worthy of a little common courtesy. Even despised individuals who call under these circumstances generally receive more consideration. One mother answers the phone and calmly says, "It's your father," and hands the phone over to the child. Another mother answers and curtly says to the child, "It's your *father*," and stiffly gives the phone to the child—conveying the message that the caller is not a former husband, but a person who is so objectionable that the mother would not want in any way to be associated with him. The implication is that the caller is a possession of the child and is in no way related to her.

One mother encourages her child to visit with the father by saying, "You have to go see your father. If you don't he'll take us to court." Nothing is mentioned about the positive benefits to be derived by the child from seeing the father. The only reason to go is for them to protect *themselves* ("...he'll take us to court") from the father's litigation. One mother, who had agreed to involve herself in court-appointed therapy in order to bring about a rapprochement between her two daughters and their father, told me early in the first session that her main purpose was to bring about such reconciliation. However, about ten minutes later she told me that she felt it was her obligation to help support her daughters' decisions not to see their father. In this case, there was absolutely no good reason for their not wishing to see their father, except that they were complying with their mother's subconscious wishes that they not do so.

There are mothers who use the "guilt trip" approach to programming their children against their husbands. For example, when the child wants to visit with the father during a scheduled visitation period, the mother might say, "How can you leave your poor old mother?" Not only is the child made to feel guilty about abandoning the mother, but in the ensuing discussion the father is also portrayed as an individual with little or no sensitivity to the mother's feelings. He has not only abandoned this poor helpless mother, but is now luring the children away, thereby increasing her loneliness. He comes to be viewed by the children as insensitive and cruel. The children then, by exaggerating any of the father's weaknesses or deficiencies, can justify their not visiting with him and thereby lessen the guilt they feel over the abandonment of their mother.

A common way in which a parent will contribute to the alienation is to view as "harassment" the attempts by the hated parent to make contact with the children. The alienated parent expresses interest by telephone calls, attempts at visitation, the sending of presents, etc. These are termed "harassment" by the mother, and the children themselves come to view such overtures in the same vein. In frustration the father increases efforts in these areas, thereby increasing the likelihood that his attempts will be viewed as nuisances. A vicious cycle ensues in which the denigrated father increases his efforts, thereby increasing the likelihood that the approaches will be viewed as harassments. Related to this view of the calls as harassments, a mother may say to a calling father (with the child within earshot): "If you keep up this pressure to see him we're going to have one of those teen-age suicides on our hands." If this is said enough times the child then learns that this is a good way to avoid seeing his father. The next step then is for the child to threaten suicide if the father attempts to visit, to which the mother can then say to the father: "He keeps saying that he'll kill himself if he has to visit with you."

The mother who moves to a distant city or state is essentially communicating to the children that distance from the father is not a consequential consideration. It is sometimes done with the implication that they are moving to bring about a cessation of the harassment and other indignities that they suffer while living close to the father. I am not referring here to situations in which such a move might be to the mother's benefit with regard to job opportunities or remarriage. Rather, I am referring to situations in which there is absolutely no reason for the move, other than to put distance between the children and their father. Sometimes parents will even litigate in order to gain permission to leave the state. However, the ostensible reasons are often unconvincing; the basic reason is to bring about a cessation of the parent-child relationship.

Another subtle maneuver commonly utilized by brain-washing parents relates to the psychological mechanism of doing and undoing. An example of this would be an individual who makes a racial slur, recognizes that the other person has been offended, and then retracts the statement by saying, "Oh, I didn't really mean it" or "I was only fooling." In the vast majority of cases the person so criticized does not "get the joke," the smiles and acceptance of the apology notwithstanding. Doing and undoing is not the same as never having done anything at all. A mother might angrily say, "*What* do you *mean* you're going to your father's house?" This may then be followed immediately with the statement, "Oh, what am I saying? That's wrong. I shouldn't discourage you from seeing your father. Forget I said that. Of course, it's okay for you to go to your father's house." The initial statement and the retraction, all taken together, are not the same as undiluted and unambivalent encouragement. The child gets the message that a strong part of the mother does not want the visitation. Some mothers may make such derogatory comments and then, when confronted with them later, will claim that they were said at a time of extreme duress and that they were really not meant. One mother threatened her husband, as he left the home, "If you leave this marriage I vow to God that you'll never see your children again." This was said to her husband in front of their four children. In subsequent custody litigation she first denied to me that she had ever made the statement. When, however, in family session her husband and four children "refreshed her memory," she reluctantly admitted that she had made the statement, but then gave as her excuse the fact that she was quite upset when her husband was leaving and she was thereby not responsible for her comment. She explained at length how, when people are upset, they will say all kinds of things that they don't really mean. Again, doing and undoing is not the same as never having done at all—and the children, at some level, recognize this.

One father, the owner of a large trucking company, dealt effectively with tough and often brutal truckers, union chiefs, and even underworld Mafia figures. He considered carrying a gun to be crucial for his own survival as well as that of his company. He described numerous encounters with violent gangland figures. His fearlessness in these situations was remarkable. Yet, this same man claimed total impotence with regard to convincing his somewhat under-weight and scrawny ten-year-old daughter to visit his former wife. His professions of helplessness were often quite convincing to his friends and relatives, but when I pointed out to him the disparity between his ability to impose his opinion on people at work as compared to his home, he still claimed that he had absolutely no power over his child: "Doctor, I can't do a thing with her."

One could argue that such subtle programming is extremely common in the divorce situation. I cannot deny this. However, in the *parental alienation syndrome* the child is *obsessed* with resentment above and beyond what might be expected in the usual divorce. It is the extent and depth of the alienation that differentiates the *parental alienation syndrome* from the mild alienation that is engendered in many divorces. In addition, there are other factors operative in producing the parental alienation syndrome that are not present in the common type of divorce programming—the most important of which are the presence of custody litigation and the threat of disruption of a strong parent-child (usually mother-child) bond.

Although the mothers in these situations may have a variety of motivations for programming their children against their fathers, the most common one relates to the old saying: "Hell hath no fury like a woman scorned." Actually, the original statement of William Congreve was: "Heaven has no rage, like love to hatred turned. Nor hell a fury, like a woman scorn'd" (*The Mourning Bride*, III, viii). Because these mothers are separated, and cannot retaliate directly at their husbands, they wreak vengeance by attempting to deprive their former spouses of their most treasured possessions, the children. And the brainwashing program is an attempt to achieve this goal. One of the reasons why such brainwashing is less common in fathers is that they, more often than mothers, have the opportunity to find new partners. Less frustrated, they are less angry and less in need of getting revenge.

It is important for the reader to appreciate that these mothers are far less loving of their children than their actions would suggest to the naive observer. Ostensibly, all their attempts to protect the child from harm by the dreaded parent are made in the service of their love of their children. Actually, the truly loving parent appreciates the importance of the noncustodial parent to the children and, with the rare exception of the genuinely abusing parent, facilitates all meaningful contact between the children and their father. These campaigns of denigration are not in the children's best interests and are in themselves manifestations of parental deficiency. But, I will take this even further. These mothers exhibit the mechanism of reaction formation, in that their obsessive love of their children is often a coverup for their underlying hostility. People who need to prove to themselves continuously that they *love* are often fighting underlying feelings of hate. On a few occasions, I have observed dramatic examples of this in my custody evaluations. On these occasions, in the midst of what could only be considered to be violent custodial conflicts—in which both parties were swept up in all-consuming anger—the mother would suddenly state that she was giving up the custody conflict and handing the child over to the father.

In one such case, in the middle of a very heated session, the mother suddenly stated to the father: "Okay, if you want him that bad, take him." When I asked the mother if she was certain that this was her decision, she replied in the affirmative. I reemphasized that the implication of her statement was that the custody litigation would be discontinued and that I would be writing a letter to the judge informing him that my services were no longer being enlisted because the mother had decided voluntarily to turn custody over to the father. At this point the mother's second husband leaned over and asked her if she appreciated the implications of what she was saying. After two or three "jolts" by her new husband, the mother appeared to "sober up again" and stated, "Oh, I guess I didn't realize what I was saying. Of course, I love him very much." She then turned to her son and hugged him closely, but without any genuine expression of affection on her face. I believe that what went on here was that there was an inexplicable relaxation of internal censorship that keeps unconscious processes relegated out of conscious awareness. My statement and that of her new husband served to "put things back in place," and she then proceeded with the litigation as viciously as ever. In short, we see another motivation for the obsessive affection that these mothers exhibit toward their children—an underlying rejection. And when these mothers "win," they not only win custody, but they win total alienation of their children from the hated spouse. The victory here results in psychological destruction of the children which, I believe, is what they basically want anyway. And they are dimly aware that their unrelentless litigation, indoctrination, and alienation will bring this about. In Chapter Seven I will discuss additional psychodynamic factors operative in these mothers, especially as they relate to the therapeutic approaches and the ways in which the courts should deal with them.

Factors Arising Within the Child

Here, I refer to factors that initially involved no active contribution on the part of the loved parent, conscious or unconscious, blatant or subtle. These are factors that originate within the child. Of course, a parent may use the child's contribution to promote the alienation and "get mileage out of" this factor, but it is a contribution that originates from psychopathological factors within the child.

The most important contributing factor that arises within the child relates to the fact that the basic psychological bond with the loved parent is stronger than that which the child has with the hated parent. The campaign, then, is an attempt to maintain that tie, the disruption of which is threatened by the litigation. The aforementioned maneuvers utilized by mothers is also an attempt to maintain the integrity of this bond. (This point will be discussed in greater detail in Chapter Seven.)

It is important also for the reader to appreciate that the weapons that children use to support the mother's position are often naive and simplistic. Children lack the adult sophistication to provide themselves with credible and meaningful ammunition. Accordingly, to the outside observer the reasons given for the alienation will often seem frivolous. Unfortunately, the mother who welcomes the expression of such resentments and complaints will be gullible and accept with relish the most preposterous complaints. Unfortunately, attorneys and even judges are sometimes taken in by these children and do not frequently enough ask themselves the question: "Is this a justifiable reason for the child's never wanting to see his or her father again?" The inconsequential nature of the complaints and their absurdity are the hallmarks of the child's contribution to the development of the parental alienation syndrome.

Related to the aforementioned desire on the child's part to maintain the psychological bond with the preferred parent (usually the mother) is the fear of disruption of that bond. And there is also the fear of alienating the preferred parent. The hated parent is only ostensibly hated; there is still much love. But the loved parent is feared much more than loved. And it is this factor, more than any other, that contributes to the various symptoms that I have discussed in this section. Generally, the fear is that of losing the love of the preferred parent. In the usual situation it is the father who has left the home. He has thereby provided for himself the reputation of being the rejecter and abandoner. No matter how justified his leaving the home, the children will generally view him as an abandoner. Most often the children subscribe to the dictum: "If you (father) really loved us you would tolerate the indignities and pains you suffer in your relationship with our mother." Having already been abandoned by one parent, the children are not going to risk abandonment by the second. Accordingly, they fear expressing resentment to the remaining parent (usually the mother) and will often reflexly take her position in any conflict with the father. This fear of the loss of the mother's love is the most important factor in the development of the symptoms that I describe in this chapter. The parental alienation syndrome, however, provides a vehicle for expression of the anger felt toward the father because of his abandonment. This expression of resentment is supported by the mother, both overtly and covertly. It is part of the maneuver by which the children become willing weapons in the mother's hands, weapons that enable her to gratify her hostility through them.

A common factor that contributes to the obsessive hatred of the father is the utilization of the reaction formation mechanism. Obsessive hatred is often a thin disguise for deep love. This is especially the case when there is absolutely no reason to justify the preoccupation with the hated person's defects. True rejection is neutrality, when there is little if any thought of the person. The opposite of love is not hate, but indifference. Each time these children think about how much they hate their fathers, they are still thinking about their fathers. Although the visual imagery may involve alienating fantasies, their fathers are still very much on their minds. The love, however, is expressed as hate in order to assuage the guilt they would feel over overt expression of affection for their fathers, especially in their mothers' presence. And their affection is also repressed because of the fear of their mothers' rejection if such expressions of affection for their fathers were to manifest themselves, especially in their mothers' presence. One boy, when alone with me, stated: "I'm bad for wanting to visit with my father." This was a clear statement of the guilt he felt over his wish that he basically wanted to visit with his father, his professions of hatred notwithstanding. This child was not born with the idea that it is bad to want to be with his father. Rather, he was programmed by his mother to be guilty over such thoughts and feelings.

Oedipal factors are sometimes operative in the alienation. A girl who has a seductive and romanticized relationship with her father (sometimes abetted by the father himself) may find his involvement with a new woman particularly painful. Whereas visitations may have gone somewhat smoothly prior to the father's new relationship, following the new involvement there may be a rapid deterioration in the girl's relationship with her father. Such a girl may say to her father: "You've got to choose between me and her." In such situations there may be no hope of a warm and meaningful relationship between the father's new woman friend and his daughter. Sometimes the mothers of such girls will support the animosity in that it serves well their desire for vengeance. These girls sometimes exhibit such rage that one is reminded again of William Congreve's:

"Heaven has no rage like love to hatred turned. Nor hell a fury, like a woman scorn'd." Elsewhere, (1986b) I describe in detail my views of the Oedipus complex.

Many of these children proudly state that their decision to reject their fathers is their own. They deny any contribution from their mothers. And the mothers often support this vehemently. In fact, the mothers will often state that they want the child to visit with the father and recognize the importance of such involvement. Yet, such a mother's every act indicates otherwise. The child appreciates that, by stating that the decision is his or her own, he or she assuages the mother's guilt and protects her from the criticism that she basically does not want the child to visit with the father. Such professions of independent thinking are supported by the mother, who will often praise the child for being the kind of person who has a mind of his or her own and is forthright and brave enough to express his or her opinions. As mentioned, in extreme cases such mothers will hire lawyers for the children and go to court in order to support what is ostensibly the child's own decision not to visit. The realities are that, with the exception of situations in which the father is indeed abusive, there is no good reason for a child's not wanting to have at least some contact with a father. Children are not born with genes that program them to reject a father. Such hatred and rejection are environmentally induced, and the most likely person to have brought about the alienation is the mother.

Situational Factors

Often situational factors are conducive to the development of the disorder. By situational factors, I refer to external events that contribute to the development of the parental alienation syndrome—factors that abet the internal psychological processes in the parents and in the child. Most parents in a custody conflict know that time is on the side of the custodial parent. They appreciate that the longer the child remains with a particular parent, the greater the likelihood the child will resist moving to the home of the other. Even adults find change of domicile to be anxiety provoking. One way for a child to deal with this fear is to denigrate the noncustodial parent with criticisms that justify the child's remaining in the custodial home. For example, a mother dies and the maternal grandparents take over care of the child. Although at first the father may welcome their involvement, there are many cases on record of the maternal grandparents then litigating for custody of the child. The child may then develop formidable resentments against the father in order to insure that he or she will remain with the grandparents, the people whom the child has come to view as the preferable parents.

In one case I was involved with, two girls developed this disorder after their mother, with whom they were living, met a man who lived in Colorado. The mother then decided to move there with the two girls. The father then brought the mother to court in an attempt to restrain her from moving out of the state of New Jersey with the children. Whereas previously there had been a good relationship with their father, the girls gradually developed increasing hatred of him, as their mother became progressively more deeply embroiled in the litigation. It was clear that the disorder would not have arisen had the mother not met a man who lived in Colorado, a man whom she wished to marry.

A common situation in which the child will develop complaints about the hated parent is one in which there has been the observation of a sibling being treated harshly and even being rejected for expressing affection for the hated parent. One boy I treated repeatedly observed his mother castigating his sister for her expressions of affection for her father. His sister was older and could withstand better the mother's vociferous denigration of her. The boy, however, was frightened by his mother's outbursts of rage toward his sister and was adamant in his refusal to see his father, claiming that he hated him, but would only give inconsequential reasons for his hostility. In this way he protected himself from his mother's animosity toward him. We see here clearly how his hatred of his father stemmed not so much from alienating qualities within the father, but from fear of the loss of his mother's affection.

One girl observed her mother making terrible threats to her older brother: "If you go to court and tell the judge that you want to live with your father, I'll have you put away as a psychotic. I'll have the child authorities put you away. You're crazy if you want to live with him." In this case the father was an unusually good parent, and the mother suffered with a moderately severe psychiatric disturbance. The older brother was strong enough to express his preference for living with the father and appreciated the fact that the mother had no powers to unilaterally and perfunctorily have him incarcerated in a mental hospital. The younger sister, however, believed that this was a possibility and therefore told the judge that she wanted to live with her mother. Again, it was fear, not love of the mother, that brought about her professions of preference to live with her. And it was fear of her mother, not genuine hatred of the father, that caused her to reject her father.

One boy repeatedly observed his father sadistically and mercilessly beating his mother. In order to protect himself from similar maltreatment, the boy professed deep affection for his father and hatred of his mother. The professions of love of his father here stemmed from fear rather than from genuine feelings of affection. This phenomenon is generally referred to as "identification with the aggressor." It is based on the principle: "If you can't fight 'em, join 'em." Those who were knowledgeable about the father's brutal treatment of the mother expressed amazement that the child was obsessed with hatred of his mother and love of his father, and they were unable to understand why the boy kept pleading for the opportunity to live with his father. Another factor that may be operative in such situations is the child's model of what a loving relationship should be like. Love is viewed as manifesting itself by hostile interaction. Father demonstrates his "affection" for mother here by beating her. In order to be sure of obtaining this "love," the child opts to live with the hostile parent. This mechanism, of course, is central to *masochism* (C. Thompson, 1959; R.A. Gardner, 1970, 1973a).

One 13-year-old girl's mother died in an automobile accident during the course of her parents' custody litigation. Specifically, she was killed en route home from a visit to her lawyer. Even prior to her mother's death, the girl had identified with and supported her mother's position and viewed her father as an abandoner. Her mother was supported in this regard by the maternal grandmother as well. At the time of the mother's death the girl manifested what I have described elsewhere (1979b) as an "instanteneous identification" with her dead mother. This is one of the ways in which children (and even adults) may deal with the death of a parent. It is as if they are saying: "My parent isn't dead; he or she now resides within my own body." In the context of such immediate identification the child takes on many of the dead parent's personality traits, often almost overnight. And this is what occurred in this case. There was a very rapid maturational process in which the girl acquired many of the mannerisms of her mother. As part of this process she intensified her hatred of her father and even accused him of having caused the death of her mother: "If you hadn't treated my mother so badly, there wouldn't have been a breakup of the marriage, she wouldn't have had to go visit with her lawyer, and she wouldn't have been killed on the way home from his office." Although there were many other factors involved in her obsessive hatred and rejection of her father, this identification factor was an important one. Prior to her mother's death she had grudgingly and intermittently seen her father; after the death there was a total cessation of visitation. Interestingly, this identification process was supported by the maternal grandmother, who began to view the girl as the reincarnation of her dead daughter. And in the service of this process she supported the girl in her rejection of her father.

CONCLUDING COMMENTS

In this chapter I have focused primarily on the manifestations of the parental alienation syndrome and described contributing factors from four areas: 1) brainwashing, 2) subtle and often unconscious programming, 3) the child's contributions, and 4) situational factors. The main emphasis in this chapter has been to describe the phenomenon of the parental alienation syndrome, but not to delve significantly into its underlying psychodynamics. In Chapter Seven I will discuss in greater depth certain aspects of the programmer's psychodynamics, especially as they relate to therapeutic approaches and the ways in which the courts can deal with parents who contribute to the development and perpetuation of their children's parental alienation syndromes.

Lawyers and judges often ask examiners who are involved in custody evaluations whether a particular child has or has not been "brainwashed." Frequently, under cross-examination, they will request a yes or no answer. Under these circumstances I generally respond: "I cannot answer yes or no." My reason for this response is that to answer simply "yes," I would only be providing a partially correct response and this would be a disservice to the brainwashing mother. The yes or no response does not give me the opportunity to describe the more complex factors, especially those originating within the child and the situation. Examiners are often asked, "With which parent does the child have a psychological bond?" Again, I usually refuse to answer this question. If I am given an opportunity to elaborate, I state that there is rarely a situation in which a child has a psychological bond with one parent and not with the other. Generally, the child has psychological bonds with both parents. What one really wants to know in custody evaluations is the parent with whom the child has the *stronger* psychological bond. And, if a stepparent is under consideration, one would want to know about the strength of the psychological bond with the stepparent, as compared with each of the natural parents. The psychological bond consideration will be discussed in greater detail in Chapter Seven.

FOUR

DIFFERENTIATING BETWEEN FABRICATED AND BONA FIDE SEX-ABUSE ALLEGATIONS IN CHILD CUSTODY DISPUTES

In the last 10 to 15 years we have witnessed a burgeoning of child custody disputes. This increase is related to two recent developments that have affected significantly such litigation. The first development took place in the mid-1970s. Prior to that time the courts generally gave preference to mothers, under the *tender years presumption*. The assumption was made that a mother, by virtue of the fact that she is female, is more likely to be a superior child rearer than a male. During that period men began to complain that the tender years presumption was instrinsically sexist, and the courts agreed. As a result, we witnessed a burgeoning of child custody litigation as fathers developed hope for success in such disputes. In the late 1970s and early 1980s, the joint custodial concept came into vogue. Under this custodial arrangement an attempt was made to provide a more egalitarian role for both parents in their children's upbringing. An attempt was made to do away with rigid schedules and to enlist both parents' involvement in the upbringing of their children. Particular emphasis was given to the equalization of the time the children spent with each parent and joint involvement in the decision-making process. The increasing popularity of the joint custodial concept was also accompanied by an increase in custody litigation as parents began to fight even more vehemently for a greater portion of time with their children.

One result of these changes was a progressive erosion of the mother's secure position in custody disputes. Prior to the development of these trends many mothers, even those who were clearly inadequate, were protected by the tender years presumption and could rest assured that custody was not likely to be wrested from them. In response to the weakening of their positions, many mothers began using various tactics (some misconceived and desperate) to gain advantages in the custody litigation. And fathers as well began resorting to a variety of devious maneuvers to strengthen their positions.

One of the outgrowths of this warfare was the development in children of what I refer to as the *parental alienation syndrome* (Gardner, 1985, 1986a). As described in detail in Chapter Three, the child exhibits vicious vilification of one of the parents and idealization of the other. It is not caused simply by parental brainwashing of the child. Rather, the children themselves contribute their own scenarios in support of the favored parent. My experience has been that in about 80–90 percent of cases the mother is the favored parent and the father the vilified one; and the opposite is true for the remaining cases.

In 1982 or 1983 I began seeing a new development, namely, the utilization of fabricated allegations of child sex abuse in the context of custody disputes. A new weapon was now being added to the parents' armamentarium in the custodial warfare. What more effective way could there be to get quick action by the courts than to allege that a parent was sexually molesting a child? Whereas other allegations did not generally gain the court's immediate attention, this one was more likely to do so. And the slowness of the legal process was clearly a factor that prolonged such litigation. The litigation was also slowed by the parent with whom the children were living—regardless of whether that parent was indeed the best one for them. Such a parent knew well that the longer the children remained with him or her, the greater the likelihood that they would choose to stay and the more reluctant the courts would be to transfer custody. A sex-abuse allegation, more than any other claim, could reverse these two factors that contributed to the protraction of the litigious process.

Prior to the early 1980s the general consensus among those who worked with sexually abused children was that children rarely, if ever, fabricated sex abuse. The main argument given was that children had no direct access to the details of the sexual encounter, and if a child was able to describe such details there had to have been an actual experience. But this is no longer the case. Sex abuse has become a common topic on television programs and in the public media. Television programs have become increasingly more explicit. I am not referring simply to R- and basically X-rated programs that can now be seen on television; even soap operas are sex-laden. Sex-abuse prevention programs have been introduced into most schools, even down to the nursery school level. Here again, children are given specific information about sexual activities. There are sex-abuse prevention coloring books and audiotapes. Well-publicized cases of sexual abuse often involve children giving testimony in which they provide the details of their alleged sexual abuses. These testimonials can also be viewed by children on television—engendering a certain amount of envy for the

widespread attention and notoriety that these children enjoy. Accordingly, children are now literally bombarded with
information about the details of sexual abuse.

The point of the child's increasing familiarity with sex
abuse was brought home recently while I was playing *The
Talking, Feeling, and Doing Game* (Gardner, 1973b) with a
seven-year-old boy. He selected the card, "What's the worst
thing a parent can do to a child?" The boy replied, "Play with
his private parts." This response was given in the year 1985,
at the time when the aforementioned exposures to sex were
becoming increasingly prevalent. At that time I had been
playing the game for 15 years, and I can say with certainty
that I had never previously received such a response. My
first reaction was that I was dealing here with the revelations
of a sexually abused child. Furthermore, the session was
being videotaped, and the implications of this were obvious.
I incredulously asked the child where he had heard about
such things. He responded, "They taught us all about that in
school. You know, a child should never let another person
touch his body. Your body is your own. You should never let
anybody touch your body. If somebody wants to touch your
body you should say no to the person. And then you go and
tell one of your parents or a teacher or somebody like that."
It was clear that the child was repeating almost verbatim
what he had been taught in school. I then asked him if either
one of his parents had ever done such a thing to him. He
replied, "Of course not. My mommy or my daddy would
never do such a terrible thing to me. They wouldn't do that
to any child."

As a result of these developments we are being confronted with a grave problem, namely, how to differentiate
bona fide from fabricated sex-abuse allegations. This is
indeed a crucial differentiation because of the terrible consequences of a false accusation. The careers of innocent people
have been literally ruined by such allegations. Even when

found not to be guilty their reputations have still been marred. Although we have accumulated a vast amount of information about the signs and symptoms of bona fide sex abuse in children and those who perpetrate sex abuses, we are just beginning to learn about the characteristics of the child fabricators and those adults who prompt and support their false allegations. Accordingly, no one can claim vast experience in this area. In this chapter I will present the criteria I have developed over the last few years, criteria I have found useful in making these differentiations. Because my experience with such fabricators has been primarily in the context of custody disputes, I will focus primarily on the differentiation in association with such disputes. However, the same criteria, I believe, can be useful in other situations in which such allegations are made.

In the early 1980s, when I first started to describe my new observations at conferences, many sex-abuse workers were quite irate with me. Many claimed that I was being deluded and that there was no such phenomenon as fabricated sex abuse by children. Most held strongly to the position that children do not fabricate sex abuse and that a child who describes a sexual encounter must have had the experience; otherwise the child could not provide such details. I was accused of not knowing about the high prevalence of bona fide sex abuse, which was certainly not the case. I was familiar with the findings of D. Russell (1983) that by the age of 18, one of every three girls described some kind of sexual abuse and that one out of every 11 boys described similar experiences (D. Finkelhor, 1979). I knew also that in 1977, M.E. Cahill had reported that 75 percent of prostitutes claimed that they had been sexually victimized as children. For more recent data on the incidence and prevalence of childhood sexual abuse the reader does well to refer to the contributions of J. Waterman and R. Lusk (1986).

Other sex-abuse workers admitted that there might be a

rare child who could be making such an allegation, but that I was doing the whole field a terrible disservice by publicly announcing their existence. They claimed that I would be giving ammunition to defense attorneys and that many bona fide perpetrators would thereby have information that might be useful for them to avoid prosecution. I believed then, and I still believe now, that this was an extremely unfortunate and injudicious position to take. We must accept basic realities, however unpleasant they may be. If some attorneys were to misuse my findings in order to protect bona fide perpetrators from prosecution, then this problem had to be dealt with. We should not, however, squelch such data because of such misguided use of it. The data is crucial to have if we are to protect those who have been falsely accused. Furthermore, all knowledge is power, and any information we may gain about the workings of the human mind cannot but be useful in advancing our understanding of psychiatric disorders.

I believe that the reluctance by sex-abuse workers to recognize and accept the increasing frequency of fabricated sex-abuse allegations relates to certain psychological factors operative in their career choice. All career choices are determined by psychological factors and even psychopathological factors—and the people who choose sex-abuse work are no exception. I believe that people who have been sexually abused themselves in childhood are much more likely to enter this field than those who have not had such childhood experiences. I believe that if one were to compare the frequency of childhood sexual molestation in a thousand sex-abuse workers with three to four matched groups of workers in unrelated fields, the percentage of sex-abuse workers who were sexually molested as children would be significantly higher than the percentages in the other three to four groups. The sex-abuse field was attractive to those who were molested because it provided them with the opportunity for working through in many complex ways residual and unresolved reactions to their early truamas. I am not claiming that these factors necessarily operate at conscious levels (but they may), nor am I claiming that the processes are necessarily pathological (but they may be).

The phenomenon is no different from the factors that operate in just about any other field. To begin with my own field, many people choose medicine because they have grown up in a home with a parent who has suffered with a chronic illness. They may deal with this childhood trauma by devoting their lives to the treatment of others with that disorder or to search for a cure for the parent's illness. Many choose psychiatry or psychology because they hope to gain understanding and even help for their psychological problems, and by treating others with similar disorders they gratify vicariously this desire for a cure of their own problems. People who frequently consider themselves to be put upon or victimized may choose law as a vehicle for protecting themselves and others from such persecutions. People who grew up in poverty may aspire to be (and even become) philanthropists. When they give to others they are basically giving to their projected selves. In all of these examples there is a range from the nonpathological to the pathological psychodynamic factors and each person's balance lies at some point along the continuum.

Among the sex-abuse workers who have been sexually molested as children, there are many who use their career experience in healthy ways in their work—much to the benefit of abused children and their families. They have been there, they know what it's like, and they can provide a degree of sympathy and empathy not often possible for one who has never had the experience. But there are others in whom pathological factors are clearly operative in their work with patients—factors that may becloud their objectivity. Some of these individuals harbor significant resentment against the original perpetrator, resentment that may not have been completely dealt with properly. They vent their pent-up hostility on present-day offenders in a work setting that provides sanctions for such pathological release. And some of these workers operate on the principle that there will never be enough perpetrators to punish, so great is their desire to wreak vengeance on those who sexually molest children. Concluding that an alleged perpetrator is indeed innocent deprives them of their vengeful gratification. It is this subgroup of sex-abuse workers, I believe, who work with exaggerated zeal to prosecute alleged abusers and resist strongly the idea that some alleged offenders are indeed innocent. They often adhere tenaciously to view that children *never* fabricate sex abuse. They must blind themselves to the aforementioned developments in recent years that makes this notion an anachronism. Such zeal and denial, I believe, has contributed to the increasing incidence of sex-abuse litigation that we are witnessing at this time.

I recognize that there will be some (especially those who work with sexually-abused children) who will conclude that what I have just stated is prejudice on my part and that I have no scientific evidence to support my conclusions. I agree that I have no such studies to support my hypothesis and that my conclusions are based on my own experiences as well as colleagues in the mental health professions (some of whom, interestingly, work in the field of sex abuse). My view of people in my own field is no less critical. There is no question that the field of psychiatry attracts some of the sickest people in medicine and this is no doubt a factor in the reputation we have as being "crazies." This phenomenon also serves as an explanation for the fact that the suicidal rate among psychiatrists is highest of all the medical specialities. Accordingly, if I am prejudiced against sex-abuse workers I may very well be considered to be prejudiced against people in my own field. However, one might also conclude that I am making accurate statements about both fields.

On a number of occasions I have been asked to see a child in order to ascertain whether or not he or she has been sexually abused. Frequently I am told that I will not be permitted to interview the alleged perpetrator. I will, however, be permitted to interview the accuser. I have *never* accepted such an invitation. To do so would be involving myself in what could not but be considered trial by hearsay. And the younger the child, the more likely my conclusions would be speculative. Accordingly, I cannot emphasize strongly enough that examiners who involve themselves in these cases should insist upon being given the freedom to see *all* concerned parties: the allegedly abused child, the adult accuser, and the alleged perpetrator. In addition, it is crucial that the examiner have the opportunity to interview these parties individually and in any combination that is warranted. To do otherwise is to conduct what can only be described as a seriously compromised, if not completely inadequate, evaluation.

Accordingly, in this chapter I will describe only the kind of evaluation that involves the child, the accuser, and the alleged perpetrator. And this is the only kind of experience I have had. Although I may choose not to interview various parties together, especially the allegedly abused child and the accused, I must have the freedom to make that decision myself and not be constrained by outside individuals from conducting such an interview if I choose to do so. It is not necessarily the case that such an interview will automatically be psychologically traumatic—and this is especially true if the allegation is fabricated. In order to insure that all parties cooperate in the different types of interview (individual and joint) and that all pertinent information becomes available to me, I require that the parties and their attorneys secure a court order in which I am designated an impartial examiner by the court. They also sign my provisions document (Addendum I) outlining in detail the aforementioned stipulations as well as other requirements that must be accepted before I begin my evaluation. Although this document may be considered stringent by many, I believe its provisions insure my being given the opportunity to conduct the evaluation in the optimum way. An evaluation conducted without these requirements is far less likely to be impartial, comprehensive, and objective.

For simplicity of presentation, I will refer to the accuser as the mother and the alleged perpetrator (or the accused) as the father. This is the more common situation. It is important for the reader to recognize, however, that there are situations (relatively uncommon) in which the father is the accuser and the mother the perpetrator. Furthermore, I use the term *father* because I will be focusing primarily on situations in which the alleged perpetrator is the child's father, rather than a stranger. I.S. Lourie and L.C. Blick (1987a) point out certain differences in children's reactions to being sexually abused by a close family member as compared to a complete stranger. It is beyond the purposes of this book to go into these differences in detail. I deal here with the question of whether the accused father did or did not sexually abuse the child. I will discuss each of these three persons (child, mother, and father) separately and, in the discussion of each, divide the differentiating criteria into three categories. The first category are those differentiating criteria that are the most valuable, that is, provide the most compelling evidence for whether or not sexual abuse has indeed taken place. The second category are those that are of moderate value in making such differentiations. Although useful, they do not provide as compelling evidence as those in the first category. Last, I present the least valuable differentiating criteria. Although less valuable than the criteria listed in the first two categories, they are still of some value in making this important differentiation and, in certain situations, have the potential for being of greater value.

THE CHILD

Very Valuable Differentiating Criteria

The Presence of the Parental Alienation Syndrome Fabricating children are more likely to exhibit manifestations of the aforementioned *parental alienation syndrome.* Children with this disorder typically involve themselves in a campaign of vilification of their fathers and idolization of their mothers. They have been programmed by the mothers to hate their fathers and also contribute their own scenarios of hostility. The fabricated sex-abuse allegations may very well be one manifestation of this disorder. Its presence strongly supports the argument that the sex abuse is fabricated. Children who have been genuinely abused do not usually manifest the signs and symptoms of the parental alienation syndrome. Although there are situations in which a child with parental alienation syndrome has suffered genuine sexual abuse, I suspect that this is rare. Accordingly, I include the presence of the parental alienation syndrome to warrant placement in this section on extremely valuable differentiating criteria.

Receptivity to Divulgence Children who fabricate sex abuse generally welcome the opportunity to talk about the abuse to mental health professionals, lawyers, judges, etc. And they are often encouraged by the accuser to present their litany to all who will listen. Many obtain morbid gratification from the attention that they enjoy, attention that they may never have received before. Some of these children are envious of youngsters whose testimonies have been shown on television. In contrast, children who have been genuinely abused are typically very hesitant to talk about their experiences. They are fearful of inquiries by professionals and often have vowed to keep the "special secret" about "our little game." Such fear may relate to the threat of the abuser that terrible harm will befall them and their loved ones if they are ever to reveal the sexual activities. Some have even been beaten as a warning of what will happen to them if they divulge the secret. Some children are bribed with material goods and money in order to discourage divulgence. Children who have fabricated sex abuse have no history of this special secret. It is an important and very valuable differentiating criterion.

Providing Specific Details   Children who have experienced bona fide sexual abuse generally have a fairly clear visual image of the experience and recall it fairly clearly when asked to do so. The lack of such an internal visual-mental image clearly differentiates the fabricator from the child who has been genuinely abused. And this difference results in the fabricator's difficulty in providing specific details of the event(s) when asked to do so. The fabricator may refer to the abuse in general terms and even utilize adult terminology, such as "I was sexually molested" or "I was sexually abused." When asked to provide details, the youngster is either unable to do so or creates a scenario for the purposes of the interview. However, in subsequent interviews a different scenario may be presented. It is common knowledge that no one's memory is good enough to be a good liar and children even less so. In contrast, the child who has suffered bona fide sexual abuse will usually provide specific details, and they will be consistently the same on subsequent interviews. Even though there may be some variations in the story because of the younger child's cognitive limitations and weak reality testing, I still consider this to be a valuable differentiating criterion because children who have been genuinely abused will still provide a much more consistent story than those who are fabricating their abuse. This relates to the aforementioned visual-mental image of the event(s) and the fact that no one's memory is good enough to be a good liar.

As will be discussed in detail below, in a joint interview in which the child and accused are present together, the accused is in an excellent position to "smoke out" the fabricator by pointing out how the details provided are inaccurate and preposterous.

Credibility of the Description   The child who is fabricating sex abuse will often describe settings that are unlikely for such activities. For example, "He did it to me while my friend went to the bathroom" and "He did it to me while my mommy was in the kitchen." It is reasonable to say that only the most simple-minded or psychotic perpetrator would attempt abuse under these circumstances; but the child is not appreciative of this obvious fact. In contrast, the child who has been genuinely abused sexually will describe settings that are much more likely and reasonable. The story provided by the fabricated accuser is often naive and simplistic. For example, one child stated, "At my father's house he played with my penis and in my mother's house he played with my hiney" and "At my father's house he did it in the daytime and in my mother's house he did it at night."

Questions regarding the ejaculate are common in sex-abuse investigations. Such focus stems from the recognition that the child who has been genuinely abused may be able to provide a credible description of the ejaculate, whereas the child who is fabricating will not be aware of its existence and is likely to become confused by a discussion of it. Accordingly, it is in the description of the ejaculate, especially, that the fabricator is likely to provide preposterous explanations.

Examiners investigating in this area do well to make certain important differentiations regarding *whose* ejaculate (the offender's or the victim's) and the age of the ejaculator (adult or child). The seminal emission of the adolescent and adult male is generally white, thick, and copious (approximately the liquid volume of a teaspoon). The ejaculate of the pre-pubertal boy (often referred to as the "stuff" that comes out of the penis) may not be produced at all at the time of orgasm ("the good feeling") or, if present, it is usually clearer (less white) than the adult's and less copious. When interviewing the child, the examiner does well to make a sharp differentiation between the discussions of the perpetrator and that of the child as well as the descriptions of each one's emissions (or lack of such).

The child who has been genuinely abused is usually aware that "stuff" has come out of the offender's penis, but may not be certain about its color. Young children, especially, may believe that it was yellow, confusing it with urine — the only penile emission they are familiar with. Older children may recognize the emission as white and sticky. But semen tends to become clearer with the passage of time, at which point the child might easily confuse it with water or urine. Or the child may not know the color because he or she may not have noticed this particular detail. This is especially the case when the abuse has been coerced and the child has submitted under duress. If the boy himself has been brought to orgasm, he may describe a "good feeling" and either describe no ejaculate or a small quantity of clear or only slightly white fluid.

The child who is fabricating may exhibit initial confusion regarding questions about the "stuff" that came out of the penis of the perpetrator. Although initially unaware of the fact that such emissions exist, the child gets the "hint" implied in the leading question and then is likely to provide fabrications. Yellow is a common response, as a first guess.

On further questioning regarding whether the yellow stuff was thick or clear, whether one could easily see through it or not, the child will generally describe a clear liquid like urine—the only penile emission the child is familiar with. If the child senses that this is not the "right" answer, then any color of the rainbow may be provided with any consistency from clear like water to so thick that one couldn't see through it. Once a programmer has had the opportunity for input, the offender's ejaculate is likely to be described as white.

With regard to the question of manipulation of the child's own genitals by the offender, the child who is fabricating is generally not aware of the "good feeling" that may be a concomitant of such manipulation. When asked about the stuff that came out of *his* penis, the same considerations apply as described above for the fabricator's concept of the offender's ejaculate: yellow, white, or any other color of the rainbow. Here again, the programmer's input may be "smoked out" when the child describes his own ejaculate as white. Both the programmer and the child are generally not aware of the fact that the pre-pubertal child's ejaculate is usually clear.

Guilt Relating to the Consequences of the Disclosure to the Accused   Fabricated sex abusers generally exhibit little if any guilt over the potential effects on the perpetrator of their disclosure. This guiltless disregard is one of the hallmarks of the fabricator. There may be even a morbid or sadistic gratification in the telling of the story. The child may recognize that the accusation is an extremely effective way of hurting the father and may hope thereby to gain the enhanced affection of the accusing mother. Children who have suffered bona fide sexual abuse may feel guilty over their disloyalty and the recognition that the disclosure is going to result in formidable painful consequences for the perpetrator. The perpetrator has often laid the groundwork for such guilt by telling the child never to reveal the secret lest there be terrible consequences. And the commotion that results from the disclosure confirms that terrible consequences have indeed taken place.

Guilt Relating to Participation in Sexual Activities The aforementioned guilt over the consequences of the disclosure should be differentiated from guilt over having participated in sexual activities with the perpetrator. The fabricating child generally feels no guilt over the sexual activities allegedly engaged in. The child who has suffered bona fide abuse may very well have enjoyed the experience and will often suffer guilt over such pleasure because the child has subsequently learned that the act is an unacceptable, sinful, or even criminal act. And interrogators, although they may try to reassure the child that he or she was the innocent victim, may still not be successful in assuaging such guilt. The fact that the interrogations are made by individuals such as lawyers, prosecutors, judges, and psychiatrists cannot dispel the notion that some heinous act has been engaged in. Fabricators, not having actually engaged in any act at all, are not likely to feel guilty in association with interrogations.

Another form of guilt that is derived from the sexual experience relates to the child's having been selected from all the other children as the one for sexual involvement. Often the perpetrator communicates to the child that he or she enjoys a special sense of superiority over the siblings for having been so chosen. The abused child gets special attention from the offender at the same time that attention is withdrawn from other siblings. This sense of exclusivity may also produce fear of jealous reprisal by the allegedly nonfavored siblings. Children who fabricate do not generally describe guilt over their having been selected nor fear of reprisals from siblings because of their allegedly exclusive relationship with the perpetrator.

Another form of guilt related to participation in the sexual activities relates to the parents' blaming the child for initiating the sexual activities. Although this is very uncommon, in my experience, it does occur and I will discuss this factor below. The perpetrator will attempt to assuage his own guilt by blaming the child, and the child, because of cognitive immaturity, will accept as valid the accusation. Children who fabricate the sex abuse will not generally describe such accusations.

Another form of guilt arises from the child's need to gain a sense of control in a situation in which he basically feels impotent. Intrinsic to the notion "it's my fault" is the concept of control. This is the same mechanism that enables children of divorce to believe that a parent's leaving the home was their fault. In such situations the child will often make statements such as: "I know you're leaving because I was bad. I promise I'll never be bad again. I promise that I'll always be good" (Gardner, 1979a). This phenomenon, although it may appear to be a form of guilt because of the child's statement that a transgression has been committed, is really not properly guilt and is preferably referred to as a *delusion of control* (Gardner, 1970). Again, fabricators are not likely to describe this mechanism.

Fear of the Alleged Perpetrator Examiners must differentiate the aforementioned types of guilt from fear. The child who is fabricating sexual abuse generally does not describe fear of the perpetrator and is usually free from tension in the perpetrator's presence. If there is any tension, it relates to fear that the perpetrator will punish the child for the false accusation. The child who has been genuinely abused will be quite fearful of the perpetrator, both inside and outside of the examiner's office. In fact, the fear may generalize to others of the same sex so that the child who was abused by a father may be fearful of being alone with any male figure—including a male examiner. This fear may result in the child's making every attempt to be away from home as much as possible, especially when alone with the offender. In extreme cases these children will run away from home in order to avoid the sexual encounters. Fabricators generally have no history of such avoidance, nor are they as likely to have run away from home. In fact, the fabricator may even describe tension-free visitations with a divorced father in the context of which the alleged abuses are said to have taken place.

Sexual Excitation   Children who have been sexually abused usually experience an early introduction into sexual activities and may become "turned on" sexually at an age much earlier than they would have otherwise. This premature introduction into sex may result in a heightened state of sexual excitation that frequently seeks relief. During the clinical interview such children may seek physical contact with the examiner, even to the point of rubbing their genitalia against the examiner in the hope of gaining some sexual gratification. Sexually abused children may talk frequently about sex, to the point of obsession. They may be preoccupied with the desire to play sexual games with other children (especially exhibitionistic and voyeuristic) and/or may become compulsive masturbators (privately and publicly). They may become preoccupied with doll play in which sexual encounters (especially their own) are portrayed. In contrast, children who are fabricating sex abuse generally exhibit no such preoccupation with sex—other than at those times when they are asked to describe the scenarios related to the sexual encounters with the alleged perpetrator.

Desensitizing Play Children who have been abused may involve themselves frequently in various kinds of play activities that are designed to desensitize themselves to the abuse. For example, in doll-house play they may frequently eject the doll that symbolizes the perpetrator and/or refuse to allow that person to enter the house. Sometimes the play will involve a reenactment of the sex-abuse experience, again for the purposes of desensitization. One such boy I saw in treatment insisted upon engaging family members in a game in which they hid themselves in the bathroom, behind the locked door, and waited there until the "bad man" went away. He would instruct the adults to peek periodically outside in order to reassure the child that the bad person was no longer there. On occasion, the youngster insisted that all participants stand in the shower stall, with the curtains closed, in order to gain further protection from the bad man.

Attitude Toward One's Genitals Children who have suffered bona fide sex abuse will often consider their genitals to have been damaged. This may result from actual trauma to the genitalia that the child has experienced and/or the social reactions to physical activities focusing on the genital area. Those who fabricate sex abuse do not generally consider their genitalia to have been damaged and will not independently describe such a complaint.

Moderately Valuable Differentiating Criteria

The Litany Mention has been made of the litany that fabricators may have created for the benefit of the parade of examiners who interview them. This has a rehearsed quality and, as mentioned, may include adult terminology such as, "Daddy molested me" and "I was sexually abused." Children who have been genuinely molested will not generally have a litany at the outset, nor will they use adult terms. However, after repeated inquiries (by the same parade of interrogators) the child may then develop a litany and even the utilization of adult terminology (now learned from the interrogators). Accordingly, examiners do well to learn how many times previously and by whom the child has been interviewed in order to assess properly this differentiating criterion.

Depression   Children who have been genuinely sexually abused are often depressed, especially if they have been frequently abused over time, and especially if there have been terrible threats made regarding disclosure of their sexual experiences. The main manifestations of the depression may be depressive affect, loss of appetite, listlessness, loss of enjoyment in play, impaired school curiosity and motivation, and difficulty sleeping. The depression may often be associated with suicidal thoughts, especially if the child has been made to feel guilty over the experiences. The depression may be related to the feelings of betrayal engendered not only by the offender, but by the passivity and/or failure of the mother to protect the child and interfere with the repetition of the abuse. Depression may be related to pent-up resentment that is not allowed expression, lest the perpetrator carry through with his threats of retaliation. Fabricators are not generally depressed, although they may profess being upset over their alleged sexual experiences.

Withdrawal   Children who have been genuinely abused may often withdraw from involvement with others. They prefer more a fantasy world that is safe and free from the traumas of their real life. Such withdrawal is observed in the interview and is described as existing in the home, in school, and elsewhere. Fabricators are not generally described as withdrawn; rather they are typically outgoing and outspoken.

Compliance Sexually abused children are often quite compliant. Their experiences with the perpetrator have often been ones in which they have been threatened that noncompliance will result in terrible consequences to themselves and their loved ones. Especially in situations where the perpetrator lives in the home, the child's life is controlled, both body and mind. It is only through compliance that the child may be protected from the realization of the threats. Many develop a cheerful facade that extends to inhibiting themselves from expressing dissatisfaction in any situation and contributes to their compliant behavior. Fabricating children generally do not exhibit such compliant behavior, because they have not had the coercive experiences suffered by the abused child. What compliance they do exhibit is generally with the request of the accuser to provide details about the encounters to anyone and everyone who may ask about them.

The Borrowed Scenario Children who have been genuinely abused describe details of their abuse and generally confine sexual discussion to these specific experiences. Fabricators, having no such experiences, create their scenarios. These may be derived from classroom presentations, video- and audiotapes about sex abuse, coloring books about sex abuse, or pornographic movies observed unknown to the parents. Examiners do well to inquire into the child's experiences with such exposures. This differentiating criterion may become weakened when the child who has indeed been abused also has similar environmental exposures to information about sex abuse.

Psychosomatic Disorders Children who have been genuinely abused are more likely to suffer with psychosomatic disorders than those who have not. Their bodies have indeed been traumatized, and they may thereby generalize from the genital trauma to other areas. Sometimes children who have been forced into oral sex will complain about nausea, vomiting, and stomach aches. Fabricators do not typically suffer with psychosomatic complaints. However, some fabricators may have such complaints (common in childhood) from other sources. This is one of the factors that weakens this differentiating criterion.

Regressive Behavior   Children who have been sexually abused are more likely to exhibit regressive behavior such as enuresis, encopresis, thumb sucking, baby talk, and separation anxieties. Having been psychologically traumatized at a higher level of development, they wish to regress to earlier levels in order to gain the securities attendant to these more primitive states. Children who are fabricators are less likely to exhibit such regressive manifestations.

A Sense of Betrayal   Children who have genuinely been abused suffer with deep-seated feelings of having been betrayed. They feel betrayed by the offender because of his exploitation of them, and they may feel betrayed by their mothers, escpecially in situations in which the latter does not provide them with protection from further abuse. I.S. Lourie and L.C. Blick (1987a) state it well: "Nonetheless, the children still feel betrayed. Someone upon whom the children have relied and in whom was placed a basic sense of trust has taken advantage of this dependency and trust in a destructive way." The children feel a loss of trust in the parent who has abused them and the concomitant sense of betrayal may be devastating. T.B. Kaufman (1987) states: "The abuse serves to rob children of the small degree of personal power they may have, leaving them helpless and defenseless in a world in which they have also lost faith in their parents, their primary protectors." The younger the child, the less specific the description of such betrayal. It is only older children who will describe it, especially with regard to the unprotecting mother. Children who fabricate sex abuse do not generally complain about the fact that their mothers did not protect them from the indignities they suffered at the hands of their fathers. This factor is lost from consideration by both the mother (who is happy to broadcast the abuse) and the child (who joins her in such public denunciation).

Differentiating Criteria of Low But Potentially Higher Value

Sleep Disturbances   Children who have been sexually abused often suffer with sleep disturbances. Fear of going to bed may be related to the fact that the abuse has occurred at bedtime and that the perpetrator has used the occasion of putting the child to sleep as an opportunity for sexual abuse. The scenario may involve the perpetrator's kissing the child goodnight: starting with the forehead, then the cheeks, the lips (lingers there), the neck, the nipples, the abdomen, and then the genitalia. The child may not appreciate that the extra pleasurable sensations associated with the genital "kiss" are not outside normal "goodnight" activities. Or the offender may "check" the vagina to see whether the child has to go to the bathroom. And this may be done with a finger or even with the penis. Again, the child may not appreciate the fact that such examinations are atypical and exploitive. However, once the child learns that these activities are "bad, wrong, or sinful," then guilt and fear are evoked and the child may fear going to sleep, suffer from nightmares, and wake up in the middle of the night fearful of the perpetrator's overtures.

Children who fabricate sex abuse do not typically describe such sleep disturbances. However, the child who is a fabricator may very well be exposed to other environmental influences that may produce sleep disturbances. Exposure to the multiple traumas attendant to the parents' divorce and custody dispute may very well lead to tensions and anxieties that can produce a sleep disturbance. Only by inquiry into the nature of the child's fears about going to sleep can one utilize this as a differentiating criterion.

Chronicity By the time bona fide sex abuse comes to the attention of others, it may have been going on for a long period. Fabricating abusers more often describe only one or two experiences, which is deemed to be enough for the purposes of the litigation. Again, this is not a strong differentiating criterion because there are children who have been sexually abused on one or two occasions. This drawback notwithstanding, chronicity still speaks more for the abuse being genuine.

Pseudomaturity Some girls who have been sexually abused by their fathers have been prematurely pressured into a pseudomature relationship with him. In some cases the abuse was actually encouraged (overtly or covertly) by the mother in order to use the child as a substitute object for the father's sexual gratification. Such mothers view sexual encounters as odious, and the child is used as a convenient replacement—protecting the mother thereby from exposure to the noxious act. Sometimes this pattern extends itself to the mother's encouraging the daughter to assume other domestic roles such as housekeeping, caring for the other children, etc. The result is a pseudomature girl who provides the father with a variety of wifelike gratifications. Girls who fabricate sex abuse are less likely to be pseudomature and/or placed in such a situation. However, pseudomaturity can result from other factors—factors having nothing to do with sex abuse—thereby weakening this differentiating criterion. Boys who have been sexually molested are less likely to become pseudomature.

Seductive Behavior with the Perpetrator The girl who has been sexually abused by her father, and who does not consider her acts to be sinful or bad, may exhibit seductive behavior in the joint interview(s) with him, in the presence of the examiner. She may not recognize that such behavior may be a source of embarrassment to him and threaten disclosure of the sexual encounters. Girls who fabricate sexual encounters are not as likely to be seductive with their fathers. However, the interrogation itself may engender such seductive inclinations, and so the value of this differentiating criterion is lessened. However, it still does have potential value. Boys who have been sexually molested are less likely to exhibit seductive behavior with the accused.

Retraction The issue of retraction of the allegation is a complex one, but it has relevance to differentiating bona fide from fabricated sex abuse allegations. Both types of children may recant. The child who has been genuinely abused may retract from the appreciation of the consequences of the disclosure. The retraction may come from a desire to protect the abuser from punishment. Sometimes the retraction stems from the fear of retaliation by the perpetrator—to the child, the mother, or others. Children who have fabricated sex abuse may also retract because of their appreciation of the consequences of their allegation. The retraction here, however, is more likely to be associated with guilt, because the child did not initially appreciate the serious implications and consequences of the allegation. In both cases the child may go back and forth between disclosure and recanting. Although the *guilt* element is more likely to produce retraction by the fabricator and the *fear* element more likely to produce recanting by the genuinely abused, one may certainly see fear in the fabricator and guilt in the genuinely abused in association with the recanting. Nevertheless, there is still some value to this differentiating criterion, because fear is more likely to be associated with the recant of the genuinely abused child and guilt with the retraction of the fabricator.

THE MOTHER

As mentioned, I will use the mother as the prototype for the accuser in that this is most often her role. However, this does not preclude females from being sexual abusers. Most workers in the field agree that males are sex abusers far more frequently than females.

We sometimes hear about the typical personality patterns and general characteristics of mothers who support or even initiate a child's fabrication of sex abuse. There are risks involved in making such generalizations because we have not had enough experience at this point to come to definitive conclusions in this area. What I present below are tentative conclusions, held by many who examine such mothers. We must recognize, however, that these conclusions will probably have to be modified as we gain more experience in this area. J. Waterman (1986a) provides a summary of the literature on the personality patterns and family dynamics of such mothers.

Very Valuable Differentiating Criteria

The Initial Scenario   It is important for the examiner to learn from the mother the exact way she learned about the sex abuse. Mothers of the fabricators will often describe a situation in which it is clear that she has created the scenario from minimal if nonexistent evidence. This is less likely to be the case for the mothers of children who have been genuinely abused. I recall one situation in which a mother, who was litigating heavily for the custody of her three- and five-year-old boys, asked them about their visit with their father. In the course of the conversation the mother learned that the father had taken both boys into the shower with him, had rubbed them down with soap, and they all showered together. The mother then went into a detailed inquiry with the boys regarding whether or not the father had washed their genitals and rear ends. They both replied in the affirmative. She then involved herself in a detailed inquiry regarding whether, when washing their genitals, he had rubbed soap on their penises. Again, they responded in the affirmative. She then asked whether he had rubbed their penises back and forth, and again they said yes. She then asked whether their penises had gotten hard and the boys initially said no. On repeated questioning as to whether they were *sure* that the penises weren't even *a little* hard, the boys responded that they might have been "a little hard."

She then turned to a discussion of the details of his washing their buttocks. She asked them whether the father's hand had gone between the cheeks, and the boys agreed that his hand had. She then tried to get details about how deeply his hand had gone, especially as to whether or not he had touched their anuses. Again, the boys replied that his hand had touched their anuses "a little bit." She then tried to learn whether his finger had been inserted *into* their anuses. Whereas initially the boys stated that they did not think so, after repeated questioning they admitted that perhaps his finger had gone into their anuses "a little bit."

The mother immediately called her lawyer, who spoke with the boys. By that time their penises were harder and the insertion of the finger into their anuses was deeper. By the time they reached the consulting psychologist (who did not see fit to call in the father and get his opinion on this matter), definite erections and deep insertion into the anus was claimed. The psychologist then called in the New Jersey Department of Youth and Family Services (DYFS), the agency responsible for investigating such matters, and the children by this time provided a full description of sexual abuse. It wasn't until the father got a call from DYFS that he learned about what had gone on. The mother's attorney reported the matter to the court, and the judge ordered an immediate cessation of visitations, pending a plenary court hearing. It wasn't until six months later that I was finally involved in the case. By the time I saw them the boys described "white stuff" to have come out of their penises when their father stroked their erections. Apparently, the person who had planted this seed (the reader will please excuse the pun) was not aware of the fact that any ejaculates pre-pubertal boys may have are generally clear. It took another six months before the court ruled that there was no evidence for sex abuse. By this time the matter was in local newspapers, and the father's reputation and business suffered irreparably.

In contrast, one does not generally see such scenarios in children who suffer bona fide abuse. One doesn't get a story in which there is evidence of the mother coercing, cajoling, and drawing out a story with the desire to transform an innocuous event into a sexual trauma. Rather, the tendency on the mother's part is to underplay it. I.S. Lourie and L.C. Blick (1987b) describe the three most common ways in which bona fide sex abuse is disclosed. The first method involves the child. The child steps forth and deliberately and intentionally tells someone, usually in the hope of some intervention. Childen who fabricate abuse rarely initiate such a disclosure. Rather, as mentioned above, it is elicited and even manufactured by the mother. The second way in which children divulge is generally unintentional. A parent notices a consistent change in the child's behavior and questions the child about what is wrong. It is from such questioning that the abuse may be revealed. This kind of disclosure may very well take place when the sex abuse is fabricated. The difference is that in the bona fide something really is wrong and in the fabricated situation, the mother is using some transient period of discomfort, unrelated to abuse, as an excuse for conducting an inquiry in the hope of eliciting information that might serve the purposes of a sex-abuse allegation. The third way in which the sex abuse can be disclosed is through actual observation of the sexual act. The mother in the fabricated scenario does not generally describe having observed the sexual acts herself; rather, she claims the child related it to her.

Shame   Many (if not most) mothers of children who have been genuinely abused are ashamed about the fact that their husbands have engaged in such reprehensible behavior with their children. Some deny the obvious in order not to "rock the boat" and thereby jeopardize the marriage. Others tolerate it silently because of the public stigma associated with such behavior on a father's part. Some of these sanctioning mothers will readily accept the father's promise that he will "never do it again." Although they may partially recognize that sexual abuse of a child is often compulsive, and thereby very difficult to control, their willingness to accept the apology and believe that the father will indeed never repeat the act is basically a statement of their compliance and their sanctioning its repetition. Some mothers may tell the child not to tell anyone lest the family suffer public mortification. Even those who are more vociferous in their reactions to the abuse do not generally advertise it to the world.

This is in direct contrast to the mothers of children who fabricate sex abuse in the context of child custody disputes. These mothers would have the world know it if they could. If they were given opportunities to vilify the father on public television, they would often do so. Their greatest desire is to publicly humiliate the father and thereby insure that he will be viewed by the court as too despicable a character to possibly be considered worthy of fathering his children. In the service of this goal they will exaggerate every scintilla of evidence the child provides or every shred of information that they have suggested the child provide. They fan every spark and make a mountain out of every molehill. This is in contrast to mothers of genuinely abused children who traditionally are likely to make light of the abuse and tend to view it as less extensive and pervasive than it may have been.

Seeking "Hired Gun" Evaluators   In the course of custody litigation, mothers of the fabricating children will seek only "hired gun" evaluators in order to insure that their positions will be supported in the courtroom. They will not risk involving the services of an impartial examiner, lest he or she see through the facade and expose the sham. Elsewhere (1982) I have elaborated on the importance of examiners serving only as impartials rather than as advocates in custody litigation.

Mothers of children who were genuinely abused may not be involved in custody disputes, and so they are not looking for hired guns. If, however, after divulgence of the abuse, they decide not to divorce, they are likely to seek the services of people whose aim is more conciliatory, that is, individuals who might be available to treat the father and/or bring about an improvement in the family situation that might have contributed to the abuse.

Attempts to Corroborate the Child's Story in Joint Interview   In joint interviews, when the mother is present with the child, the child will often "check" the sex-abuse description with the mother through side glances and other gestures to be sure that the "correct" story is being related. The mothers are actively involved in transmitting the proper signals. And the child actively seeks the mother's corroboration. It is as if they are working as a team. Often it is hard to keep such mothers quiet—so pressured are they into insuring that the child comes up with the complete story with all its details. Children who have been genuinely abused do not usually involve themselves in such behavior. They know well what has happened, and they do not need any assistance in helping them remember the details.

Moderately Valuable Differentiating Criteria

Appreciation of the Psychological Trauma of Repeated Interrogations   Mothers of children who fabricate sex abuse do not generally appreciate the psychological trauma to the child of repeated interrogations by mental health and legal professionals. This trauma is sometimes referred to as *legal process trauma*. They are so enraged at their husbands, and so determined to wreak vengeance on him, that they blind themselves to the detrimental effects of the interrogations on their children. In contrast, mothers of children who have suffered bona fide sex abuse are usually more hesitant to subject their children to these inquiries. This does not simply relate to their reluctance to have the abuse divulged but to their appreciation that the interrogations are likely to be psychologically traumatic. I consider this a moderately valuable differentiating criterion because there are some mothers of children who have been genuinely abused who become so enraged that they blind themselves to the detrimental effects of the legal and psychological interrogations.

Appreciation of the Father-Child Relationship   The mothers of children who are fabricating sex abuse are generally so angry that they ignore or deny the importance of the father-child relationship and welcome every opportunity to exclude the father completely from the child's life. They welcome the facility with which the courts may interrupt visitation, pending the outcome of the investigations, and seem to be oblivious to the fact that the removal of the father completely from the child's life may be psychologically detrimental. They will use the alleged sex abuse as justification for denying any possible benefit the child might derive from the father-child relationship. In contrast, mothers of children who have been genuinely abused may still recognize that, the abuse notwithstanding, the father may still provide valuable input into the child's life. I include this criterion under the category of the moderately valuable ones, because there are some mothers who are so incensed over bona fide sex abuse that they will attempt to exclude the father entirely from the child's life and deny that he can now provide any beneficial input.

Childhood History of Sex Abuse   The mothers of youngsters who fabricate sex abuse were not typically sexually abused themselves as children. Mothers of children who are genuinely abused are more likely to have been abused themselves as children. Sometimes, mothers who were sexually abused as children may have set up a situation to increase the likelihood that the father will abuse the child. They may do this as a way of mastering their own abuse trauma. They may secretly and/or unconsciously hope that the child's resistance or successful working through will vicariously enable them to do the same for themselves. Or, they may have responded to the abuse by frigidity or sexual unresponsivity and use the child as a substitute source of satisfaction for their husbands. I consider this a moderately valuable differentiating criterion because some mothers of the children who fabricate may indeed have been sexually abused themselves but, as mentioned, such a history is more likely present in the parent of the child who has been genuinely abused.

Passivity and/or Incapacitation The mothers of children who have been genuinely involved in incestuous relationships with the father are more likely to be passive, incapacitated, disabled, or even absent frequently from the home. In contrast, the mothers of fabricating youngsters are more likely to be aggressive and outspoken. Because the opposite characteristics are possible (but less probable) in each category, I include this as a moderately valuable differentiating criteria.

Differentiating Criteria of Low
But Potentially Higher Value

Personality Characteristics Mothers of children who were sexually abused are more likely to be social isolates, whereas the mothers of the fabricators are less likely to be so. In addition, mothers of the fabricators are more likely to be hysterical, paranoid, or delusional. In contrast, the mothers of the bona fide category are less likely to exhibit these personality characteristics. I include these diffentiations to be of low value because one may certainly see hysteria, paranoia, and delusional thinking in the mothers of the bona fide category and one may see social isolation in the mothers of the fabricators; however, such characteristics are less likely.

My comments here relate directly to my previously stated warning that it is dangerous for an examiner to conclude that there are typical personality patterns of the parents of sexually abused children and/or the parents of the fabricators. The word *typical* is too strong considering the wide variety of personality traits that parents in both of these categories may exhibit. However, there are some patterns that may prove useful, and these have been described herein.

THE FATHER

The fathers who are bona fide abusers are often said to fall into certain personality categories. I believe such generalizations are dangerous. There are surveys that indicate that 15–20 percent of all children have suffered some form of sexual abuse during their childhood. If this is the case, then one is making statements about the personality characteristics of 15–20 percent of abusers. Accordingly, there must be a wide variety of personality characteristics in this population, and generalizations are thereby made much more difficult. Each father must be evaluated individually in an attempt to ascertain what factors operated in his case to contribute to his sexually abusing his children. J. Waterman (1986a) provides a good overview of the literature on personality characteristics of fathers who sexually abuse their children.

Very Valuable Differentiating Criteria

Bribes and/or Threats   Children who have experienced genuine sex abuse have often been bribed by the abusing father. Accordingly, there will be a past history of frequent gifts and other indulgences. Children in the fabricating category generally have not been so indulged. Other children are warned that terrible consequences will ensue if they reveal the sexual activities to others. The child who fabricates sexual abuse does not generally present with a past history of such threats. Sometimes the bribes and/or threats play on the child's guilt with resulting feelings of disloyalty over the divulgences. Again, children who fabricate their allegations do not generally exhibit guilt related to such indoctrination.

Indignation   The fathers who have been falsely accused generally suffer with extreme indignation. This is not feigned. They can often be considered to be in the category of the innocent man who has been accused of a crime. There is a sense of impotency, and in joint interview with the children they may plead with them to be honest. Many will be quite willing to take a lie detector test and spontaneously request it. (I will comment below on the lie detector test.) Sometimes their indignation will develop into rage, but it is more often a sense of impotent rage that one observes. In contrast, fathers who have genuinely involved themselves in such incestuous behavior may put on a facade of false indignation, but one can generally detect their lack of conviction. More commonly, one sees passive silence, which cannot be viewed as the reaction of an innocent man who is being accused of a crime. There is an artificiality to their prostestations of innocence. There is a play-acting quality to their denials that lessens considerably their credibility. The important aspect of this differentiating criterion is whether or not there is a sense of bona fide indignation and whether the father demonstrates the manifestations of an innocent man being accused of a crime.

Presence of Other Sexual Deviations   Another important differentiating criterion is the presence of associated sexual deviations. Men who involve themselves in pedophilia often exhibit other sexual deviations such as exhibitionism, rape, voyeurism, sado-masochism, and homosexuality. There are some who might take issue with my inclusion of homosexuality here as a sexual deviation. As described elsewhere (Gardner, 1982, 1986a), I consider *obligatory* homosexuality to be a psychiatric disorder. Whether or not the reader agrees with me on this subject, the realities are that a father with homosexual inclinations is more likely to sexually abuse a male child than a father who is heterosexual.

Moderately Valuable
Differentiating Criteria

Childhood History of Sex Abuse Fathers who have been sexually abused themselves in childhood are more likely to abuse their own children than fathers who have not. Fathers of the fabricators are less likely to have been sexually abused in childhood. Those fathers who have been sexually abused in childhood may utilize sexual abuse of their own children as a way of working through the trauma of their own childhood abuse. Moreover, they may view parent-child sexuality as the model, as the natural and expected mode of sexual experience.

Receptivity to Taking a Lie Detector Test Fathers of children who fabricate sex abuse are much more likely to be enthusiastic about taking a lie detector test than the fathers of children who have been genuinely abused. One would think that the former group would be quite enthusiastic and the latter group extremely resistant. However, occasionally the father of a fabricator expresses some reluctance, not because he feels guilty or he has anything to hide, but because of his appreciation that the technique is not 100 percent foolproof. Those fathers who have genuinely abused their children basically do not want to take their chances with the test and, if sophisticated about it, may use the test's occasional inaccuracy (especially with psychopaths) as an excuse for not taking it. Accordingly, I consider receptivity to taking a lie detector test to be a moderately valuable differentiating criterion. If the test were 100 percent foolproof I would put it in the section on very valuable differentiating criteria.

History of Drug and/or Alcohol Abuse   Sexually abusing fathers are much more likely to have a history (past of present) of drug or alcohol abuse. Such utilization is a manifestation of greater psychopathology in the abusing fathers than in the fathers of the fabricators. People who abuse drugs and alcohol tend to be immature, with impaired ability to delay gratification and tolerate frustration. They tend to be dependent, childlike individuals who in many ways have never grown up. Psychologically they relate better to children, with whom they can easily identify. When this psychological bond with the child is combined with adult biological needs, the incest situation is likely to arise (I.S. Lourie and L.C. Blick, 1987a). The fathers of fabricators are not only less likely to be drug abusers, but less likely to have the aforementioned personality characteristics that contribute to the substance abuse as well as the sexual abuse of children.

Self-Esteem   Fathers who abuse their children are more likely to suffer from feelings of low self-worth than those who have not. Often, the fathers in the bona fide group do not feel they can handle an adult egalitarian sexual relationship, especially because they fear female rejection. They welcome the child's passivity, adoration, and unquestioned acceptance of their overtures. In contrast, the fathers of the fabricators generally have a past history of egalitarian heterosexual relationships and can tolerate female rejection to a reasonable degree. I include this as a moderately valuable differentiating criterion, because there are certainly fathers of fabricators who may have had problems with egalitarian relationships with a woman and have had difficulty tolerating female rejection, but such problems are far more common in fathers who are genuine abusers.

Regression   Another manifestation of greater psychopathology in the bona fide abuser is the tendency to regress in stressful situations, especially heterosexual disappointment. They then regress to sexuality with a child—the less threatening sexual experience. Fathers of the fabricators are less likely to manifest a history of regression in response to stress. But divorce is an extremely stressful situation, and fathers of fabricators may very well regress under such circumstances. Because of this I place regression as a moderately valuable differentiating criterion. It is still, however, an important criterion, because fathers who are sexual abusers are more likely to provide past and present histories of regression (especially following stress) than fathers of fabricators.

Career Choice   Fathers of children who have genuinely been abused may select a career that enables them to come in close contact with potential candidates for child sex abuse. Some common career choices that are particularly attractive to men who sexually abuse children are scout leader, coach, summer camp officer, clergyman, choir director, big brother, school janitor, and school bus driver. Teaching at the lower grades of elementary and even nursery school is also an attractive career choice for such abusers. In my elementary school days in New York City, it was against the policy of the New York City Board of Education to allow men to teach below the sixth grade. Although we were not told the reason for this, I suspect strongly that the policy related to the fear that men might sexually molest the children. Although this policy has long since been inoperative, it may not have been completely misguided. I am not recommending that we go back to the old system and prohibit men from teaching at the lower grades; I am only stating that we must be aware that allowing them to do so is associated with certain risks. My reason for stating that we continue the practice relates to the recognition that many children grow up in homes without fathers, and having a male teacher can serve as a form of valuable compensation.

Social Isolation   Sexually abusing fathers are more likely to be social isolates. Having few friends outside the home, they are likely to turn to their children for companionship and even sexual gratification. The fathers of the fabricators are not as likely to be social isolates. I include this as a moderately valuable differentiating criteria because there certainly are fathers of fabricators who may be socially isolated, and there are fathers of the genuinely abused who may be more outgoing. However, the initial generalization still has merit.

Differentiating Criteria of Low But Potentially Higher Value

Stepfathers   Stepfathers are more likely than fathers to be sex- abuse offenders. Stepfathers generally exhibit less of an incest taboo than fathers. They have not grown up with the child over years and have not become desensitized somewhat to the child's sexual attractiveness. In addition, stepfathers have a lower sense of loyalty to their stepchildren than fathers have to their children. Accordingly, a father may squelch sexual impulses toward a child from the recognition of the detrimental effects it could have on the children. Stepfathers are less likely to have such loyalty. In addition, children are less likely to be seductive with their fathers than their stepfathers; this child initiation factor is less likely to be operative with fathers than stepfathers. (I will discuss below in greater detail the issue of the child's initiation and contribution to the sex abuse.) I consider this a differentiating criterion of low but potentially higher value because there are certainly fathers who do sexually abuse their children but, in my experience, stepfathers are more likely to.

Personality Characteristics   Some fathers who abuse their children are rigid and controlling. They need to have total control of their families, not simply their children but their wives as well. Their dominating control includes utilizing family members to service them and provide them with a multiplicity of gratifications and indulgences, one of which is sexual gratification—regardless of the age (and even the sex) of the gratifier. Fathers of the fabricators are less likely to exhibit the personality characteristic of rigid demand for complete obedience from all members of the family.

Interestingly, some fathers who sexually abuse their children are very moralistic, especially regarding sex. They may moralize to an obsessive degree. Some even become clergymen, an occupation that provides them with a socially acceptable vehicle for their moralizing. Such an obsession may relate to the mechanism of reaction formation: It is not so much others they are trying to convince to be "pure," but themselves. Preachers are more often preaching to themselves than to their congregations. When this fragile defense mechanism breaks down, they become "the sinners" they have basically always wanted to be and may become child molesters. And, if choir boys are available, they become easy victims because of the reverence these youngsters may have for their abusers. Because nonabusing fathers may still exhibit qualities of controlling behavior and moralism, I include this as differentiating criterion of low but potentially higher value.

CLINICAL EVALUATION

Preliminary Considerations

Before I agree to evaluate a child who is fabricating sex abuse, I insist that I do so under the aegis of the court. This enables me to be sure that all of the involved parties: the child, the accuser, and the alleged perpetrator will be interviewed. Without such an order I cannot be certain that all parties will be available; without such an order, one or more of the parties may decide to withdraw from the evaluation before it is completed. In addition, the court order is so worded that I am chosen to serve as an impartial examiner, rather than as an advocate of either side. Under such circumstances I am viewed by the court as the judge's appointee and answer directly to him or her. Because I am not serving as a hired-gun advocate of either side, my findings and conclusions are more likely to be viewed as credible by the court. These provisions of my involvement are described in detail in my provisions document: *Provisions for Accepting an Invititation to Serve as an Impartial Examiner in Sex-Abuse Litigation* (Addendum I).

Evaluating the Child Without the Alleged Abuser   On occasion I am asked to conduct an evaluation of an allegedly abused child, and I am told that I will not be permitted to evaluate the alleged perpetrator. I have never agreed to evaluate a child under such circumstances. Interviewing a child alone and then stating whether or not the child has indeed been abused is certainly possible in many situations. But there are other situations in which it may be very difficult, if not impossible. An examiner is much more likely to be able to make a statement about such abuse if he or she has the opportunity to evaluate the accused person. But more important, if one is to ascertain whether it was the accused or some other party who abused the child, it is crucial that that party be interviewed. The referring sources usually have some particular individual in mind when they make such a request, and the examiner's statement that the child was indeed abused is tantamount to making an accusation by hearsay and may contribute to the alleged perpetrator's being tried by hearsay. Such procedure for ascertaining guilt and innocence was commonly used in the days of the Spanish Inquisition. I would like to think that we have gone beyond those times. Seeing a child alone and then making a statement about abuse is a throwback to that tragic era.

Joint Interviews   Because of the serious compromise that the aforementioned evaluation of the child alone causes in a sex-abuse evaluation, I require a court order in which all parties involved in the abuse are required to be interviewed by me, individually and in any combination that I consider warranted. It is important for the reader to appreciate that I do not automatically place the child and the alleged perpetrator in the room together. I only insist upon the freedom to do so if I consider it warranted. I recognize that such a confrontation may be extremely traumatic for some children and, in such cases, I may not conduct such an interview. It is because of the recognition that such a confrontation may be potentially traumatic that many investigators will attempt to protect the child from this trauma and absolutely refuse such permission. I believe that this is misguided benevolence, because to implement it as a blanket rule may deprive the examiner of an important source of information. It deprives the examiner of direct confrontation between the accused and the victim, a confrontation that may be the richest source of data pertinent to the question of whether or not the abuse actually occurred. The alleged perpetrator is the one who is in the best position to respond specifically to the allegation. He was presumably at the site(s) where the abuse allegedly took place, and he can thereby conduct a cross-examination far better than the lawyers, judges, and mental health professionals. He is in a better position than all of the other involved parties to "smoke out the truth," and the presence of the examiner can assure that the alleged perpetrator's inquiry is humane and nonpunitive.

Proponents of the adversary system claim that one of its strongest points is that it insures that the accused will be faced by his or her accuser. This, they claim, is an advantage over the inquisitorial system, in which people were often condemned without any opportunity to know what the charges were against them and who made them. I certainly am in agreement with the principle of the accused facing the accuser. However, the adversary system does not allow for such confrontations in the optimum way. The two face one another in a courtroom in which each is required to provide testimony under extremely restricted and constrained conditions. Proponents of the system do not appreciate fully the drawbacks of such an artificial type of confrontation. Each party comes with prepared presentations, and each party generally has a roster or an agenda of data that he or she will not present to the court. It is an extremely artificial and unnatural kind of confrontation. The kind of confrontations I conduct in my office are much more natural and spontaneous. They allow for a free flow of communication between the two parties and give the accused a much greater opportunity to prove his or her innocence. Neither is protected by a system designed to provide the judge with selected information. I recognize that there may be situations in which the confrontation between the accused and the accuser might get carried away to the point where someone's life might be endangered. Under such circumstances one could still conduct such confrontations with other parties being present to protect them from one another. I can envision a situation in which they might have to be separated from one another by a glass partition and communicate through microphones. But still, such an arrangement is far superior to the restricted confrontations of the courtroom.

The Length of the Evaluation   The provisions document also insures that I will have the opportunity to conduct as many interviews as I consider warranted. Many investigators confine themselves to one or two interviews in sex-abuse cases. Sometimes this is dictated by the pressures of their positions and the great number of cases that need to be investigated. The acquisition of information about such a delicate issue as sex abuse is best accomplished when there has been a relationship formed between the evaluator and the child—and this is especially the case when the child has *genuinely* been sexually abused. The greater the number of sessions allowed for the inquiry, the greater the likelihood that such a relationship will develop. This is the same principle that holds in treatment: One is much more likely to get accurate data from a patient who has formed a relationship with the therapist, trusts him or her, and has had the living experience over time that divulgences will not result in humiliation or rejection. I would generally consider three or four interviews to be a minimum for the development of the kind of relationship that is going to prove useful in ascertaining whether or not sexual abuse has indeed taken place. This is especially the case for children who have been genuinely abused because of their fears of the consequences of disclosure. Although one may be able to diagnose a parental alienation syndrome in the first interview—and conclude thereby that the allegation has a high likelihood of being fabricated—there is still the possibility that bona fide abuse has taken place. Furthermore, even in those cases in which the abuse has indeed been fabricated, one wants to ascertain whether or not changes take place over a series of interviews in order to confirm one's initial conclusion. So here, too, multiple interviews are necessary.

Audiotapes and Videotapes   In many cases it is a good idea to make audiotapes and even videotapes of the interviews. Courts are becoming less reluctant to utilize videotapes because of their increasing appreciation that they can be extremely valuable sources of information. Videotapes are especially useful for comparing original statements with subsequent ones—in order to pick up alterations and discrepancies that are valuable in differentiating the bona fide from the fabricated sex-abuse allegation. An important further benefit of the videotape is that it can protect the child from the psychological trauma of multiple interviews. If the court will permit the videotape to be shown in evidence, it will protect the child from direct interviews with the judge, attorneys, mental health professionals, and others. It may even be used in lieu of the child's giving testimony directly. Courts vary with regard to their receptivity to the use of such taped interviews. I believe, however, that they are becoming increasingly appreciative of their value and are thereby becoming more receptive to their utilization.

The argument that a tape can be tampered with (and therefore risky evidence) is not, in my opinion, a good one. If one suspects tampering, one can have the tape examined by an expert qualified to detect the presence of such. But even a nonprofessional can often detect an unnatural interruption or break in the smooth flow of the videotaped interview. The fear of such tampering is a throwback to the times when only audiotapes were available. Tampering with them was much less likely to be recognized easily by the average person, and even experts might have difficulty if the tampering was done by an extremely skilled technician. In my office I generally tape two videotapes simultaneously. One of these is mine, and one of these is brought in by the patient or client. I use this practice for therapeutic purposes, in order to enable patients to view their sessions at home. But the same procedure can be used to insure that tapes are not tampered with. The litigant him- or herself takes the copy at the time it is made, and each copy serves as insurance that the other has not been tampered with. One problem with videotapes is that they are extremely time-consuming to review, edit, and transcribe. This drawback notwithstanding, their advantages far outweigh their disadvantages. K. MacFarlane and S. Krebs (1986a) have written a useful review of this issue.

Interviewing the Child

Preliminary Considerations Prior to the interview with the child, it is important for the examiner to learn from the parents what the particular words are that are used by that child to designate various body parts, especially genital parts. It is also important for the examiner to determine how many previous interviews there have been. The greater the number of previous interrogations the greater the likelihood the child will have developed a litany, and this creates problems regarding differentiating bona fide from fabricated sex-abuse allegations. Also, in the early interviews the child is likely to use terminology that is natural to the home and uncontaminated by professional jargon. With subsequent interviews the child is more likely to pick up professional terminology to the point where, in later interviews, the child might present him- or herself as one who has been "sexually molested" or "sexually abused." Obviously, these are not the kinds of terms that normal three- or four-year-olds are likely to use. Children who fabricate sex abuse may use such terms in the first interview because they have been programmed to do so. Also, successive interviews generally entrench feelings of guilt and disloyalty. Many children, especially those who have been abused at ages two and three, may not have initially considered their sexual activities to have been bad, wrong, or sinful. They may have considered themselves fortunate to have had a parent who provides them with such gratification. Generally, once the disclosure is made to a third party, new attitudes toward the activity develop. Of course, when the child has been sexually coerced from the outset and warned about the terrible consequences of disclosure, then the notion that the activity is wrong and sinful will have been inculcated from the beginning.

Ideally, the child should be brought to the interview by a neutral third person, that is, someone who is neither the accused nor the accuser. In situations in which the sex-abuse allegation is part of a parental alienation syndrome, the child is likely to describe and elaborate upon the sex abuse if the accuser is present in the waiting room and is likely to underplay and possibly even deny it if the alleged perpetrator is in the waiting room. In the severer cases of parental alienation syndrome, however, the child may be comfortable making the accusation under circumstances in which the accused is nearby and even brought into the consultation room. In situations of genuine sex abuse, the presence of the perpetrator in the waiting room may be such a source of fear in the child that little information about the abuse will be forthcoming. The presence of the accuser, however, may make it more likely that the child will reveal the information. In all these situations the child appears to operate on the principle that what is said to the examiner will be immediately revealed to the person waiting outside. Or the child may recognize that the parent who is outside may "grill" him or her regarding what has been said.

In order to prevent these potential contaminations, the

examiner does well to arrange that a neutral third party bring the youngster to the individual interviews. Sometimes the so-called neutral third party may not be so neutral in that the individual may have been selected by a parent and has a particular position with regard to the allegation. The examiner must take into consideration this person's beliefs or biases when conducting the interview. In some cases a neutral third party may not be available to bring the child. Under these circumstances the examiner should alternate interviews so that the child is brought to one or more interviews by the mother and one or more by the father. Under such circumstances it is crucial that the examiner ascertain whether the story varies in accordance with which parent is sitting in the waiting room.

An Important Data-Collection Interview Sequence When interviewing children in order to determine whether or not they have been sexually abused, the examiner does well to follow the specific sequence outlined below. I am not as firm with this sequence when interviewing children who have not been sexually abused, but I do believe that the proposed sequence is extremely important when interviewing children under consideration for sex abuse. The sequence follows a progression from the elicitation of material that is least likely to be contaminated by stimuli provided by the examiner to material that is most likely to be so contaminated. In this way the examiner is most likely to obtain useful data. The more the examiner digresses from this sequence, the greater the likelihood that contaminated data will be evoked.

Direct Verbal Inquiry with the Child   The best kind of information to obtain from the child in the inquiry regarding sex abuse is that which is derived from directly verbal discussion. I recognize that this may not be possible because of the child's verbal immaturity and/or inhibitions regarding disclosure of the sexual abuse (in cases where it has been genuine). However, the examiner does well to recognize that it is the optimum kind of information. The fabricating child, of course, will be happy to provide this information directly and will quickly present his or her litany. The genuinely abused child is less likely to provide a little speech. And the child who has been genuinely abused may be extremely reluctant, fearful, and so guilt-ridden that direct verbal communication of the abuse is extremely difficult, if not impossible, to obtain.

At the outset of the interview with the child who is being evaluated for possible sexual abuse, it is extremely important for the evaluator to keep in mind an important principle of the psychoanalytic interview. I am referring here to the concept of the psychoanalytic "blank screen." In order to avoid any potential contamination of the child's comments by anything the examiner may say, it is crucial that he or she refrain from any comments that might direct the child's verbalizations into a specific area, sexual or otherwise. In the ideal situation the examiner need say nothing, and the child spontaneously begins verbalizing. The fabricators, who recognize that this is the time for their litany, directly go into their little speeches. Those who have been genuinely abused are less likely to do so, especially if the evaluator is one of the first. But even in later interviews, those who have been genuinely abused may be quite reticent to talk. One wants to determine what is occupying the child's mind. One wants to find out what thoughts are spinning around. One wants to avoid saying anything that might stimulate and pull forth a particular line of thinking. The best way to do this is for the examiner to make only the most vague catalytic comments necessary to elicit spontaneous verbalizations.

Accordingly, I much prefer a "pure" verbal interchange at the outset. Adult patients in analysis know well that the analyst will not be saying anything at the beginning of the session, and so they will generally start in without any comments at all from him or her. Children may need a little more encouragement. Generally, I will often start the interview by asking the child his or her name, age, address, and other statistic-type questions. I have not found these to be contaminating. Rather, they progressively reduce the child's tension and anxiety because the child will generally get the right answers. It is as if each time the child gets a right answer tension and anxiety is reduced. Following this I may then ask a more general, open-ended question such as: "So how are you today?" "So what's been happening to you lately?" "What would you like to talk to me about?" If such general introductory questions do not result in the child's talking about the sex abuse, then the examiner might broach the subject in a general way. The less specific, the less "food for thought" the question provides, the greater the likelihood it will not contaminate the child's responses. I would consider the following to be good questions to pose to a child at this point, especially a child who the examiner suspects will be receptive to talking about the sex abuse: "I understand from your mother that some unusual things have been going on between you and your father. I'd like you to tell me about them." "I understand that some special things have happened to you recently. I'd like you to talk about them to me." "What do you understand to be the reasons why you are here?" "I understand there are some things that have been happening to you that are particularly hard for you to talk about. I know it may be difficult for you, but it's important that we discuss these things. I think this would be a good time to start talking about them." When using these questions, the examiner is particularly careful not to mention specifically the sex-abuse issue. The more the question makes specific reference to sex abuse, the greater the likelihood it will serve as a contaminant.

Leading questions, that is, questions that are designed to lead more directly to the sex-abuse issue, should only be used *after* the child has been given the opportunity to freely express him- or herself on any topic. If one does ask leading questions, then one must recognize that they may serve as a contaminant and may provide false answers because of the child's suggestibility. The leading question communicates to the child (correctly) that the examiner wants the child to answer in a specific way. I present now some examples of questions that could be considered leading questions if posed when the sex-abuse issue had not been admitted or had been denied by the child. "What was the color of the stuff that came out of your father's penis when he rubbed it back and forth?" The assumption here is that the father masturbated in front of the child, and all the child is being asked to do is describe the color of the ejaculate. It is a kind of "trick question" designed to get the child to admit the abuse. By answering the simple question about the color of the semen, the assumption can reasonably be made that the father did indeed masturbate in front of the child. However, there are children who have had no such experiences, but who will provide a color in order to ingratiate themselves to the examiner. Another example: "How many fingers did your uncle put into your vagina?" Again, the assumption is made that the uncle did indeed insert his finger(s) into the child's vagina and the only question is the number of fingers inserted. All the child need do is state a number and the implication is strongly made that the uncle did indeed sexually abuse the child. Another example: "Tell me about the things your father did with his penis when he put you to bed at night." Again, the implication here is that the father did indeed perform sexual acts and all the child need do is to fill in the details.

Lawyers who defend alleged offenders are justifiably suspicious of leading questions. They recognize the child's

suggestibility and susceptibility and believe that many innocent parties have been convicted of sex abuse because of
them. I am in agreement that such miscarriages of justice
have taken place because of leading questions posed by
overzealous examiners who "feed" the child answers incorporated into their questions. Mental health practitioners, as
well, should be wary of such questions and do everything
possible to avoid using them. Such specific questions do,
however, have a place when the child has admitted sexual
experiences and the examiner justifiably wants to obtain
details, especially corroborative details in order to insure that
the admission is bona fide and not fabricated.

When the examiner does get into more specific details
about sexual encounters, it is important to appreciate that
questions regarding *when* the alleged activities occurred are
of little value because the younger the child, the less the
likelihood he or she will be able to pinpoint the particular
time when the event occurred. It will confuse the child and
result in misleading and false answers, which then only
complicate the problem of differentiating bona fide from
fabricated sex-abuse allegations. Prosecutors and other legal
investigators commonly use *when* questions as a carry-over
from criminal investigations. They certainly serve well with
regard to crimes perpetrated by adults, but obfiscate the
interrogatory process when utilized with children who have
been sexually abused. Better questions relate to *where* and
what has gone on—with the request for specific details about
the setting, scene, and events. In addition, the examiner
does well to appreciate that children are not likely to give
accurate data when asked questions about the *number* of
times they were sexually abused. This principle is not
foolproof, however. A child may well appreciate one or two
events as opposed to a long series, but not know much about
the number if the number of experiences was 10, 15, 20, or
more.

Many examiners consider it important to establish early in the interview whether or not the child knows the difference between the truth and a lie. Lawyers, especially, may get involved in such inquiries because of statutes that require the establishment of the child's cognitive capacity in this area before determining whether or not the child's statements should be given credibility. This is simplistic thinking if one is interviewing children below the age of six or seven. And the younger the child is below these ages, the less meaningful such differentiation is going to be. Most three-year-olds can generally differentiate between a boy and a girl. Accordingly, if one shows a three-year-old child a picture of a boy and asks whether it is *a lie* to say that the picture is of a girl, the child will generally say that the examiner is lying. If then one asks whether it is *true* that the picture is of a boy, again the child will correctly state that the examiner is telling the truth. It would be simplistic, however, to conclude from this and possibly similar questions that the child can *generally* differentiate between the truth and a lie. For example, the same child may believe in the existence of Santa Claus. If the examiner asks the child whether it is true or a lie that Santa Claus exists, the child is generally going to say that it is true. The same considerations hold for the Easter Bunny, God, monsters, possibly super-heroes, and a variety of fictional characters from various children's books. And the longer the time span between the alleged abuse and the time of the interrogation, the greater the likelihood the child him- or herself will not be able to make the differentiation between details that are true and those that are lies. Accordingly, I generally recommend that examiners not spend time on making this differentiation.

Recently I saw in consultation a four-year-old girl whose parents were litigating for her custody. One afternoon the girl told her mother, among other things, that her father had killed Santa Claus, killed the Easter Bunny, and put his finger in her vagina. This was reported to the proper state investigatory authorities. It was clear that they did not call the North Pole to find out whether Santa Claus had indeed been killed, nor did they send out search parties to find the dead body of the Easter Bunny. They did, however, descend upon the poor father, and they brought him up on charges of sex abuse. In the *in camera* proceedings with the judge and attorneys, they first had to decide whether or not the child could tell the difference between the truth and a lie. They were complying thereby with state statutes that required them to establish that the child could tell the difference between the truth and a lie before accepting as potentially valid the child's statements about alleged sex abuse. They satisfied themselves that the child did know the difference when the child was able to correctly state that calling a picture of a boy a girl was a lie, and so on. In order to establish this they all had to ignore the fact that the child believed in the existence of Santa Claus and the Easter Bunny, and probably even believed that her father might have killed both of these illustrious figures.

The examiner does well to ask the child about the various events of the day: from the time the child gets up in the morning until the time the child goes to sleep at night. There are two periods, however, that are particularly important to investigate, because they are the times when sex abuse is most likely to take place. These are at *bath time* and *bedtime*. I will discuss each of these separately. As might be expected, the bedtime scene is probably the one in which sex abuse is most likely to occur. A common scenario involves a father's lying down with a little girl, hugging and cuddling her, and relaxing her. This may be associated with telling stories or playing games. Then the time comes to kiss the child goodnight. The father starts with the forehead, then kisses the eyelids, the cheeks, and then the lips. There may be lingering at the lips with tongue kissing. The child may not be aware that this kind of kiss is generally considered improper. The father may then proceed down to kissing the neck, chest, the nipples, the abdomen, and then the genitalia. Kissing the genitalia goodnight may serve as an entree into performing cunnilingus. The child may begin to experience sexual pleasure, but not appreciate that an act considered improper in our society is being perpetrated. The pleasure experienced by the child may serve as an impetus for requests in the future that the father kiss her goodnight again, especially where it "feels good." The child may even be brought to orgasm by this practice. Sometimes another excuse is given for fondling the child's genitalia. The father may "check" the vagina to determine whether or not the child needs to go to the bathroom. Sometimes a father will use his finger for such checking and on occasion his penis. Again, the child may not appreciate the fact that this is an improper act and that it is no way to determine whether or not someone needs to urinate.

With regard to bath time, one should ask specific questions about the bathroom routine: Who gives the bath? Who undresses the child? Who is in the bathroom with the child? Does the person who is giving the child a bath have clothing on? Exactly what places are washed? If the bather gets into the tub or shower with the child, then the likelihood of abuse may be enhanced. However, there are certainly parents who do this who are not abusers. One wants to get specific information about special attention given to cleaning the genitalia.

The dressing and undressing scene is also a common one for sex abuse. Here too one must get specific details, especially with regard to any kind of genital stimulation that may take place in the course of dressing and undressing.

If, in the course of such discussions, the child does divulge directly the sex abuse and feels guilty and/or disloyal, these feelings must be explored. A common cause of guilt is the recognition that the child enjoyed the activity. Such children must be reassured that the examiner has known others who have had similar experiences and that pleasurable response is not uncommon. This will help such children feel less loathesome over their enjoyment of an activity that they have now learned is criminal and/or sinful. Attempts must also be made to assuage the child's guilt over disloyalty for having divulged the activity in situations in which the perpetrator has sworn the child to secrecy. Guilt over the consequences of the divulgences of the perpetrator must also be assuaged. In situations in which the child has been threatened by the offender, the examiner does well to reassure the child that the threats are exaggerated and, with rare exception, not likely to be implemented. But even in those cases in which there is a possibility that attempts will be made to carry out the threat, the child has to be reassured that protection is going to be provided, either by the mother or other authorities who will take measures to remove the father, monitor the father's behavior and so on. Near the end of the interview the examiner does well to ask the child again to describe the sexual encounter. This helps determine whether or not inconsistencies have already manifested themselves. However, it is preferable that the examiner have the opportunity for a few interviews, because he or she will then be in a better position to ascertain whether changes or inconsistencies are common.

The Freely Drawn Picture   A freely drawn picture is a good object on which to project fantasies, because at the outset there are no stimuli at all to potentially contaminate the fantasy. The stimuli that serve as foci for the projections are drawn by the child—are self-created—and are projected out onto the blank paper. When a self-created story is elicited around the picture, even more information can be obtained. Such a picture provides, therefore, a truer and less contaminated reflection of the child's inner psychic life than a doll does. Accordingly, examiners do well to start with this superior form of facilitation by giving the child drawing paper and asking him or her to draw a picture of anything and then make up a story about it. The freely drawn picture does have intrinsic limitations because the child might want to limit his or her story to the figures or objects depicted in it. The examiner does well to encourage the child to go beyond the picture's borders, so to speak, and to elaborate on the story in any way whatsoever. In this way the examiner can circumvent this limitation. Most children have little difficulty providing such expansions and elaborations. The child who has been genuinely abused is more likely to tell a story about sex abuse—primarily as a method of desensitization to the trauma.

The Draw-a-Person Test For patients five to six years and above, I sometimes use the *Draw-a-Person Test*. First, I begin by asking the child to draw a person, and I do not specify sex or age. I then ask the child to tell me a story about the person drawn. Following this, I ask the child to draw a person of the opposite sex. Last, I ask the child to draw a picture of a family and then tell a story about the family. As described elsewhere (Gardner, 1986b), I consider the stories that children create about their pictures to be a more valuable source of information about underlying psychodynamics than data obtained from the picture itself. The interpretations in both areas are speculative, but I believe that those made from the picture are generally more valuable than those derived from the story. With regard to the picture, some sexually abused children may demonstrate anxiety when drawing sexual parts, with the result that there may be shading in or covering of these areas (S.C. Esquilin, 1987). Esquilin also describes attenuated hands and fingers as a common manifestation in the drawings of sexually abused children. She speculates that such attenuation may relate to the manual fondling that these children have been exposed to. Some children will draw sexual parts at this point. I cannot say whether this is more likely to be done by the fabricator than by the child who has been genuinely abused. The fabricator may consciously draw sexual parts in order to provide him- or herself with an excuse for presenting sexual material. The child who has been genuinely abused may draw the sexual organs in an attempt to facilitate desensitization and working through of the sexual trauma. Accordingly, such explicitly sexual drawings are of little differentiating value, but they are valuable in serving as a point of departure for a discussion of sexual issues. It is in the discussion that the examiner must attempt to ascertain whether or not the abuse is bona fide or fabricated. What is important here is that the examiner in no way suggests the drawing of the body organs, and its spontaneously being done is a manifestation of the child's reduced anxiety over and special concern with this subject.

The Use of Dolls   There is a general principle in child therapy that the ideal doll is no doll at all. By this I refer to the fact that the ideal fantasy for learning about a child's inner psychological life is the one that is projected out into space, with no potential contamination by an external facilitating stimulus such as a doll. A doll has a form, a shape, a size, and identifying details that can draw the fantasy onto it and channel it into specific directions. Many (if not most) examiners use dolls to facilitate the child's talking about the abuse. Children naturally project their fantasies onto these dolls and often do not recognize that they are revealing themselves in their doll play. Most child therapists find these fantasies extremely useful as rich sources of information about the child's conscious and unconscious psychological processes. The younger the child, the less the likelihood that the child will appreciate that the fantasies so revealed are referring to his or her own experiences. There is a kind of self-delusion operating here that appears to be part of the child's natural cognitive world. In the course of a child's sex-abuse evaluation, the examiner must be extremely cautious regarding the interpretation of these fantasies. They are projections, and they may very well introduce distortions, wish fulfillments, etc. Just because a little girl presents a fantasy of her father's involving himself with her sexually does not necessarily mean that the father did so. It may be simply a verbalization of a wish. And, at a time when young children are being exposed significantly to such material, the wish can be engendered from stimuli other than an actual experience with a perpetrator. The more detailed, personal, and idiosyncratic the projective fantasy is, the greater the likelihood that it relates to a particular incident of bona fide sex abuse. The examiner does well to present the child with a tray or box of a *large assortment* of dolls and allow the child to select one or more. To present a specific limited number, especially figures that relate to a sex-abuse experience (for example, an adult man and a little girl), is to "load the dice" and makes the information elicited thereby less credible.

Anatomically Correct Dolls   With increasing frequency, examiners in sex-abuse cases are using *anatomically correct dolls*. Their utilization is based on the principle that children can delude themselves into believing that they are not the ones to whom the events are occurring, but to the fantasized characters—out there. These have the advantage of drawing the child into a discussion of sexual issues that relate to the abuse—without the child's realizing that the fantasies refer to him- or herself. They are generally viewed as being quite efficient in that they get to the sex-abuse issue quickly, and this is especially useful for examiners who work under time constraints. I have significant reservations about the use of such dolls. They are so obviously different from traditional dolls that they may draw the child into focusing on the genitalia when sex abuse may not have taken place. Defense lawyers complain that the dolls draw the child into discussing sexual issues that might not otherwise have been related. They thereby "load the dice" and increase the likelihood that sexual activities will be described. And this may result in false accusations.

I am in agreement with this position. This does not mean, however, that I would recommend their not being used at all. Rather, I would recommend that they be used *only as a last resort*, only after traditional dolls have been tried. At this point, I do not own anatomically correct dolls. On those occasions when I have felt the need to focus the child's attention on a doll's genitalia, I have used a piece of clay to form a penis or breasts and apply these to the doll. I may also mark a vulval slit or pubic hair. The power of the projective processes are such that they generally do not need organs that are more accurate. The clay appendages and the vulval slit still provide a unique kind of doll that is predictably going to attract the child's attention. Children who have been genuinely abused may become a little more receptive to talking about their experiences via the catalyzation by the explicit presence of genital parts on the doll. Those who fabricate are likely to speak about their alleged abuse directly in inquiry and do not need the dolls as facilitators for their telling about the abuse. Accordingly, the dolls can serve as a differentiating criterion. However, with regard to their use in eliciting information from children who have been genuinely abused it may not be until after a few sessions that the child may be comfortable talking about the abuse, even through the vehicle of projective play with anatomically correct dolls.

Final Comments on the Interview Sequence, Dolls, and Drawings The sequence then should be direct talk, followed by blank screen projections (such as a blank piece of paper), followed by the *Draw-a-Person Test,* followed by presentation with a large collection of dolls. If this still does not provide useful information regarding the sex abuse, then one might want to get more specific and structure the doll play by providing the specific number of individuals in the alleged abuse scenario, such as a little boy and an adult male. If this does not work, one might then, as a last resort, utilize anatomically correct dolls—either those that can be purchased commercially or those created by the examiner with clay and markings. But the examiner should appreciate that the closer he or she gets to recreating the sex-abuse situation, the less valid the data will be.

In situations in which the assailant is unknown, the child might be asked to draw a picture of the alleged perpetrator in order to assist in the identification process. This may be especially helpful when there is a question of which one of two or three accused individuals was responsible. (From what I have said previously, in such situations I would not agree to conduct an evaluation unless I have the opportunity to interview all of the alleged perpetrators.) Some children will find it easier describing the sex-abuse experience while drawing it and then verbalizing to the pictures they have drawn.

A.N. Groth (1984) has introduced anatomical drawings that are to be used in the assessment and treatment of children who have been sexually abused. These can be useful in ascertaining what terms the child uses for the various bodily parts as well as facilitating stimuli for talking about sex abuse. I view these cards to play approximately the same role as anatomically correct dolls and have the same reservations about them. S. Conerly (1986) and K. MacFarlane and S. Krebs (1986b) have written useful contributions on interviewing sexually abused children, even though their comments are biased against the possibility that the allegation may be fabricated.

Time Considerations   It is important for examiners to appreciate that the longer the passage of time between the sex abuse and the time of the evaluation, the more blurred will be the events in the mind of the child. Also, the younger the child, the greater the likelihood that confusion will distort the events even further. There is even the likelihood in many cases that the child will reach the point where he or she does not actually know any more whether or not the abuse actually occurred. All of us have had the experience at times of not being sure whether or not an event really happened or whether we imagined it happened. In fact, we will sometimes create a scenario about something occurring and then years later actually believe that it did indeed take place when it hadn't. Adults who speak with their parents about their childhoods will invariably learn about distortions. The adult will be certain that an event occurred in one way and the parents will insist that it occurred in another way. I am not claiming that the older individual's recollections are necessarily more likely to be valid than the younger, but it is more likely that they are. We all distort and transform reality to some degree in compliance with our wishes. And this phenomenon is more likely to take place in children of three or four years of age. The ability to differentiate fact from fantasy in a three- or four-year-old is very limited.

I once received a call from a judge who asked me to evaluate a four-year-old girl who was allegedly abused at the age of two. Since that time there had been two years of ongoing litigation and interrogations. He wanted me to see the child in therapy to find out once and for all what "the truth" was with regard to the question of whether the child had indeed been sexually molested. He told me that the parents consistently gave different stories with regard to the alleged abuse, the father insisting that he had never abused the child and the mother insisting that the child had told her that she had engaged in various sexual activities with the father. I informed the judge that he was asking me to do something that was probably impossible. He was not receptive to my refusal, believing that therapy somehow would be able to accomplish this task. I told him that he had more respect for therapy than I had. He was unconvinced, and the conversation ended with his stating that he was sure he could find a therapist who was good enough to learn "the truth." I believe he is going to have a long and futile search.

Detrimental Effects of the Interrogations on the Child

Most agree that prolonged legal and psychiatric interrogation cause additional psychological trauma to these children, sometimes unnecessarily. Sometimes the psychological damage done by the investigation is greater than that done by the abuse, especially if the abuse was transient. Formidable tensions and anxieties are created by the interrogatory process. Loyalty conflicts are engendered, especially when the child is being asked to testify against a family member. Whereas an examiner may choose to protect the child from a face-to-face confrontation in the course of the evaluation, the legal process is far less likely to protect the child from such a confrontation in the courtroom. The adversary system is based on the theory that the accused has the right to be confronted by the accuser in the courtroom setting. (As mentioned, it does not allow for a free and spontaneous interchange, which, in my opinion, compromises significantly the value of such confrontations.) And even when the child is seen alone in the judge's chambers he or she is aware that the information so provided may become known to the accused.

The interrogations interfere with the natural desensitization process necessary for working through the trauma.

Such desensitization normally takes place via the child's repeatedly thinking about the trauma, talking about it, and reiterating the experience in fantasy play (with or without dolls). It is as if each time the child relives the experience in fantasy it becomes a little more bearable. Finally, after varying periods of time the trauma loses its power to affect the child adversely. The interrogatory process interferes with this process. The child may be continually reminded of the trauma long beyond the time when natural desensitization processes might have buried the whole incident, or at least reduced its capacity for creating tension and anxiety.

If the interrogation and investigation are being conducted in a typical adversary fashion, they are likely to intensify the psychological trauma even more. The alleged perpetrator's attorney is likely to interrogate the child repeatedly, as is the accuser's lawyer. The legal professionals are basically trained in direct and cross-examination techniques. Whereas these may be quite applicable to the adversary courtroom setting, they are most often psychologically traumatic to children, because they attempt to zero in and focus on the most difficult material from the outset. Therapists know well that the confrontational approach is often the most anxiety provoking and may be the least likely method for getting at "the truth." Furthermore, some legal professionals hammer away, badger, and attempt to wear down the witness to the point where an individual will say anything—just to get off the stand. And many such individuals do not consider children exempt from such inquiries. If the alleged abuse has been brought to the attention of community authorities (most often required by law), these individuals (especially prosecutors) are also going to subject the child to one or more interviews. And then if mental health professionals are brought in, they too are going to subject the child to further interrogations. Examiners who serve as impartials may thereby reduce the number of interrogations. And the more videotapes made of these interviews, the greater the likelihood that one can reduce the number of interrogations and, by implication, the extent of the psychological trauma.

CHARACTERISTIC MEDICAL FINDINGS

Medical evidence may provide the most compelling confirmation that a child has been sexually abused. There are certain medical findings that may be present in the child who has been sexually abused that will not be found in the child who fabricates the abuse. Often, by the time an evaluator is called in, these findings may no longer be present and they have to be obtained from doctors' reports, hospital charts, etc.

>   1. Abrasions, inflammation, and other evidences of damage to the genital or rectal tissues. A common warning sign of such trauma is blood-stained panties.
>   2. General trauma to the body related to beatings by the perpetrator, often associated with threats that this is only a sample of what will happen to the child if the abuse is revealed.
>   3. The presence of foreign objects in the genital, rectal, or urethral openings. Sometimes these are placed by the perpetrator, sometimes by the child him- or herself in imitation of the abuser.
>   4. The presence of a sexually transmitted disease.
>   5. Pregnancy (obviously, this criterion is for older victims).

When such evidence is present, the aforementioned criteria can provide additional data—generally confirmatory; but in rare instances, nonconfirmatory. When medical evidence is not present (more often the case), the differentiating psychological criteria may be the primary sources of information about whether or not the sex-abuse allegation is valid. M. Durfee et al. (1986) provide a useful and thorough review of the medical findings in sexually abused children.

THE CHILD AS INITIATOR

In the early 1980s, before the present epidemic of fabricated sex-abuse allegations, I generally met with incredulity and even antagonism when I spoke at meetings of the increasing frequency of fabricated sex-abuse allegations I was observing. Sex-abuse workers especially claimed that I didn't know what I was talking about— that if a child professes sex abuse he or she must be telling the truth—because children do not have explicit information available about the specific details of sexual acts. Accordingly, if they described such activities, they must have had such experiences. And they would present me with pamphlets put out by various agencies at the federal, state, and local levels confirming this principle. In addition, they were incensed at me for what I was saying because of their belief that my comments would be used by defense attorneys to protect perpetrators. Their vision was that as a result of my comments, many perpetrators would be set free to roam the streets and abuse other children. My response was that it is our duty to describe the truth as we see it and not to deny any facts because of their unpleasantness and/or possible misutilization. More important, I insisted that we had to learn more about differentiating bona fide from fabricated sex-abuse allegations; this would be the best way to protect innocent parties from being falsely accused, as well as to insure that people who were genuinely guilty would be properly prosecuted and dealt with. From 1982 to 1985 there was a progressive increase in receptivity to my warnings about the epidemic. By 1986 few were claiming that I was delusional.

More recently, I have been talking about the issue of the child as initiator. At the present time, the sexually abused child is generally considered to be the victim. I believe that there are situations in which the sexually abused child has been the initiator. I am not claiming that this is the most common way in which sex abuse takes place; in fact, it may be relatively uncommon. However, it certainly does exist. Many believe that young children do not have strong urges and that they are therefore unlikely to be initiators in any kind of sexual encounter with an adult. This assumption is not necessarily valid. I have seen many children whom I would consider completely normal who developed strong sexual urges during the first few years of life. The ubiquitousness of masturbation in these early years is just one confirmation of this phenomenon. Such potential for the initiation of sexual encounters is now being increased by children's surreptitiously watching pornographic movies on television as well as some of the standard R-rated movies that are now easily found on television.

It is probably the case that there have always been children who have initiated sexual encounters with adults. I am not claiming that this is common; nor am I claiming that when sex abuse occurs it is most often the child who is the initiator, rather than the adult. I am only claiming that child initiation does take place on rare occasion. One need not bring in the theory of the Oedipus complex to explain such initiations. It may simply be explained as a manifestation of the child's desire to gain a mild degree of sexual gratification in association with normal biological needs. (Elsewhere [1986b], I have discussed in detail my concept of the Oedipus complex.) I believe, however, that there is probably more initiation taking place in recent years than there was in the past. This is partially the result of the increasing exposure that children have had to sex abuse in the public media, in their schools, in the games they play, and so on. Furthermore, the child who is abused by one person may be prematurely turned on and may seek sexual gratification from others. I have already mentioned this phenomenon as one of the criteria for differentiating bona fide from fabricated sex abuse.

Whenever I mention the child's initiation factor in my lecture presentations, it is met with horror and resistance. Sex-abuse workers are especially upset when I talk about this factor in public. Some deny vehemently that this has ever occurred in their experience; others somewhat reluctantly admit that they have occasionally seen situations in which they have suspected that the child was the initiator. However, they generally believe that bringing this contributing factor to public attention will complicate significantly the prosecution and conviction of sex-abuse offenders. They claim that once a precedent is established in which children can be the initiators, then every attorney will seize upon this fact to help his or her client disprove the allegation. They anticipate the nightmare of this being a routine defense, with attorneys supporting their positions with questions to the examiner such as "Is it possible that the child initiated the sex abuse?" "Wouldn't you agree, Doctor, that if the child had not initiated the abuse, then my client might have not have become involved?"

My response to this criticism is this: The fact that some (and even many) attorneys may take advantage of the initiation factor and try to exonerate bona fide sex abusers should not be a reason for covering up a reality. The realities are that some children do initiate the sexual encounter. Although they are relatively rare, they do exist. As mentioned, this is no excuse for an adult to become involved. Accordingly, it is not a justifiable defense. The healthy, stable adult recognizes that the child has limited responsibility for appreciating the consequences of his or her behavior and does not participate. I would go further and state and that *no weight at all* should be given to such a defense. An adult, who may be an incipient sex abuser, may very well be tempted into a sexual activity with an initiating child. Such individuals have indeed been "seduced." However, some people are more easily seduced than others. The child's initiation should not serve as an excuse for the adult's compliance. A child may ask an adult to play with a loaded gun; this cannot be used as an excuse to justify the adult's giving the child a loaded gun. A child may ask an adult to play with matches; this does not justify the adult's giving the child matches. When the sexual encounters are divulged in these situations, the child is likely to fabricate so that the adult will be blamed for the initiation. This is another situation in which fabricated claims of sexual abuse can arise. And, if such sexual encounters occur in the context of a family situation in which there is custody litigation, one can be certain that the litigating parent will blame the spouse and deny completely any initiation by the child. To the degree that the child's initiation becomes revealed, to that degree will the nonabusing parent's case be weakened. I predict that within the next few years this factor in childhood sex abuse will become increasingly apparent to mental health professionals as well as the general public.

I recall one situation recently in which a five-year-old girl was referred to me because of preoccupation with sex. She would try to touch men's penises as well as women's breasts and vaginas. She became preoccupied with playing sexual games with other children and repeatedly requested of her parents to take her to locker rooms, both for men and women. She frequently tried to put her hand under women's dresses or into their brassieres. She would ask men if she could see their penises and often tried to pull down the zippers of their pants. The preoccupation began about three weeks after starting kindergarten. On inquiry the mother learned that the woman who was driving the school bus was frequently finding excuses to alter her traditional route in order to bring the little girl home last. Often she was late, with a variety of excuses that didn't seem to carry weight. The mother learned from other sources that this woman had a reputation for being a lesbian. Accordingly, she hired a detective and learned that the woman was parking in an isolated area and involving the child in sex play. These activities initiated a period of high sexual excitation that appeared to be in need of indiscriminate gratification. She became very friendly with a 14-year-old retarded boy in the neighborhood and began involving herself in sexual play with him. It was clear that she had initiated the sexual encounters, and the boy, being retarded, had little appreciation of the implications of what he was doing. This was a clear-cut case of the child's serving as initiator; in this situation, the initiating child had been turned on prematurely by having been sexually abused. I believe it is likely that we will see an increase in the percentage of cases in which the child is the provocateur or provocateuse, because of the general increase in child sex abuse that we are witnessing.

BONA FIDE SEXUAL ABUSE IN THE CONTEXT OF CUSTODY DISPUTES

It has been one of the primary purposes of this book to emphasize the point that a sex-abuse allegation may very well be fabricated if it is made by a child whose parents are involved in a custody dispute. However, it would be an error for the reader to conclude that children whose parents are litigating for their custody are not likely to be sexually abused. It would also be an error to conclude that children who are suffering with parental alienation syndromes are immune from such abuse. This is not so. My main point here was to demonstrate that the fabricated sex-abuse allegation is likely to take place within the context of a custody dispute, especially when the child has developed manifestations of the parental alienation syndrome. One must still consider the possibility that bona fide abuse may still occur in the context of such a custody dispute. In such cases the afore-mentioned criteria should still be used to help make the differentiation. The abuse may have taken place prior to the separation, and the child may have been fearful of divulging it because of the omnipresence of the father. A custody dispute may increase a child's animosity and thereby in-crease the likelihood that the abuse will be revealed, espe-cially if the child has developed a parental alienation syn-drome. Here the child is using the abuse allegation as another form of *real* ammunition rather than as a fantasized one.

Just as the divorce situation is likely to precipitate the child's divulgence of a pre-existing pattern of abuse, the divorce situation may actually precipitate sex abuse on the part of a parent when it did not exist previously. Divorce is one of the more important and severe stresses of life. Under this stress some parents may regress and involve themselves in pedophilia. Contested divorces are even more stressful, and custody litigation adds even further to that stress. The child offers innocent and unconditional acceptance of a potential abuser. There is little chance of rejection. Rejected by a spouse, the parent may then turn to a child. In the context of a weekend visitation, in a one-bedroom apartment with an adoring child, the parent may be unable to resist the pedophilic urges.

I recognize that my comments here may serve to introduce a note of confusion to examiners who are trying to differentiate between bona fide and fabricated sex abuse. In response I can only say once again that it is crucial that we not deny reality because of our need to make things simple or to avoid confrontation with unpleasantness. I still believe, however, that when a sex-abuse allegation can be used as a convenient weapon in the litigation, it is much more likely to have been fabricated. The situation in which it has really occurred in the context of custody litigation is probably rare.

CONCLUDING COMMENTS

My purpose here has been to provide criteria that will enable evaluators to differentiate better between bona fide and fabricated sex-abuse allegations. The focus here has been primarily on fabricated sex-abuse allegations that occur in the context of child custody litigation. My hope here is that the criteria presented will be useful in other situations (less common) in which such differentiations are important. In the next chapter I will describe a scale I have devised that will enable the examiner to objectify these differentiating criteria.

FIVE

THE SEX ABUSE LEGITIMACY SCALE (SAL SCALE)

INTRODUCTION

I found the differentiating criteria described in Chapter Four to be extremely useful for helping me ascertain whether or not a sex-abuse allegation was bona fide or fabricated. In most (but certainly not all) cases the conclusion would "jump out of the page" when I reviewed my data. However, there were certainly cases in which the findings were inconclusive. My major finding was that, when the abuse was fabricated, very few if any of the criteria were satisfied. In contrast, when I concluded that the abuse was bona fide, at least some of the criteria were satisfied, with a range varying from 25 to 75 percent of the items. Because of the large number of criteria it is unlikely that all or even most of them will be satisfied—no matter how apparent and prolonged the abuse. The crucial question then was to find cutoff points to differentiate the levels at which the abuse was fabricated, inconclusive, or genuine.

It was from these considerations that I first began to think about the creation of a scale that might help examiners objectify their findings in order to be more certain as to whether or not a sex-abuse allegation was false or genuine. Ultimately, the *Sex Abuse Legitimacy Scale (SAL Scale)* was devised. This scale is reproduced in its entirety in Addendum III. In this chapter I discuss in detail the scale's use, especially with regard to the criteria that the examiner can utilize to respond to each item. The first instruction given the examiner warns that the guidelines for scoring to be found in this book *must* be used if the scale is to be used in a meaningful way. I cannot emphasize this point strongly enough. The failure to use these guidelines may result in erroneous conclusions which, obviously, may be extremely detrimental to the parties being evaluated.

The differentiating criteria in the SAL Scale are most applicable when the sex abuse has taken place in a family situation in which the father (or stepfather) is the alleged offender and the mother is the accuser. It is also applicable when the alleged offender is someone who is known to the family and can be interviewed. This would include such parties as a relative or family friend (especially someone who has frequent opportunities for being with the child alone) and a babysitter. It may also be useful, but less so, when the alleged offender is unknown or unavailable for interview. This would include situations in which the alleged offender has absconded or is one of many possible individuals, all of whom cannot be reasonably interviewed. The proper utilization of the scale depends so heavily on the opportunity for *joint* interviews (so often emphasized in this book) that the absence of the alleged offender represents a serious compromise in the scale's proper utilization. Without that party there is no opportunity for the child to be confronted with the accused's refutations, denials, and arguments in defense. The child's fantasies then are free to elaborate upon themselves, often with suggestions and elaborations provided by the accuser.

The items are worded so that the greater the number of *Yes* answers, the greater the likelihood the sex abuse is genuine. In contrast, the greater the number of *No* responses, the greater the likelihood the sex abuse has been fabricated. I could have worded the questions in the opposite way, so that *Yes* answers indicated fabrication and *No* answers suggested bona fide sex abuse. I believe that such an orientation would have introduced a possible element of confusion when answering the questions. Furthermore, structuring the items so that *Yes* responses are associated with genuine abuse "loads" the scale slightly in the direction of bias toward concluding that the allegation is genuine. Accordingly, if the findings indicate that the allegation is fabricated, the results are slightly more convincing. Under such circumstances, an accused might say, when defending him- or herself, "Of the 50 items on the scale (covering all three parties), I only satisfied three of them. This is certainly not indicative of bona fide sex abuse."

In order to give greater weight to the more valuable criteria, point scores are given for *Yes* answers in each of the three categories:

Part A. Very Valuable Differentiating Criteria—3 points for each *Yes* answer
Part B. Moderately Valuable Differentiating Criteria—2 points for each *Yes* answer
Part C. Differentiating Criteria of Low But Potential Value—1 point for each *Yes* answer

The child, accuser, and accused are scored separately. Each of these individual's scores are divided into the aforementioned three categories. In this way, the more valuable differentiating criteria are given greater weight than the less valuable. To the right of each item are three columns: *Yes*, *No*, and *Not Clear or Not Applicable*. The examiner is asked to place a check in the appropriate column. The scale is not designed to serve as a checklist or questionnaire to be filled out in the interviewee's presence. Rather, it is designed to be completed *after* all the interviews have been conducted, individual and joint. This is especially important with regard to the items related to the interviews with the child, because it is often not possible to respond to a particular item simply from information derived from the child. Input from adults is sometimes crucial if one is to provide a meaningful response. The examiner is advised to refer to the scale during the course of the evaluation (especially as it nears completion) in order to be sure that all the items have been covered. The examiner is warned against asking the interviewee for direct input into answering an item in order to avoid the inevitable bias that will be introduced by using the scale in this manner. After all the interviews have been conducted (individual and joint), the examiner does well to refer to the guidelines provided in this book (especially in this chapter) before placing a check in the appropriate column. It is hoped that few if any checks will be placed in the *Not Clear or Not Applicable* column. Obviously, the more checks confined to the *Yes* and *No* columns, the more valid will be the conclusions derived from the scale.

For the purposes of determining whether the abuse is bona fide or fabricated, only the *Yes* responses are calculated. The total number of *Yes* responses in each category (A, B, and C) is multiplied by the appropriate factor for that category (3, 2, or 1) to obtain a weighted score for that part. The sum of the weighted part scores (Part A + Part B + Part C) is referred to as the *Sex Abuse Legitimacy Score (SAL Score)*. Separate SAL Scores are calculated for the child (maximum

60 points), the accuser (maximum 27 points), and accused (maximum 27 points). A cumulative SAL Score of all three parties together is not calculated because I do not believe that such a cumulative score would serve any useful purpose. In fact, it might introduce confusion and distortion in that high loading by one party and low weighting by another might result in some kind of a normative value that might hide a particular individual's high or low contribution to the score. Accordingly, such a calculation might result in a false conclusion regarding any individual person's role in the alleged abuse.

Mention has been made of my experience that in situations in which the sex abuse has been fabricated, the scores on this scale are extremely low, often approaching the zero level. After reviewing my clinical data collected from families in which I concluded that the sex abuse was fabricated, I found that in just about all of them very few if any of the criteria for bona fide sex abuse were satisfied. In order to be sure that the results of the SAL Scale might not be misleading, I decided to designate a cutoff point of 10 percent of the maximum score to represent the upper limit of the fabricated range. I do not believe that future studies designed to assess the validity of this scale will conclude that this figure is inappropriate. In fact, my suspicion is that the 5 percent level might even prove workable. It was more difficult finding a cutoff point above which the examiner could conclude that the sex abuse was genuine. Some of the bona fide abusers obtained scores in the vicinity of 30 to 40 percent of the maximum range. In order to diminish the likelihood that innocents might be falsely considered bona fide offenders, I decided to use the 50 percent level as the cutoff point.

This conservative approach to the setting of the cutoff point for bona fide sex abuse is based on the American legal principle that "it is better to let 100 guilty men go free than to convict one innocent man." One could argue that such a bias, when applied to sex-abuse investigations, would exonerate many bona fide perpetrators—who would then be free to molest other children. One could also argue that the false conviction of an innocent party can destroy his or her life (a common situation at the time of this writing). Both of these arguments have merit. After giving both of these positions serious consideration, I have chosen to recommend a cutoff point at a level that *might* indeed exonerate bona fide perpetrators in order to protect innocents who might be falsely considered guilty. There are two primary reasons for my taking this position. First, I am in sympathy with the aforementioned American legal principle. Second, and more pertinent to this scale, many perpetrators are so shaken and sobered by the investigations into their sexual activities that they "cease and desist" from further molestation of children, even though exonerated.

Accordingly, scores between the 10 percent and 50 percent levels should be considered inconclusive. However, the closer the score is to the 10 percent level, the higher the likelihood the sex-abuse allegation is fabricated; the closer the score is to the 50 percent level, the greater the likelihood the allegation is genuine. Examiners are advised that the cutoff levels and their significance should be viewed as preliminary and tentative. It is my hope that more extensive studies will be conducted and that the criteria presented herein will be either substantiated or modified if necessary. My plan is to include such modifications, if warranted, in future editions of the scale.

Examiners are warned that they should not use this scale independently of other data. Especially important are medical findings. These have been described in detail in Chapter Four. Medical reports should be reviewed as well as reports from other examiners. The examiner may wish to interview other parties besides the aforementioned three central individuals. Such other parties might include professed witnesses or others who might provide useful input. At this point I will direct myself to the scale and present to the reader guidelines for responding to each of the items. Examiners do well to refer not only to the material presented here but to pertinent material presented in Chapters Three and Four, especially the material in Chapter Four relating to the differentiating criteria. It is crucial that the reader appreciate that these scoring criteria are presented as guidelines only, and that the examiner's clinical judgment must be considered as well when deciding how to score an item.

THE CHILD WHO
ALLEGES SEX ABUSE

Part A
Very Valuable
Differentiating Criteria

1. *Very hesitant to divulge the sexual abuse* Children who have been genuinely abused often feel quite ashamed to reveal their sexual experiences and may have even been threatened or bribed not to tell about the abuse. Accordingly, it is unlikely that they will discuss the abuse spontaneously. Even when the examiner brings it up peripherally, they may avoid the subject. Some abused children will directly state that they don't wish to talk about their experiences with the accused. For these children, a few interviews may be necessary before the examiner will be able to obtain direct information relating to the abuse. A *Yes* response is indicated for such children.

In contrast, children who are fabricating will be quite pleased to talk about the terrible indignities they have suffered at the hands of the accused. It is not uncommon for them to begin the interview with their little speeches. Often they have been told beforehand by the parent who is programming them that the examiner is a very important person and that it is vital that they provide *all* the details of the abuse. A *No* response is warranted for such children. Some children who have been abused are not ashamed of their sexual activities. A *No* response is indicated for such children. The scale, however, is likely to reveal the abuse via other items.

2. *Fear of retaliation by the accused* This item is most applicable to the child who has been abused and who has been threatened by the offender with terrible consequences for divulgence. Such consequences might include threats of killing the child's mother, killing the child, or the perpetrator's committing suicide. Such a child may exhibit significant fear in the course of the interview – without any corresponding verbalizations. If the examiner is successful in eliciting statements about what the child is afraid of – and these statements relate to threats of significant retaliation by the alleged offender – then a check is placed in the *Yes* column. If, however, the child is frightened and the examiner is not certain what the child is afraid of, then it is not proper to put a check in this column. For example, if the child describes other fears, which are unrelated to retaliation by the accused, then a check should be placed in the *No* column. If no fears are described and/or the child shows no manifestations of fear, a check is placed in the *No* column. If the child's responses do not give the examiner a clear indication whether the child is afraid, then a check should be placed in the *Not Clear or Not Applicable* column.

3. *Guilt over the consequences to the accused of the divulgences* Children who fabricate sex abuse often manifest little

if any guilt over the consequences to the accused of their divulgences. This is especially the case initially, and may even be the case after the child comes to appreciate how much trouble the parent has been caused by the allegation. A *No* response is warranted for such guiltless children. Children who have been genuinely abused may feel guilty over the disclosure at the outset, because they may have been warned in advance about the terrible consequences to the accused of divulgence. A *Yes* response is warranted for such guilty children.

A crucial determinant of whether the child will feel guilty at the outset is the mother's attitude about the divulgence. Children who fabricate are often programmed by their mothers to divulge and describe in detail their sexual experiences, while the two together relish in the suffering of the accused. In contrast, children who have been genuinely abused are not often programmed by their mothers to wreak vengeance on the accuser (although they may be). Such children's mothers more often appreciate the importance of the parent-child bond, the abuse not withstanding. The child who fabricates may ultimately come to feel guilty over the recognition of the consequences, but this is a late-phase development. Accordingly, the examiner does well to find out about the duration of the guilty feelings, especially with regard to their presence or absence at the time of the divulgence. If such guilt has manifested itself at the outset a *Yes* answer is appropriate. If the guilt is a late development or is not present, then a *No* response is warranted. If the examiner is not certain in which category the child lies with regard to this kind of guilt, then a check should be placed in the *Not Clear or Not Applicable* column.

4. *Guilt over participation in the sexual acts* Children who have been genuinely abused may not recognize in the early phases of their abuse that they are doing anything "wrong" or "bad." By the time of the disclosure, however, they

generally appreciate that what they have been doing is considered reprehensible behavior in our society. Accordingly, they are likely to feel guilt at the time of the divulgence and afterward. For such children a response of *Yes* is indicated. It is important for the examiner to appreciate that there are some sexually abused children who do not feel guilty over their experiences; this is especially the case when it has been sanctioned by the mother, either overtly or covertly. Although a *No* response is warranted here for such sexually abused children, other items on this scale are likely to reveal the abuse.

Children who fabricate generally do not feel guilty over their alleged sexual acts because there were no actual sexual acts over which to feel guilty. More commonly, children who fabricate sex abuse express feigned anger and artificial indignation over their alleged abuse. They do not feel bad about themselves over what they have allegedly done; they feel angry over what they claim was done to them. For such children a *No* response is indicated.

5. *Provides specific details of the sexual abuse* Children who have experienced bona fide sex abuse will have a specific mental image of their experiences, which they can call upon when providing descriptions. And when asked to elaborate, they can give specific details—often without difficulty if they have been brought to the point of describing their experiences. With such children a *Yes* response is indicated. Children who fabricate have no such internal visual display to serve as a reference point for their description. Because there was no such experience, they cannot provide specific details. They usually, however, do have a "story" to tell, one that may have as a nucleus some realistic experience. But this tale will be elaborated upon significantly, especially with the prompting of the accuser. For example, a father may have, indeed, brushed up against his boys' genitalia in the course of a

wrestling match with them. Elaborations provided by mother's prompting may include manual playing with their genitals, erections, and even ejaculation. They may also include the child's playing with the father's genitalia, again an elaboration of the inevitable body contacts involved in wrestling. Because these elaborations never actually occurred, the child does not have an internal visual image as a reference and so is not likely to be able to provide the specific details. Such details not only relate to the sexual encounter per se, but to details about the places where these encounters allegedly took place and their circumstances. Children who cannot provide such details warrant a *No* response.

6. *Description of the sex abuse credible* Children who have been genuinely abused will usually provide credible descriptions. For these children a *Yes* response is indicated. Those who fabricate may not appreciate how preposterous are the elaborations that have been built into their scenarios. These preposterous and absurd elements are generally not suggested by the brainwashing parent; rather, they are created by the child. The child wants to provide ammunition against the alleged offender and is not sophisticated enough to differentiate between reasonable and unreasonable allegations. A common preposterous element relates to the color of the ejaculate. This is a frequent area of focus in sex-abuse investigations, because of the recognition that children who have been genuinely abused are likely to provide credible (or reasonably credible) descriptions of the perpetrator's semen, whereas those who are fabricators are more likely to provide preposterous responses to questions in this area. In Chapter Four I have discussed this issue in detail, with particular emphasis on the importance of the examiner's differentiating between the emissions of the perpetrator and that of the victim, as well as the differences in color and consistency of each one's seminal fluids. In Chapter Four I have given a

number of other examples of absurd elements in the fabricating child's descriptions. The presence of these simplistic and obviously fabricated elements indicate a *No* response to this item.

7. *If the description of the sex abuse* does not *vary over repeated interviews, check* Yes. *If the description* does *vary, check* No. Children who have been genuinely abused, as mentioned, have an image in their minds about their experiences that they can use as a reference point when describing their experiences. And this internal visual display can be relied upon to provide a reasonable degree of consistency over repeated interviews. Because of this lack of variation, such children warrant a *Yes* response to this item. The child who fabricates does not have such a visual reference and so will often exhibit variations from rendition to rendition. Such children warrant a *No* response for this item.

It is important for the examiner to appreciate, however, that the younger the child, the weaker this internal display and the greater the likelihood that distortions will creep in — distortions that the child may actually believe. Furthermore, children generally like to please their interviewer, especially if the interviewer is in a position of authority, e.g., a lawyer, judge, prosecutor, or mental health practitioner. This may even result in alterations of the description, even by the child who has genuinely been abused. Furthermore, all of our memories get somewhat blurred over time, and this is especially the case with younger children. When the litigation is protracted, the likelihood of such blurring of memory is enhanced significantly. Accordingly, the examiner does well to take these factors into consideration when interviewing the child and to recognize that the shorter the time gap between the interview and the alleged abuse, the greater the likelihood this criterion will be a useful one. In contrast, the longer the time gap between the alleged abuse and the interview, the greater the likelihood of variation—especially for younger children. These drawbacks notwithstanding, this item still warrants inclusion among the criteria that are very valuable, because rendition variation is a powerful differentiating criterion in the early phases following the divulgence.

8. *Frequent episodes of sexual excitation, apart from the abuse encounters* This is one of the items that requires parental input. The child who has been genuinely abused may be prematurely "turned on" sexually and may frequently be in need of sexual gratification. This may result in frequent masturbation, obsessive desires for sex play with other children (and even adults), and compulsive rubbing of the genitals against people, furniture, or other objects. When the examiner observes such behavior in the consultation room a *Yes* answer is readily warranted for this item. A *Yes* answer might also be justified if the examiner has good reason to believe that the parent's description of such behavior is credible. The fabricating child does not manifest such behavior, nor is the fabricator's prompter generally aware of this phenomenon. Such children warrant a *No* response to this item.

9. *Considers genitals to have been damaged* Some children who have been sexually abused have indeed suffered physical damage to their genitals, and such trauma will generally be verified in medical reports. However, there are children who have been abused who have not suffered any physical damage to their genitals, but still feel that their genitalia have been damaged because of their appreciation of the cultural attitudes toward their sexual activities. Accordingly, we have two categories of sexually abused children for whom a *Yes* response is warranted for this item.

Children who are fabricating sex abuse have not suffered any physical trauma to their genitals. Nor do they usually describe feelings that their genitals have been damaged by their alleged sexual encounters. Such children warrant a *No* response to this item. However, the programmers of fabricating children may have gone to the point of bringing the child for physical examination in the hope that the physician might provide supporting evidence for sexual abuse. Their hope is that the physician will agree with the parent that a minor blemish is indeed a sign of sexual trauma. Under such circumstances, it is important that the examiner get a medical report. But even these fabricating children do not report *ongoing* feelings that their genitals have been in any way altered or disfigured by their experiences. Such children warrant a *No* response for this item.

10. *Desensitization play engaged in at home or during the interview* This is another item that may warrant parental input before it can be properly answered. Children who have suffered bona fide sexual abuse have been traumatized. Often, they will deal with the trauma by the process of desensitization. As is true with other forms of trauma, each time the child relives the experience, he or she becomes a little more desensitized to it. For these children, such desensitization is often accomplished in the process of play, in which games are created that allow for repeated reenactment of the sexual experience, either overtly or symbolically. Sometimes others are brought into these games. A common scenario involves getting rid of a "bad man" or protecting oneself from monsters and other malevolent creatures who are trying to harm the child. Often the child's fantasies provide symbolic protection from these malevolent creatures. Another common scenario involves the child's recreating the sexual scene, but successfully rejecting the offender rather than complying with his requests or demands. Often, the examiner can observe such play within a few interviews, if not the first. It is easy for the child to provide descriptions

of sexual abuse through the symbolic and disguised vehicle of play. The mothers of children who have genuinely abused may also describe such play at home.

A *Yes* response is indicated for this item when the examiner is convinced that such desensitization play is indeed taking place, either within or outside of the consultation room. Children who fabricate are not sophisticated enough to appreciate this phenomenon and so will not generally provide this kind of play for the examiner. Also, the mothers of those who fabricate may not appreciate this phenomenon and so may not describe it. A *No* response is warranted when there is no evidence for such play.

11. *Threatened or bribed by the accused to discourage divulgence of the abuse* Children who have been genuinely abused have often been threatened that there will be terrible consequences to themselves and their loved ones if they ever divulge the special "secret." Others may be bribed to keep quiet. And some children are exposed to both methods of getting them to "keep the secret." Children who describe such experiences warrant a *Yes* response to this item.

Children who are fabricating sex abuse have not been exposed to such threats or bribes and are generally not sophisticated enough to describe them. Their absence warrants a *No* response for this item.

It is important for the examiner to appreciate that there are situations in which the offender does not attempt to preserve secrecy. This will be seen in offenders who are very sick psychologically, who may be intellectually impaired, or who may suffer with such disorders as alcoholism or drug abuse. Under the influence of these substances they may not be aware of what they are doing; or, if they are, they have such poor judgment that they do not appreciate the consequences of their acts. In such cases the examiner has no choice but to respond *No* to this item, even though the child has been sexually abused. If this scale is a valid one, the abuse will be indicated by so many other criteria that the child's score will warrant the conclusion that sexual abuse has indeed taken place. As mentioned, even in cases of proven abuse it is rare that all of the items will indicate that such abuse has taken place.

12. *If a parental alienation syndrome is not present, check* Yes. *If a parental alienation syndrome is present, check* No. When responding to this item the reader does well to be familiar with the manifestations of the parental alienation syndrome that I have described in detail in Chapter Three. When a parental alienation syndrome is present, the likelihood that the sex-abuse allegation is fabricated is quite high and that it is a manifestation of the disorder. Accordingly, a *No* response is warranted under these circumstances. If, however, a parental alienation syndrome is not present, then the likelihood that the sex-abuse allegation is bona fide is high and so a *Yes* response is warranted here.

13. *If the complaint was not made in the context of a child custody dispute or litigation, check* Yes. *If there is such a dispute, check* No. When a child custody dispute is *not* present, the sex-abuse allegation is more likely to be genuine, and so a *Yes* response is warranted. The presence of the dispute increases the likelihood that the allegation is fabricated, and so a *No* response is warranted for this item. There are situations in which the parents are embroiled in a vicious child custody dispute in which the child does not develop a full-blown case of parental alienation syndrome. The child may still seize upon a sex-abuse allegation as a convenient weapon in the dispute. Such a child appears to have skipped over the step of the parental alienation syndrome and has seized upon one of the most powerful weapons that he or she can utilize to assist the supported parent. Such a child also warrants a *No* response to this item.

Part B
Moderately Valuable Differentiating Criteria

14. *If the description* does not *have the quality of a well-rehearsed litany, check* Yes. *If it* does *have a litany quality, check* No. Children who have been genuinely abused are not creating any stories. They are telling the truth about an actual experience. Their renditions have the quality of credibility, rather than a rote repetition of a well-rehearsed scenario. Such children warrant a *Yes* response for this item.

In contrast, children who fabricate are creating a tale. In order to be successful when they relate their stories to evaluators, they make sure to "memorize their lines." They may also have been subjected to many rehearsals by the programming parent to insure that they have learned their lines. Because children are generally not skilled actors and actresses, their rehearsed presentations have an artificial quality that lessens their credibility. Children who demonstrate such a litany warrant a *No* response.

It is important for the examiner to appreciate that, as time goes on, even the child who has been genuinely abused may develop a litany. The child has presented the story to many examiners and comes to recognize which items are important and which are not. The description, then, may become memorized and take on a litany quality. Under such circumstances a *No* response is indicated for this item. This is one of the reasons why it is so important to see the child soon after the allegation has been made. Otherwise, an important differentiating criterion may lose its value. Accordingly, we have here another situation in which a child who has been genuinely abused will receive a *No* response. If the scale is indeed valid, the examiner will still be able to conclude that the abuse has taken place, because the child will have so many other *Yes* answers on other items.

15. *If there is* no *evidence of a "borrowed scenario" (description taken from other persons or sources), check* Yes. *If the description appears to have been taken from external sources, check* No. The child who has been genuinely abused will not use adult terminology; rather the child uses descriptive terms appropriate to the idiosyncratic terms used in that child's home, e.g., "He touched my 'gina," "He kissed my pee-pee," and "He put his big pee-pee where my doo-doo comes out." Such children warrant a *Yes* response to this item.

The child who is fabricating sex abuse will often use terms "borrowed" from others, especially the programmer. The examiner must be alert to such phraseology, e.g., "I've been sexually molested" and "I've been sexually abused." Sometimes the phraseology of the child fabricator is taken from school programs on sex abuse, e.g., "He touched me in private places," "He touched my private parts," and "He touched me in bad places." When such terminology is present, a *No* response is warranted for this item.

It is important for the examiner to appreciate that the longer the time span between the alleged abuse and the examiner's inquiry, the greater the likelihood the abused child will begin to incorporate standard adult terminology when describing the abuse. Accordingly, in the early phases of description the *Yes* is warranted when there is *no* evidence for "borrowed" terminology. The *No* response is indicated when these terms are present. Consequently, a *No* response may be warranted for a child who has been genuinely abused. It is hoped that other criteria in this scale will reveal the abuse. My experience has been that this is most often the case.

16. *Depression* Children who have been subjected to ongoing sexual abuse may become depressed. The indignities they suffer over time result in a general deadening of their personalities. They lack the sparkle, vivacity, and

optimism of normal children. Rather, they may exhibit listlessness, loss of appetite, impaired motivation and curiosity in school, little interest or enjoyment of play, and, on occasion, suicidal thoughts. Some of the psychodynamic factors that may contribute to their depression have been described in Chapter Four.

Children who have been exposed to ongoing custody litigation may also become depressed, but the onset of the depression usually dates to the beginning of the litigation. However, such children's depression may also extend back further if they have been exposed to ongoing parental hostilities in the context of the marriage. Careful questioning of the child might enable the examiner to differentiate between these two causes of the child's depression, namely, sex abuse and exposure to the parental hostilities. If the examiner is confident that the depression is a result of sexual abuse, then a check should be placed in the *Yes* column. If the examiner concludes that the depression is the result of exposure to ongoing parental hostilities, then a check should be placed in the *No* column. If the examiner cannot clearly differentiate between the two causes of depression, then a check should be placed in the *Not Clear or Not Applicable* column.

Some sexually abused children are not depressed. In such cases a check is placed in the *No* column. It is my belief that other items checked *Yes* will more than compensate for this loss, with the result that the scale will still reveal the sex abuse. Generally, children who are fabricating sexual abuse are not depressed, and so the check in the *No* column enhances the likelihood that the examiner will conclude that they are fabricating.

17. *Withdrawal* Children who have suffered bona fide sex abuse often withdraw from the abuser because of the trauma they anticipate when involved with him. They tend to

generalize and assume that others, especially those of the same sex as the abuser, will subject them to indignities as well. And such withdrawal may exist in school, at home, and elsewhere. And the examiner may observe such withdrawal in the interview. Children subjected to ongoing parental animosity may also withdraw in order to protect themselves from the psychological trauma of such exposure. Questioning the child may enable the examiner to ascertain the sources of the child's withdrawal. If the examiner is certain that the withdrawal is related to ongoing sex abuse, then a check in the *Yes* column is warranted. If the examiner is certain that the withdrawal is related to ongoing exposure to parental hostilities, then a check in the *No* column is indicated.

If no withdrawal is present, then a check in the *No* column is warranted. This may result in a child who has been sexually abused receiving a *No* response. However, other items on this scale are likely to reveal the abuse. Most children who fabricate the sex abuse do not withdraw, because they have not actually been exposed to the psychologically traumatizing abuse. For such children a check in the *No* column is warranted.

18. *Compliant personality* Commonly the abusing father is a very domineering individual who subjects all members of the family to his demands and whims. And the sexual abuse is just one manifestation of such subjugation. These children often develop compliant personalities in association with the fear of invoking the wrath and rejection of the only father they have. And they may be compliant, as well, in imitation of their mothers. Such children warrant a check in the *Yes* column. Children who fabricate are less likely to be compliant. More often the fabricating child is an assertive and angry one who is wound up by his mother to express vociferously his or her vilifications of the father. Such children warrant a check in the *No* column.

19. *Psychosomatic disorders* Children who have been genuinely abused have suffered bona fide body trauma. Although the trauma is primarily directed to the genital or rectal areas, somatic complaints often extend to other areas as well. In addition, such children may develop formidable tensions and anxieties—which may have somatic components such as nausea, vomiting, and stomach aches. Such children warrant a check in the *Yes* column.

Fabricators do not typically suffer with psychosomatic complaints. Accordingly, children without such complaints warrant a check in the *No* column. However, fabricators are often subjected to many tensions and anxieties in the context of the parental hostilities. Such children might develop somatic complaints as a result of such exposure. These children would warrant a check in the *Yes* column. This might result in a misleading score for the fabricator in favor of the child's being considered to have been genuinely abused. However, I believe that the total scale will ultimately make the differentiation, their misleading scores notwithstanding.

20. *Regressive Behavior* In response to the trauma of sexual abuse, many such children exhibit regressive manifestations such as thumbsucking, baby talk, enuresis, encopresis, and separation anxieties. Such children warrant a check in the *Yes* column. Children who fabricate are less likely to exhibit such regressive manifestations and so many of them will warrant a check in the *No* column. However, some children who have been exposed to ongoing parental hostilities may also exhibit such regressive manifestations. These children also, although they have not been sexually abused, still warrant a check in the *Yes* column. Again, the misleading score here should be outweighed by scores confirming fabrication when the whole scale is considered.

21. *Deep sense of betrayal, especially regarding the sex abuse*

Children who have been genuinely abused often suffer with deep-seated feelings of having been betrayed by the offender. He has exploited them and has used them for purposes that society generally considers reprehensible. They may also feel betrayed by their mothers, especially in situations in which she has not provided them with protection from the father's abuse. Such children warrant a check in the *Yes* column. However, younger sexually abused children may not describe betrayal because they are not appreciative that they have been exploited. The child has to learn of the exploitation. Accordingly, some genuinely abused children will not warrant a *Yes* check on this item. Rather, they would warrant a *No* response on this item. It is likely, however, that other criteria in this scale will be satisfied, and so the sexual abuse will ultimately be revealed.

Children who fabricate sex abuse do not generally describe this sense of betrayal over being sexually abused. They may describe other indignities they suffer, especially the absurd ones incorporated into the parental alienation syndrome. But these children do not describe betrayal over sexual abuse and so warrant a check in the *No* column. Children who fabricate may describe feelings of betrayal over the divorce, the abandonment that they feel has taken place, and the father's betrayal of the mother. Because such children's sense of betrayal does not focus on the sex abuse, a *No* response is still warranted. Also, children who fabricate sex abuse do not generally complain about the fact that their mothers did not protect them from their fathers' exploitation of them. Rather, they are usually quite laudatory of their mothers and, if a parental alienation syndrome is present, have no complaints at all about them. The failure to include the mother as a figure who has betrayed them lends support to the examiner's placing a check in the *No* column for these children.

Part C

Differentiating Criteria of Low

But Potentially Higher Value

22. *Sleep disturbances* Because putting the child to bed is commonly used as an opportunity for sexually abusing children, it is not surprising that children who are genuinely abused may fear going to sleep. The tensions and anxieties associated with going to bed may contribute to the development of sleep disturbances. These children warrant a *Yes* response for this item. Children who fabricate sex abuse are not as likely to develop sleep disturbances from the fear of being sexually abused at bedtime. They may, however, develop sleep disturbances in association with the psychological traumas attendant to their parents' hostilities, especially if the parents are litigating over their custody. My experience has been that children who fabricate are less likely to have a sleep disturbance than those who are genuinely abused. If a fabricator does warrant a *Yes* response in this category, it is likely that other criteria will ultimately support the conclusion that the allegation is not genuine.

23. *Abuse took place over extended period* By the time a child's sex abuse is brought to the attention of others, it has been generally going on for a long period. When this is the case, a *Yes* answer is warranted for this item. In contrast, the fabricated allegation is often confined to a few specific incidents, more commonly after the time of the onset of the litigation. Such descriptions warrant a *No* response for this item. There are fabricators, however, who have described ongoing sexual encounters over time. When this is the case, a *Yes* response is warranted for this item. In such cases the scale is likely to reveal the fabrication with other items.

24. *Retraction with* fear *of reprisals by the accused, rather than retraction with* guilt *over the consequences to the accused of the divulgences* Children who have been genuinely abused are

more likely than fabricators to have been threatened with dire consequences if they divulge their sexual experiences. After the child who has been genuinely abused reveals his or her experiences, the fear of such consequences may become enhanced. And such fear may contribute to a retraction of the allegation. Children who retract with fear warrant a *Yes* response for this item.

Children who fabricate sex abuse have not been exposed to such threats, and so they are not as likely to anticipate dire consequences for their divulgences. However, they may still retract after becoming aware of the terrible consequences of their divulgence to the accused. They may feel guilty over what they have done. Children who retract with guilt warrant a *No* response for this item. And such response increases the likelihood that the scale will indicate such youngsters to be fabricators. A check in the *Not Clear or Not Applicable* column is warranted when the examiner is not certain whether the fear or the guilt element was the most important contribution to the retraction.

In many cases there is no recanting. In these situations a check in the *No* column is warranted.

25. *Pseudomaturity (girls only)* Sexual abuse of some girls by their fathers is sometimes consciously or unconsciously sanctioned by their mothers. In such cases the mothers may foster other wife-surrogate behaviors in their daughters. This will result in a pseudomature child who will involve herself in the housework, care for other children, and act in many ways like she is the wife of her father. Such youngsters warrant a *Yes* response for this item.

Girls who fabricate are less likely to have developed this behavioral pattern and so will generally warrant a *No* response for this item. Boys who have been sexually abused are far less likely to exhibit pseudomature behavior. If they do, it is likely to be the result of other family influences, unrelated to their having been sexually abused.

26. *Seductive behavior with the accused (girls only)* Girls who have been sexually abused may exhibit seductive behavior with the accused in joint interview. Or this may be described by the mother. When the examiner observes such behavior in joint interviews, then a *Yes* response is warranted. If the examiner considers the mother's description of such seductivity to be credible, then a *Yes* response is also warranted. If there is any question about whether or not such seductive behavior with the accused is being exhibited, then a check in the *Not Clear or Not Applicable* column is warranted.

Fabricators are not likely to have been sexually aroused, have little if any experiences with sexual behavior with the accused, and so are not as likely to exhibit seductive behavior in joint interview. When no such behavior is described or observed by the examiner, then a check in the *No* column is indicated. Again, boys who have been sexually abused are not likely to exhibit seductive behavior toward their abusers. Accordingly, this item is not used for males.

Because items 25 and 26 are not used when the alleged victim is a boy, a minor deficiency is introduced into this scale. Accordingly, the maximum score for boys is 58 points, whereas the maximum score for girls is 60 points. This discrepancy could have been obviated if I were able to find two differentiating criteria that were applicable for boys and not girls. In addition, such criteria would have had to warrant placement in the Part C category. I was unable to find such criteria, nor did I consider it proper to try to "dream up" such items in order to introduce an element of balance in the scale. At one point, I considered dropping these two items entirely. I finally decided to retain them with the justifications that they are valid criteria (even though of low but potentially higher value) and that their l-point value would not significantly affect the child's total SAL Score. In those rare situations in which these two items do indeed change the total SAL Score category, then it behooves the examiner to make note of this when discussing the conclusions.

THE ACCUSER

(Especially when the accuser is the mother)

Part A
Very Valuable Differentiating Criteria

1. *Initially denies and/or downplays the abuse* If the mother has demonstrated denial or downplaying of the abuse, then place a check in the *Yes* column. If the child states that the mother was informed and did nothing about the child's complaints about being abused, then a *Yes* check is also warranted. In contrast, if the mother has immediately reported the father's abuse to outside authorities, especially in the context of pressing charges and litigating, then a check in the *No* column is warranted. There are situations in which the abuse was genuine and the mother immediately reported the abuse to outside authorities. And there are also fabricating mothers who quickly report the abuse to authorities in order to wreak vengeance on their husbands. Under such cases a check in the *No* column is warranted. When the abuse has indeed been genuine, and a check has been placed in the *No* column because the mother reported it to authorities, this item will not serve to support the sex-abuse allegation. However, if the abuse did indeed occur, it is likely that the total scale will reveal its presence.

2. *If the complaint was* not *made in the context of a child custody dispute or litigation, check* Yes. *If there is such a dispute, check* No. The scoring criteria presented under Part A, item 13, of the child's scoring criteria are applicable here.

3. *Shame over revelation of the abuse* If the mother has been hesitant to tell others about the abuse, has kept it

secret, in the situation in which she has not denied its existence, then place a check in the *Yes* column. In contrast, if the mother has freely discussed the abuse with a wide variety of people, especially in the course of litigation, then a place a check in the *No* column.

4. *If she* does not *want to destroy, humiliate, or wreak vengeance on the accused, check* Yes. *If such attitudes* are *present, check* No. If the mother has reported the father to outside authorities, with the goal of causing him pain, punishment, or humiliation, then a check in the *No* column is warranted. Mothers of fabricators are more likely to want to wreak vengeance on the father. In contrast, if no such attitudes are present then a check in the *Yes* column is warranted. There are, however, mothers of children who have been genuinely abused who wish to wreak vengeance on their husbands. In such cases a check in the *No* column will be warranted. If the abuse has genuinely taken place, it is likely to be revealed through other items in this scale.

5. *If she has* not *sought a "hired gun" attorney or mental health professional, check* Yes. *If such professionals have been or are being sought, check* No. Mothers of fabricators are more likely to institute litigation and bring in professionals who will support the charges against the father. In such situations, a *No* response is warranted. Mothers of genuinely abused children who have been genuinely abused are not as likely to quickly bring in such outside authorities. In such situations, a *Yes* response is warranted. However, there are mothers of sexually abused children who do indeed bring in such authorities. In such cases a *No* response is warranted. However, it is likely that in such situations the abuse will be revealed through other items in this scale.

6. *If she* does not *attempt to corroborate the child's sex abuse description in joint interview(s), check* Yes. *If she* does *exhibit such behavior, check* No. This item can only be answered after one or more joint interviews in which are present the child

and the accuser (with or without the accused, as warranted). When children who have been genuinely abused tell their stories, they know what has happened and they do not need any hints or reminders from their mothers. They may need some support from their mothers to reassure them that they will be protected from any anticipated repercussions from the accused, but they will not need to check their stories' veracity with their mothers. Such children warrant a *Yes* response to this item.

In contrast, children who fabricate will often "check" their stories with their mothers through side glances and other manifestations of the need for reassurance from the accuser that the child has the "right story." And the accuser herself will often actively attempt to provide such communications, either overtly or covertly. In such situations, a *No* response is warranted to this item.

Part B

Moderately Valuable Differentiating Criteria

7. *Appreciates the psychological trauma to the child of repeated interrogations* Mothers of children who have been genuinely abused are often hesitant to expose the child to a series of interrogations by outside authorities, because of the recognition that such inquiries may be psychologically damaging to the child. They may hesitate to involve the child in such inquiries and, if involved, they will request that the authorities minimize their number and duration. Such mothers warrant a check in the *Yes* column. In contrast, mothers of children who are fabricating will often relish the opportunity for as many interviews as possible in order to strengthen the case against the father. In such cases a *No* response is warranted.

8. *Appreciates the importance of maintenance of the child's relationship with the accused* Although pained and even indig

nant over the sex-abuse divulgence, mothers of genuinely abused children often hope that the relationship between the child and the abusing father can be salvaged. Often they will express such desires in interview. In such situations a *Yes* response is warranted.

In contrast, mothers of fabricating children often take the position that the child would be better off without any contact whatsoever with the father. One of the aims of their litigation is to reduce contacts between the child and the father as much as the court will allow. They have no problems with a court-ordered cessation of visitation pending a plenary trial. The fact that this might last months or even years does not seem to bother them at all. Such mothers warrant a check in the *No* column.

9. *Childhood history of having been sexually abused herself* If the mother reports having been sexually abused herself as a child and/or in adolescence, a check is placed in the *Yes* column. Mothers of children who have been genuinely sexually abused are more likely to have been sexually abused themselves in childhood. In contrast, mothers of fabricating children are less likely to have been abused themselves, and so a check in the *No* column is warranted for these mothers.

There are certainly mothers who have not been sexually abused themselves, but whose children have been abused. Although such mothers will warrant a *No* response for this item, other items in the scale should counterbalance this response and indicate that the child has been sexually abused. Also, there are certainly mothers of fabricating children who have been abused. In such cases, a check in the *Yes* column is warranted. This scale, however, should ultimately result in the conclusion of fabrication, even though a *Yes* check for this item lends support to the bona fide argument.

10. *Passivity and/or inadequacy* Mothers of children who have been genuinely abused are more likely to be passive

and/or inadequate individuals. They are often meek, dependent, and inhibited in asserting themselves. If the mother exhibits such personality traits, then a check in the *Yes* column is warranted. Mothers of children who are fabricators are more likely to be assertive, domineering, and overt in their complaints and denunciations of the father. In such cases a *No* response is warranted. Of course, there are situations in which the mother does not fall into either of these two categories. In such situations a check in the *Not Clear or Not Applicable* column is indicated. Also, there are mothers who are passive and/or inadequate, whose children are fabricators. A check in the *Yes* column is still warranted for these mothers. The scale, however, should still indicate fabrication when all items are considered. And there are mothers who are not passive and/or inadequate whose children are genuinely abused. Although such mothers will warrant a check in the *No* column, other *Yes* items on the scale should still result in the conclusion that their children have been abused.

Part C
Differentiating Criterion of Low
But Potentially Higher Value

11. *Social isolate* Mothers of children who have been genuinely abused are more likely than fabricating mothers to be withdrawn from society. In such cases a check in the *Yes* column is indicated. Mothers of fabricating children are more likely to be outgoing and involved with others (even though often pathologically so). In such cases a *No* response is warranted. When a mother does not fit clearly into either of these categories, then a check in the *Not Clear or Not Applicable* column is indicated.

Of course, there are mothers who are isolates who may

still be fabricators. For such mothers a *Yes* response is indicated for this item. This misleading indicator of abuse should be counterbalanced by other items on the scale that will ultimately reveal the fabrication. Also, there are mothers who are not isolates whose children have been abused. The misleading *No* response on this item should be more than offset by other items in the scale that will result in the conclusion that their children have indeed been abused.

THE ACCUSED
(Especially when the accused is the father)

Part A
Very Valuable Differentiating Criteria

1. *Bribed and/or threatened the child to keep the "secret"* Fathers who sexually abuse their children often threaten them with dire consequences if they reveal the abuse (often referred to as "our special secret"). In such cases a *Yes* response is indicated. Some fathers who sexually abuse their children bribe them with gifts, again to keep the secret. If such bribing has occurred, then a *Yes* response is warranted. If neither bribing nor threatening has occurred, then a *No* response is indicated. There are fathers, however, who sexually abuse their children and do not bribe or threaten them. This is sometimes seen in fathers who are severely disturbed, such as those who suffer with psychosis. Or, if the perpetrator is of borderline or of retarded intelligence, such suppressive maneuvers may not have been utilized. Sometimes the abuse will take place when the father is under the influence of alcohol or drugs. Bribing and threatening may not then occur. In such situations a *No* response is warranted. The scale, however, is likely to reveal the abuse via other items.

2. *Weak and/or feigned denial* Fathers who have genuinely abused their children often give very weak or feigned denials that are not very convincing. Such fathers warrant a *Yes* response. Fathers of fabricating children usually exhibit significant frustration and indignation. They manifest the attitudes of the innocent man who has been falsely accused. Such fathers warrant a check in the *No* column. There are situations, however, where the examiner cannot be certain about the father's response, whether it has the quality of feigned denial or righteous indignation. In such cases a check in the *Not Clear or Not Applicable* column is indicated.

The examiner must also be aware of the fact that psychopaths can be extremely convincing liars and may be able to put on such a good show that the examiner will actually believe that the bona fide perpetrator is exhibiting genuine righteous indignation. Unfortunately, in such cases a *No* response will be indicated. Examiners who have been so duped may gain some reassurance from the belief that the scale will ultimately "smoke out" such duplicity and will differentiate between the bona fide and the fabricated accusation.

3. *If the complaint was* not *made in the context of a child custody dispute and litigation, check* Yes. *If there* is *such a dispute, check* No. The scoring criteria presented under Part A, item 13, of the child's scoring criteria are applicable here.

4 *Presence of other sexual deviations* Fathers who have sexually abused their children are more likely to manifest symptoms of other sexual deviations such as exhibitionism, voyeurism, sado-masochism, and homosexuality. The homosexual deviation is especially likely to be present if the abused child is male. The presence of such deviations warrant a *Yes* response. If such deviations are not present, then a *No* response is indicated. Of course, there are fathers who sexually abuse their children who do not exhibit such deviations. In such situations a *No* response will be indicated. However, if the abuse has indeed occurred, the scale is

likely to reveal it through other items. And there are fathers who exhibit such deviations who do not sexually abuse their children. In such situations, a *Yes* response is warranted. Again, other items on the scale should ultimately indicate that there was no sexual abuse.

Part B
Moderately Valuable
Differentiating Criteria

5. *Childhood history of having been sexually abused himself* Fathers who abuse their children are more likely to have been sexually abused themselves as children. Sexual abuse has been part of the family pattern, and it is not surprising that it is carried down to another generation. If such a history is present, then a check is placed in the *Yes* column. If the father provides no history of childhood sexual abuse, then a check should be placed in the *No* column.

There are, however, fathers who have not been sexually abused themselves as children, but who sexually abuse their own children. Such fathers will warrant a check in the *No* column. If the abuse has indeed taken place, it is likely that the scale will reveal it through other items. And there are fathers who have been sexually abused as children, who do not abuse their own children. Such fathers warrant a *Yes* response. It is likely that other items in the scale will indicate that no abuse has taken place.

6. *Reluctance or refusal to take a lie detector test* Fathers who genuinely abuse their children usually are quite reluctant to take a lie detector test. They recognize that the test may reveal them to be lying when they deny the abuse. If such refusal is present then a check in the *Yes* column is warranted. Fathers of fabricators more commonly ask for a lie detector test and are quite enthusiastic about taking it. This is especially the case if they are not aware of the fact that

the test is not foolproof. They fear they will find themselves in the category of "false positives." Such fathers warrant a check in the *No* column.

There are, however, fathers of fabricators who are reluctant to take the test because they are aware of the fact that it is not foolproof. Such fathers, however, are not common. Most fathers of fabricators are quite willing to take the test, its inadequacies and risks notwithstanding. However, the father who does exhibit reluctance, for whatever reason, warrants a check in the *Yes* column. If such a father is being falsely accused, the fabricated allegation is likely to reveal itself through other items.

7. *History of drug and/or alcohol abuse* Bona fide sexual abusers are more likely to have a history of drug and/or alcohol abuse than fathers of children who fabricate the abuse. When such a history is present, a *Yes* response is indicated. When such a history is absent, a *No* response is indicated. There are, however, fathers of fabricators who have a history of drug and/or alcohol abuse. In such cases a *Yes* response is warranted. If the abuse, however, is fabricated, it is likely to be revealed through other items on this scale. And there are certainly sex abusers who do not have a history of alcohol and/or drug abuse. Such individuals will warrant a *No* response in this item. However, it is likely that the scale will reveal their sex-abuse behavior through other items.

8. *Low self-esteem* Fathers who abuse their children are more likely to suffer with feelings of inadequacy. This will be revealed through such symptoms as low self-assertion, low motivation, repeated job failures, and impaired interpersonal relationships. Their choice of an immature child, a person who cannot reject them, a person whom they can overpower, is just one manifestation of their low self-esteem. They may or may not express verbally their feelings of inadequacy. Sometimes these are conscious and sometimes

unconscious. Fathers who exhibit these symptoms warrant a *Yes* response.

Fathers of fabricators are less likely to exhibit symptoms of low self-esteem. They are more likely to be outgoing, assertive, and effective in the world. This does not preclude underlying feelings of inadequacy, with which all people suffer to a certain degree. However, whatever their internal feelings of inadequacy, they are not so deep-seated that they interfere with successful functioning in the world. Such fathers warrant a *No* response. If the examiner cannot be certain regarding the category of response, then a check in the *Not Clear or Not Applicable* column is warranted.

9. *Tendency to regress in periods of stress* Fathers who have genuinely abused their children are usually immature individuals who cannot tolerate the stresses of adult egalitarian relationships. In stressful situations they are likely to withdraw, regress, and become fixated at earlier levels of development. In such situations they may exhibit symptoms such as dependency, petulant and demanding behavior, inability to work, and substance abuse. When such symptoms are present, a *Yes* response is warranted.

In contrast, fathers of fabricators are less likely to exhibit such regressive manifestations. When such symptoms are not present, a *No* response is warranted. If the examiner is not clear regarding which category of response to provide, then a check in the *Not Clear or Not Applicable* column is warranted.

It is important for the examiner to appreciate that divorce is an extremely stressful experience, and if custody litigation is taking place, the stresses are even greater. Under such circumstances, some regression may occur—even in relatively mature individuals. In such cases it is possible that sex abuse may take place. (This was described in greater detail in Chapter Four.) The *Yes* response here for such fathers will lend weight to the argument that they have indeed sexually abused their children. There are, however, fathers who regress in response to the divorce and custody litigation who do not sexually abuse their children. The *Yes* response for such fathers will result in weight being given to the argument that sex abuse has indeed taken place. Other items in the scale, however, should support the conclusion that the sex-abuse allegation is fabricated.

10. *Career choice which brings him in close contact with children* In Chapter Four I described various careers toward which bona fide sex abusers tend to gravitate. If the father is in such a career, then a *Yes* response is warranted. There are, obviously, fathers of fabricators who are engaged in such careers. In such cases a *Yes* response will still be warranted. If the sex abuse has not indeed taken place, it is likely that other items in this scale will support such a conclusion. Fathers who do not have such a career warrant a *No* response. Of course, there are fathers who sexually abuse their children who are not involved in such a career. They still will warrant a *No* response. Again, it is likely the scale will reveal the abuse through other items.

Part C
Differentiating Criteria of
Low But Potentially Higher Value

11. *Moralistic* Some fathers who are abusers tend to be very moralistic with their families. They may subscribe to very high standards of behavior in a very domineering way. Such attitudes may serve as compensation for their deep-seated thoughts and feelings that they are extremely immoral. This is one of the factors operative in clergymen who sexually abuse their children, or children in their houses of worship. If such moralistic attitudes are present, then a *Yes* response is warranted. Fathers of fabricating children are

less likely to be so highly moralistic. Such fathers warrant a *No* response.

There are, of course, highly moralistic fathers who are not sex abusers. Such fathers will still warrant a *Yes* response for this item. However, other items should reveal the fact that they have not abused their children. Also, there are fathers who are not moralistic who abuse their children. Such fathers will warrant a *No* response for this item. Again, their abuse should be revealed via other items in this scale.

12. *Controlling* Many fathers who abuse their children are domineering and controlling of their families. Sexually abusing their children is one manifestation of this pattern. Fathers who exhibit such controlling behavior warrant a *Yes* response. Fathers of children who fabricate sex abuse are less likely to exhibit these personality traits. Such fathers warrant a *No* response for this item.

However, there are certainly fathers of fabricating children who do indeed exhibit controlling and domineering behavior. Such fathers warrant a *Yes* response. In such situations, if the abuse is indeed fabricated, it is likely to be revealed through other items in this scale. And, there are certainly fathers who do not exhibit controlling behavior who still sexually abuse their children. Such fathers will warrant a *No* response for this item. Again, their sexually abusing their children should be revealed via other items in this scale.

13.*Stepfather or other person with frequent access to the child* Stepfathers are in a high-risk category for sexually abusing their stepchildren. Without the sexual desensitization which takes place over years of familiarization, stepfathers are more likely to give in to sexual feelings toward their stepchildren. Stepfathers have less of an incest taboo than natural fathers. Accordingly, if the accused is a stepfather, a *Yes* response is indicated. Of course, there are stepfathers who are subjected to fabricated allegations of sex abuse. They, too, will warrant a *Yes* response in this category. If the sex abuse has indeed not taken place, it is likely that other items in this scale will support that conclusion. The same considerations hold for accused individuals who are close friends, relatives, or others who have frequent access to the home. If the accused is the child's father, then a *No* response is indicated. If such a father has indeed sexually molested the child, then other items on this scale should certainly reveal it.

CONCLUDING COMMENTS

It is important that examiners who use the *Sexual Abuse Legitimacy Scale* adhere strictly to the scoring criteria presented above. It is crucial also that they not score the scale until all interviews, individual and joint, have been completed. Otherwise, the scale's value will be seriously compromised. It is also important for the examiner to appreciate that the cutoff points utilized are tentative and preliminary. The items have face validity only and their classification into the three categories of importance are based on my clinical experience only. Moreover, the cutoff points are similarly based on my clinical experience during the five years prior to the preparation of the scale.

Fabricated allegations of sex abuse as a widespread phenomenon is a recent development. Accordingly, few can claim vast experience with such children. Many can claim vast experience with children who have been genuinely abused. But very few can claim formidable experience with large populations of *both* categories, i.e., those who have been abused and those who fabricate such abuse. It is probable that with further experience I will introduce modifications of this scale, with regard to its format and the cutoff points. Examiners who are not appreciative of these weaknesses and drawbacks of the scale may come to erroneous conclusions, much to the detriment of the parties being evaluated.

The scale should be viewed as part of a total evaluation. When medical evidence is present that supports the conclusion that sex abuse has indeed taken place, then the scale can provide adjunctive information, usually confirmatory (but possibly nonconfirmatory). When medical evidence is of no value regarding whether or not the sex abuse has taken place, the scale may be the most important source of information the examiner has for ascertaining whether or not the abuse has taken place. But even then it should not be used in isolation; interviews with other parties and reports from other examiners should be taken into consideration. Last, I wish to emphasize again that the scoring criteria presented here should serve as guidelines; the examiner's clinical judgment must also be considered when scoring each item.

SIX

JUDGES INTERVIEWING CHILDREN WITH PARENTAL ALIENATION SYNDROME AND/OR THOSE WHO ALLEGE SEX ABUSE

INTRODUCTION

I have described elsewhere (1982) the techniques that evaluators can utilize when interviewing children in child custody disputes. The special considerations necessary for interviewing children with parental alienation syndrome have also been presented (1986a). In Chapters Four and Five of this book I have described techniques evaluators might find useful when examining children who allege sex abuse. Although my publications are designed primarily for use by mental health professionals, the techniques described therein have proven of value to attorneys, especially those who are serving as guardians ad litem, and/or who are called upon to interview children. Elsewhere (Gardner, 1986a) I have presented some guidelines that might prove useful to judges when interviewing children with parental alienation syndrome. Here I provide further details on interviewing such youngsters as well as those who allege sex abuse. I believe that judges who utilize these techniques will be in a better position to make decisions regarding their custody as well as whether or not they have been sexually abused. And such enhanced knowledge of these children will place them in a better position to consider and implement the recommendations presented in Chapter Seven.

It is important for judges to appreciate that when they interview children in their chambers, they are doing so under significantly compromised circumstances. An appreciation of these compromises can help the judge place in proper perspective the information so gained. The court's primary question in custody/visitation litigation is this: Who would be a better parent for this child to live with, the mother or the father? This question is not likely to be answered reasonably unless data is collected from all *three* parties referred to in the question. Furthermore, the data-collection process will also be compromised if the parties are seen only alone and not interviewed in various combinations. Restricting oneself to interviewing the child alone compromises the data-collection process significantly because it deprives the evaluator of obtaining data in joint interviews, which are often the most valuable part of the data-collection process. Family interviews also enable the interviewer to "smoke out" fabrications in a situation in which children traditionally say to each parent what they think that parent wants to hear at that moment. In custody-/visitation evaluations, observing the parent-child relationship is the best source of information for ascertaining which parent has the better relationship with the child. The present structure of courtroom proceedings generally precludes the court's conducting such parent-child and family interviews. It must rely on the information provided by mental health professionals who conduct these interviews elsewhere.

Another compromise relates to the fact that intervie-wees, regardless of the circumstances, are more likely to reveal themselves to known parties than to strangers. And the longer and deeper the relationship with the interviewer, the greater the likelihood the interviewee will provide dis-closures. The greater the "dangers" of such revelations, the greater the likelihood that valid information will not be obtained in a short period. Interviewing a child only once does not provide the court with the opportunity to develop the kind of relationship in which such divulgences are likely to be obtained. Judges rarely have the time for multiple interviews, which provide the optimum setting for the kinds of revelations the court is looking for. Furthermore the child generally enters the judge's chambers in a state of fear. Although *in camera* interviews are less frightening than courtroom testimony, the judge is still held in awesome regard by most children and many adults. The fear element is likely to compromise significantly the data-gathering pro-cess, and this cannot but make the information so obtained of dubious value.

The child's level of cognitive development is also an important consideration. Obviously, the younger the child, the less meaningful his or her verbalizations. In the individ-ual interview the court does not have the opportunity to get "translations" from a parent who understands better the child's terminology, innuendos, and gestures. Accordingly, judges must appreciate that the person they are interviewing is the one of the three (mother, father, and child) who is least likely to provide valid data—who believes in the existence of Santa Claus and the Easter bunny. The younger the child, the less the capability of differentiating fact from fantasy—a differentiation to which courts pay particular attention. The purpose of the judge's interview is to find out what "the truth" is with regard to various aspects of the custody dispute. The assumption is made that the child knows what the truth is regarding a variety of pertinent issues. All of us distort the truth somewhat in accordance with what our wishes are, and children even more so. Time generally blurs reality, and the younger the person is at the time of a particular event, the greater the likelihood that time will distort its recollection. By the time a judge sees a child in chambers, the events under consideration may have taken place months or even years previously. It is reasonable to say that for many of the events being discussed with the judge, many children no longer know the truth and could not tell what the truth was, no matter how honest they were trying to be.

TECHNICAL CONSIDERATIONS

Many judges will tell children, at the beginning of their interviews with them, that what the children say will be held strictly confidential and that their parents will never learn what they speak about. Unless the court can be 100 percent certain that this promise will be fulfilled, it is a risky one to make. Generally, this reassurance is given under circumstances in which a transcriber is recording every word. The transcripts that are ultimately made of the interview are usually sent to the attorneys, who may or may not be instructed to reveal their contents to the parents. It is but a short step to the child's learning as well that the judge has not kept the "secrets." Under these circumstances the child cannot but feel betrayed—especially betrayed by someone who is held in high esteem. It is yet another betrayal added to the betrayal of a parent's leaving a home or sexually abusing the child. Accordingly, I generally discourage judges from making such promises. Rather, judges should proceed without such a promise and hope that the child's need to communicate important issues will override the fear that the parents may learn of the disclosures. If the child does ask about whether the divulgences will be revealed, the judge does well to tell the child that his or her comments may be available to the parents or that the judge must be given the freedom to decide which information will be revealed and which not.

The court does well to begin the interview by asking the child simple questions that the child can answer with ease and freedom from anxiety, e.g., name, address, age, telephone number, and so on. Each time the child gets the "right" answer, the initial tensions and anxieties are reduced and make it easier for the child to answer the more anxiety-provoking questions that will inevitably ensue. The court does well to avoid questions that could be answered by either yes or no. Of course, this is just the opposite of what is done in cross-examination, where the yes-no question has a deep-seated heritage. Although this form of inquiry may be useful in "nailing down the facts," I do not hold it in as high regard as my legal colleagues. When one asks a person a question that could be answered either yes or no, one does not really know whether the response is valid. A quick answer of yes or no may be an easy way for the responder to "get off the hook" with regard to providing a meaningful answer. Much more valid material is obtained with questions that elicit sentences and descriptions self-derived by the respondent. For example, if one asks a boy whether he loves his mother, one is likely to get a yes answer—even if she has been brought up on charges of physical abuse. Or if the child says no, one still has very little information. However, if one asks questions like, "Tell me about your mother" or "I'd like you to tell me the things about your mother that you like and the things about her that you don't like," the responses are likely to be far more revealing. In the context of such discussions the court does well to get specific details about each of the items described. One wants the child to verbalize from concrete imagery being mentally visualized.

The court does well to avoid questions relating to *time*. To ask a child about *when* a particular event took place is not likely to produce meaningful data. The younger the child, the less appreciative he or she is of the passage of time, and the less capable the child is of pinpointing the exact time a particular event occurred. Time questions only invite fantasized answers that only compromise the data-collection process. The court does well to ask questions that begin with *what, where, who, and how*. These require the formation of a specific mental image from which the child can relate a response.

When providing examiners with guidelines for the kinds of questions to ask children involved in custody/visitation conflicts, I generally recommend they use what I refer to as *grandma's criteria*. These are the parental manifestations that grandma's ghost would consider if it were free to roam the house and then report its findings to the court. If she is like most grandmas, she doesn't have an M.D. or Ph.D. degree and has very little formal so-called "psychological sophistication." She would observe the child from the minute it got up in the morning until it went to sleep. She would determine who wakes the child up in the morning, who gives it breakfast and prepares it for school. Of course, if father's work requires him to leave so early that he cannot involve himself in these activities, this cannot be considered a deficiency on his part. This is similarly the case for spending lunch time with the children and being available after school. It is the after-work hours, when both parents are traditionally home, that grandma would get her most useful information. She would want to observe who helps the children with their homework and if this is done smoothly or whether there are typically power struggles, tears, fits, tantrums, threats, impatience, and other manifestations of a poor parent-child relationship. She would observe disciplinary measures, especially whether they are humane, consistent, and benevolently administered. She would pay close attention to the bedtime scene. Are bedtime stories read? Are the children lulled into sleep in a loving manner or is it typically a time of threats and punishments? What happens during the night may also be important. Who gets up to change the diapers? To whom does the child turn to for consolation after nightmares? Which parent has traditionally taken the child to the Emergency Room or the doctor's office when there have been evening and nighttime accidents and/or other medical emergencies? The judge does well to get information in these areas by discussing directly with the child the day's events, from arising in the morning to going to sleep at night, and finding out who are the adults who are involved in these various activities.

Another important area of inquiry is parental attendance at school activities, both curricular and extracurricular. The court should find out who attends teacher conferences and what the parental reactions are to report cards. Who attends the various plays, concerts, recitals, and open-school activities? Is there pride and/or emotional reactions or complete indifference? These are among the most valuable criteria for ascertaining parental capacity and the nature of the parent-child relationship.

The court may learn much by asking the child about the details of the visitations: what is done, who was present, where did they go, etc. A child, for example, might describe a father who brings along every transient date, thereby fulfilling two obligations at the same time. Some children describe the visiting parent as dropping them off at the home of third parties (aunts, grandparents, and an assortment of other individuals) and then pursuing their own interests. Many children describe the visiting parents' cross-examining them on visitation days to extract information that might be useful in litigation. Other children go on a round of circuses, rodeos, zoos, etc. Although such overindulgence may serve the purposes of guilt assuagement or rivalry with the custodial parent, in excess it is a parental deficit.

Sometimes questions about the reasons for the divorce may provide the court with useful information. The child's description of the nature of the marital conflict may include information about parental capacity. For example: "My mother couldn't stand my father's drinking anymore. I used to help her find the bottles that he would hide." One can ask about each parent's receptivity to friends visiting the home and the parental tolerance of the noise, rambunctiousness, horseplay, and the minor household damage that inevitably occurs when children are visiting the home. Do the child's friends like each of the parents or not? Is the parent receptive to the child's visiting other homes? Although none of the aforementioned questions are in the category: "Who do you want to live with, your mother or your father?" they clearly provide vital information for the court in making its decision regarding parental preference.

The child should be invited to talk about anything he or she wishes. Although the child's comments may initially appear irrelevant to the court's purpose, there are times when useful information regarding parental capacity can be obtained. Such discussion might be introduced with questions such as "What would you like to talk about now?" and "So tell me something else." In response to such a question a boy might start talking about his interest in baseball. In the context of his discussion he speaks with pride about his accomplishments in Little League and how proud he is that his father is one of the coaches. He expresses regret that the rules do not permit him to be on the team that his father is coaching. Or a 14-year-old girl, again after professing to the judge that she does not want to state her parental preference, may start talking about the fact that she goes shopping with her mother, who is quite expert at selecting perfumes, lipstick, and make-up and with whom she can discuss such personal matters as her period and her feelings about boys. Time does not generally permit the court to indulge itself to a significant degree in this kind of inquiry, but it does well to appreciate its value and recognize that its investigations are compromised by its omission.

The court does well to recognize that the child's comments may be colored by individuals who are outside the judge's chambers during the course of the interview. Children embroiled in custody/visitation disputes suffer with terrible loyalty conflicts. They generally say to each parent that which will ingratiate them to that parent at that time, regardless of their true beliefs and regardless of the consequences of the fabrications they may provide. And this principle extends itself to the *in camera* interview wherein the child is likely to support the parent who is close by. Moreover, the parent who brings the child and/or the parent who takes the child back home is also likely to have an influence on what is said in chambers. Furthermore, children have short memories. A father who brings the child to the court on Monday morning, after a weekend of fun activities, may very well be viewed as the preferable parent. And a mother who brings the child to court on Friday afternoon, after a difficult week in which the child was forced to do homework, chores, and was disciplined for normal childhood transgressions, is likely to be viewed with disfavor. Accordingly, the court does well to have both parents bring the child together and both parents bring the child home, or have a neutral third party accompany the child to the courthouse. But even under such circumstances the court does well to make inquiries regarding the aforementioned considerations of recent parental involvement.

It is important for the judge to appreciate that by the time he or she interviews the child in chambers, there have probably been numerous earlier interrogations extending over many months and even a few years. Under such circumstances the child may no longer know what he or she wants, so mind boggling have been the child's experiences with lawyers and mental health professionals. Lying may become a *modus vivendi*, so much so that the child has long forgotten what he or she really wants or believes. Under these circumstances many children operate on the principle that they will say whatever is most expeditious at that particular time, that which will ingratiate them to the person with whom they are speaking at that moment. The pattern has become so deeply ingrained that the bona fide preferences and opinions have long been suppressed and repressed from conscious awareness.

INTERVIEWING CHILDREN WITH PARENTAL ALIENATION SYNDROME

Children suffering from a parental alienation syndrome may present the judge with a convincing picture. By the time the child reaches the judge, he or she has usually developed a well-rehearsed litany of complaints against the presumably hated parent. This can be quite convincing, especially because the script has probably been rehearsed many times over with the allegedly preferred parent. Also, by the time the child reaches the judge, he or she has probably presented the scenario to a variety of attorneys and mental health professionals. This has given them the opportunity to practice and sharpen their speeches. I have seen a number of occasions when judges have been completely taken in and have not appreciated that they were being handed a "bill of goods." These children have a way of "snowballing" even experienced psychologists and psychiatrists, so I cannot be too critical of judges here. Before interviewing such children, the judge does well to be familiar with the manifestations of the disorder (described in Chapter Three): complete lack of ambivalence, the dwelling on frivolous and inconsequential "indignities," the total removal from the extended family of the hated parent, the absolute denial of any positive input on the hated parent's part at any time in the child's life, and the definite statement that the child wishes never to see the hated parent again throughout the remainder of his or her life. It is hoped that judges will increasingly appreciate what is occurring when they see such children and will rectify the situation in accordance with the guidelines in Chapter Seven.

I present below a series of questions that judges should find useful when interviewing children exhibiting manifestations of the parental alienation syndrome. It is important to appreciate that the questions provided here relate to the more common situation, the one in which the father is the hated parent and the mother the loved one. However, when the situation is reversed (the mother the hated one and the father the loved one), I obviously reverse the questions.

Describe your mother to me. Children with parental alienation syndrome typically provide only positive responses. If any negatives are provided, they will usually be minimal. If asked to elaborate upon the negatives, only inconsequential criticisms will be provided. Children who are normal or suffer with other kinds of psychiatric disturbance will generally be able to list both positives and negatives about each parent. The complete idealization of a parent is a clue to the presence of this disorder.

Describe your father to me. The child with parental alienation syndrome will enumerate various criticisms at great length. These will be both present and past. Often the past indignities will be about experiences that other children would consider normal or would have forgotten long ago. Sometimes a complaint will be about an event that the child has not actually observed him- or herself, but that the mother has described. The child will accept as valid the mother's rendition and not give any credibility to the father's refutation. When it is pointed out to the child that few if any positives have been described, the child will claim flatly that there are none. Inquiries into past good times between the child and the father will be denied as nonexistent, or the child will claim that these events were painful and the child's professed enjoyment of them stemmed from the fear of punishment for not doing so. It is this complete one-sidedness of the response, the total absence of normal ambivalence, that should alert the interviewer to the fact that one is probably dealing with a child suffering with parental alienation syndrome.

How do you feel about your father's family?   The child with a parental alienation syndrome will generally respond that all members of the father's extended family—even the child's own grandparents and previously loved aunts, uncles, and cousins—are somehow obnoxious and vile. When asked for specific reasons why there is absolutely no contact at all with any of these individuals, no compelling reasons are provided. Often inconsequential reasons are given. Attempts to impress upon the child how important it is to have relationships with these loving relatives is futile. The child extends the view of the father as noxious to the father's extended family. The child will describe no sense of loss or loneliness over this self-imposed removal from the father's extended family. If a potential or actual stepmother is involved with the father, this hatred will extend to her and her extended family as well.

Does your mother interfere with your visiting with your father?   Generally the child will describe absolutely no interference on the mother's part. Often the child will proudly describe the mother's neutrality and state that the decision not to visit is completely his or her own.

Why then don't you want to visit with your father? The child may give very vague reasons. When asked to give *specific* reasons these children may describe horrible abuses in a very convincing way. In addition, they often provided gross exaggerations of inconsequential complaints. They make "mountains out of mole hills" and will dwell on frivolous reasons for not visiting. Often they will claim that they want absolutely no contact at all with the father for the rest of their lives, or at least not before they are adults. When it is pointed out to these children that the vast majority of other children would not cut their fathers off entirely, forever, for such "indignities," they insist that their total rejection is justified.

Does your mother harass you? Healthy children generally will give some examples of "harassment," such as being made to turn off the television, do homework, or go to bed earlier than they want. Children with parental alienation syndrome describe no such harassments. They often will describe their mother as being perfect and as never asking them to do things they don't want. This is obviously a fabrication and is a manifestation of the whitewash of the mother. I use the word *harassment* with these children because it is a common expression utilized by mothers of parental alienation syndrome children. The father's overtures for involvement with the child are generally referred to as harassment by the mother. If the child is unfamiliar with the word harassment, I substitute "bother you a lot."

Does your father harass you? These children are likely to describe in great detail the father's "harassments." Generally, they involve attempts on his part to gain contact with the children. Letters, telephone calls, and legal attempts to gain visitation are all clumped under the term "harassments." Although the father's initial overtures may have been spaced reasonably, with mounting frustration over rejection and alienation, the father's overtures increase in frequency and intensity. The love and affection that is at the foundation of these overtures is denied completely by both the mother and the parental alienation syndrome child. Rather, they are viewed simply as onerous harassments.

The above questions are general ones. The judge does well to ask more specific questions pertinent to the particular case. These might include questions regarding why the child wants to change his or her name back to the mother's maiden name, why the father's Christmas presents were thrown in the garbage (usually in the mother's presence), why the child wants to have the father still contribute to his or her education even though he or she never wants to see the father again, what the brother's and sister's reasons are for not wanting to see the father (these too often prove inconsequential).

INTERVIEWING CHILDREN
WHO ALLEGE SEX ABUSE

Children who claim that they have been sexually abused present judges with further problems. Children with parental alienation syndrome are generally not accusing the hated parent of any punishable crimes. This is not the case with children who allege sex abuse. The Sixth Amendment of the U.S. Constitution guarantees the right of the accused to be confronted by the accuser in an open courtroom. And the Constitution does not differentiate between a child and an adult with regard to this right. There are many cases in which prosecution is not possible because children are either barred from testifying or their testimonies do not have credibility. Most often children who allege that they have been sexually abused are required to appear in court and face the defendant if any legal action is to be taken. Although most of the mental health and legal professionals involved recognize that such testimony may be psychologically traumatic, they see themselves as having no other options if the alleged perpetrator is to be brought to trial. Recently, various modifications have been introduced that attempt to provide some kind of a compromise that will at the same time allow the accused to be confronted by the accuser and yet protect the accusing child from the psychological trauma attendant to providing open courtroom testimony. Some courts are allowing videotapes of interviews with others to be submitted as evidence. Some courts allow interviewing with one-way mirrors, without the child's knowledge that he or she is being observed by various parties involved in the litigation. Yates (1987) describes a situation in which a psychiatrist, serving as a court examiner, directly questioned a child while both were being viewed through a one-way mirror. Throughout the course of the interview, the psychiatrist responded to attorneys' questions and requests via a tiny transmitter in his ear. The constitutionality of all of these modifications has yet to be tested. All of them are attempts to protect the child from psychological trauma, but they all deprive the accused from direct confrontation with the accuser in an open courtroom. Basically, the videotape of the child making the accusation is being used instead.

Judges have the discretion of interviewing such children in chambers. Such interviews, however, are not generally considered to replace open courtroom testimony. Judges must appreciate that the child's having a good relationship with the interviewer is crucial if the information obtained in interview is to be valid. Single interviews in chambers are not likely to satisfy this important proviso. Accordingly, to the degree that the judge has the freedom, time, and flexibility for multiple interviews, will his or her data be valid. Children are generally awestruck by a courtroom. The judge's chambers may be more reassuring. However, even *in camera* interviews usually cause considerable fear in most children. If the judge has the opportunity to interview such children in other settings (such as the home), then this contaminant to accurate data collection may be reduced. If it is possible to have the two attorneys and the court reporter in a separate room, viewing the interview through a one-way mirror, then anxiety and tension might also be reduced.

Many children who have been sexually abused consider themselves to have committed a crime and may fear that they will be put in jail. Judges do well to inquire of the child as to whether or not such a concern is present and, if so, to reassure the child that such incarceration will not indeed occur. Children who have been genuinely abused are often threatened with terrible consequences for divulging their experiences. The judge should explore this area and reassure the child that every precaution will be taken to protect the child from such retaliation. Unfortunately, the courts may not be fully capable of fulfilling such a promise completely because, in some situations, only years of imprisonment (if not life incarceration) of the perpetrator may genuinely protect the child. Some children fear that they will be punished if they cannot answer all the judge's questions. The child should be reassured that such a punishment will not ensue.

In many jurisdictions the court is asked to first ascertain whether the child can differentiate truth from falsehood before inquiring about sex abuse. If the child does not appear to be able to make this distinction, then no further inquiry is conducted, and the child is not considered a source of viable information. As mentioned earlier in this chapter, such determinations may be very difficult, if not impossible, especially with younger children. If statutes require the judge to make this determination before proceeding, and preclude continuation of the interview if this fact has not been established, then the judge's interview may be seriously compromised. The child may not be able to answer questions about such capacity to the satisfaction of the court, and yet still be able to provide useful information in areas related to the sex abuse. For example, a child who still believes in Santa Claus has not reached the point, ipso facto, of differentiating fact from fantasy in the area of Santa Claus. Such a child, however, may still be able to differentiate quite well between facts about sexual abuse and fantasies about sexual abuse.

The judge is often required to make some assessment of the child's competence to stand trial before the trial commences. This may be extremely difficult, if not impossible, in many cases. The child's story may change over time. What the child has said previously may be significantly determined by the interviewer's expectations, leading questions, and parental influences, both subtle and overt. Accordingly, the child may present the judge with a very different story from that given to previous examiners. Children often try to please adults and will frequently give an answer that they suspect the adult wants to have. Children are easily taken in by astute interrogators who will ask yes-no questions and otherwise attempt to extract the responses that will support their positions. This may play a role in the child's providing the judge with a story different from that given to previous interviewers.

The judge must appreciate that children's capacity to pay attention is limited and that prolonged inquiries are likely to be progressively less and less revealing as the child becomes increasingly fatigued. Under these circumstances the child is likely to provide perfunctory responses that are often meaningless at the end of a long inquiry. Although one long interview may appear to be more efficient than a series of shorter ones, they are not judicious for judges to utilize when interviewing children.

Judges must appreciate that a number of factors operate simultaneously in determining whether or not the child is going to discuss the event. Children's memories are generally short. Accordingly, the longer the time gap between the alleged sex abuse and the interview, the greater the likelihood the child will not remember the details. However, children will generally remember traumatic events more accurately than those that have little psychological significance. However, denial mechanisms often operate to suppress the memory of the very same traumas that may be recalled accurately if the child would allow him- or herself to discuss them. And fear of retaliation by the alleged offender may also interfere with the child's recall and/or willingness to discuss the issue. The child may feel guilty over the allegation, and such guilt may also interfere with discussion of the alleged abuse. (In Chapter Four I have described in detail the various forms of guilt these children may have, both those who have been genuinely abused and those who fabricate.)

I believe that judges would do well to review the interviewing techniques that I have presented for mental health professionals in Chapters Four and Five of this book. To the degree that they have the sophistication to use them and to the degree that they have the time to implement these principles, will their interviews be productive. They also do well to review carefully the reports provided by previous examiners in order to enable them to focus on the most pertinent areas. This will enable them to conduct their interviews in the most efficient manner. However, judges must recognize that what they may thereby gain in efficiency may be offset by the compromises related to the fact that a relationship with the child who is alleging sexual abuse has not been established. The judge would do well to learn from previous reports what names the child uses to designate various genital and body parts. He or she does well to utilize as much as possible "blank screen" questions and to stay away, as much as possible, from yes-no questions. Questions regarding *when* the abuse took place are not likely to be useful, and their utilization is a carryover from legal inquiries with adults. Also, questions about the number of times a certain event has occurred are often of little value. However, children can often differentiate between a few and a lot. Better questions relate to *where* the events occurred and exactly *what* took place. It is here that discussions about bath time and bedtime are important, because these are the times in which the sex abuse is most likely to take place. Children who fabricate sex abuse are likely to have their litany prepared at the time of the first inquiry and have them well sharpened by the time they reach the judge, usually many interviews later. Children who have genuinely been abused do not generally have a litany at the outset, but will usually develop one in the course of their series of interviews. However, they will exhibit fear of revelation for a long time. The judge must be sensitive to these clues of whether the allegation is genuine or fabricated. In Chapter Four I described the use of various instruments such as the freely drawn picture, the Draw-a-Person Test, and the use of dolls (traditional and anatomical) in interviewing children who allege sex abuse. I believe the court does well to stay away from the utilization of these techniques. They are different enough for trained mental health professionals to use properly; they are bound to cause even more trouble for those who are less knowledgeable about their utilization.

CONCLUDING COMMENTS

Judges must appreciate that their feeling constrained by the kinds of interrogations they are permitted when evaluating children in custody disputes and those who allege sex abuse is the result of the system within which they are working. The compromise is only one of many that the system causes. Mental health professionals do not operate within the constraints imposed by the adversary system. Judges do not have the opportunity to conduct joint interviews and to place together in the room any and all of the concerned parties. Judges do well, therefore, to give greatest credence to the evaluations of mental health professionals who conduct such joint interviews. Mental health practitioners who do not conduct such interviews are voluntarily and unnecessarily compromising their evaluations. Mental health professionals have certain skills and opportunities that judges do not have; courts have powers that mental health professionals do not enjoy (I am not suggesting that we mental health professionals be given these powers). We complement one another. The courts can separate individuals who are causing one another harm, either physically or psychologically. It can remove programming parents from the children they are brainwashing. It can remove abusing parents from the children who are subjected to their abuse. It does not have the interviewing skills that provide the kind of information necessary for the courts' decisions and the utilization of its powers. It behooves all of us to recognize our limits and not to attempt to assume each other's roles or enter into each other's domains.

Finally, my hope is that judges will come to act more quickly in custody cases. My experience has been that courts are notoriously slow in these matters. Cases drag on for years, during which time the pathology continues to become entrenched. I had one case that lasted nine years. In the course of the litigation, the children become adolescents—by which time the original recommendations had little relevance. But more important, over this period it was the delays, more than anything else, that brought about ever deepening psychopathology in all family members. My repeated requests that judges act quickly have generally been ignored.

As to be discussed in detail in Chapter Seven, in many cases of parental alienation syndrome the best "cure" is immediate removal from the so-called loved parent and immediate transfer to the home of the so-called hated parent. The longer the delay, the less the likelihood that such a change can be effected. If one delays too long (and a few months may be long enough) then removal will be impossible because the fear of the hated parent may have risen to such proportions that the child is placed in an unlivable situation. Similarly, court delay has resulted in significant psychopathology in cases in which sex abuse has been alleged. Frequently, the courts err on the side of removing the alleged perpetrator awaiting further investigation and a plenary hearing. This quick action may very well serve the interests of children who have been continually abused; however, it can cause significant psychological damage when the abuse is fabricated. The time lag between the time of removal of the child from contact with the alleged abuser and the trial is generally many months and, in many cases, even longer. During this time both parent and child are deprived of what might otherwise have been valuable input to each other. And these privations can be psychologically damaging. Again, my requests to the courts that quick action be taken is most often not heeded.

SEVEN

LEGAL AND THERAPEUTIC APPROACHES TO THE PREVENTION AND TREATMENT OF THE PARENTAL ALIENATION SYNDROME AND FABRICATED SEX-ABUSE ALLEGATIONS

INTRODUCTION

In this book I first traced the development of the adversary system. I then described its utilization in divorce/custody disputes. Next, I discussed the ways in which the utilization of the system in such disputes has contributed to the development of a wide variety of psychiatric problems, among which is the parental alienation syndrome (the one selected for focus in this book). Then I described how fabricated sex-abuse allegations may not only be one manifestation of the parental alienation syndrome, but can serve as a powerful weapon when custody disputes are dealt with in adversarial proceedings. I then discussed the ways in which judges could prove useful in dealing with children who exhibit manifestations of the syndrome as well as those

233

who claim they have been sexually abused. In this chapter I will focus on changes in the judicial process that might contribute to the prevention and alleviation of the grief that many divorcing families suffer. Again, there is a selective process here, with particular emphasis on changes in legal education, judicial procedure, and the laws. There is little focus in this chapter on therapy, because I consider the therapist to be "picking up the pieces" after unnecessary damage has been done. If the recommendations presented in this chapter are implemented, then many of the disorders described in this book will not arise. Obviously, it is much more judicious to prevent a disorder from taking place than to treat it after it has arisen and after much damage may have occurred.

TEACHING LAW STUDENTS ABOUT THE DEFICIENCIES OF THE ADVERSARY SYSTEM

Prevention is best accomplished if one's attention is directed to the earliest manifestations of the processes that bring about a disorder. With regard to the parental alienation syndrome and other disorders that arise from protracted adversarial proceedings, one does well to start at the law-school level, where lawyers first learn about adversarial proceedings. Although all law schools teach that the adversary system is not perfect, most professors teach their students that it is the best we have. Law students are taught that the system has evolved over centuries and that it is the best method yet devised for determining whether or not a defendant has indeed committed an alleged crime. It is based on the assumption that the best way of finding out who is telling the truth in such conflicts is for the accused and the accuser each to present to an impartial body (a judge or jury) his or her argument, in accordance with certain rules and guidelines of presentation. More specifically, each side is permitted to present any information that supports its position and to withhold (within certain guidelines) information that would weaken its arguments. Out of this conflict of opposing positions, the impartial body is allegedly in the best position to ascertain the truth. Many in the legal profession have never given serious consideration to the system's weaknesses and blindly adhere to its tenets. Essential to the system is the principle that the impartial body attempts to rule on and/or resolve the dispute through the application of some general rule of law. Although this principle certainly serves to protect individuals from misguided justice, it produces in many legal professionals what I consider to be an exaggerated deference to "the law." This may result in a blind adherence to legal precedents, statutes, and laws—often with little consideration to whether they are just, honorable, or fair. I would like to focus in this section on what I consider to be some of the grievous weaknesses of the adversary system, weaknesses that directly contribute to the kinds of family psychopathology already described.

Lies of Omission and Lies of Commission

The adversary system basically encourages lies of omission. It encourages withholding information that might compromise a client's position. This is lying. The same attorneys who routinely justify such omissions in their own work would not hesitate suing a physician for malpractice for the omission of information that could be detrimental to a patient. Many lawyers get defensive when one tries to point out that lies of omission are still lies, and that teaching law students to utilize them is a deceitful and despicable practice. The argument that this is how the adversary system works is not a justifiable one. It is a rationalization. Psychiatrists, and physicians in general, work on the principle that all pertinent information must be brought to the doctor's attention if he or she is to make the most judicious decisions regarding treatment. The same principle holds with regard to the solution of other problems in life. The more information one has, the better is one's capacity to deal with a problem. The adversary system encourages the withholding and covering up of information. The argument that the other side is very likely to bring out what is withheld by the first is not a valid one. The other side may not be aware of the fact that such information exists. Furthermore, the procedure encourages nitpicking and other time-wasting maneuvers, delays, and interrogatory procedures that usually impede rather than foster the divulgence of information.

It is unreasonable to expect that one can teach law students how to lie in one area and not to do so in others. These practices tend to become generalized. Attorneys have been known to say to clients, "Don't tell me. It's better that I don't know." The next step, after a client has unwittingly provided the compromising information, is for the attorney to say, "Forget you told me that" or "Never tell anyone you said that to me." And the next step is for the attorney to say, "You know it and I know it, but that is very different from their *proving* it." This "deal" is, by legal definition, collusion: an agreement between the lawyer and the client that they will work together to deceive the other side. Like chess, it is a game whose object is to trick and entrap the opponent.

Professors at many law schools may respond that such criticism does not give proper credit to or demonstrate respect for the "higher" principles taught at their institutions. They claim that their students are imbued with the highest ethical and moral values known to humankind. Although they may actually believe what they are saying, my experience has been that the graduates of these same institutions are still prone to involve themselves in the aforementioned kinds of deceitful maneuvers with their clients. Moreover, even these institutions teach the adversary system. When one begins with a system that is intrinsically deceitful, one cannot expect those who implement it to use it in an honest manner. To use it is to deceive. Furthermore, to utilize it risks an expansion of deceit into other areas. If one teaches a child to steal pennies and only pennies, one should not be surprised when the child starts stealing nickels. To say I only taught him or her how to steal pennies is no defense. If one teaches a child to lie to the butcher but not to the baker, one should not be surprised when the child lies to the baker as well. If one teaches a child to lie to the butcher and the baker but not to the parents, one should not be surprised when the child also lies to the parents.

The Failure to Allow Direct Confrontation Between the Accused and the Accuser

It amazes me that after centuries of utilization, adherents of the adversary system do not appreciate that they are depriving themselves of one of the most valuable and predictable ways of learning the truth. I am referring here to the placing of the accused and the accuser together in the same room in order to observe a direct confrontation between the two. Proponents of the system will immediately take issue with me on this point. They will claim that one of the reasons for the development of the adversary system was the appreciation that the inquisitorial system left accused parties feeling helpless. At least during its early utilization, the accused often were not permitted direct confrontation with their accusers, and frequently did not even know who they were. This insistence upon the right of the accused to face their accusers is considered to be one of the strongest arguments for perpetutating the adversary system. What many of the system's proponents fail to appreciate is that the confrontations that are insisted upon in the system are not as free and open as they would like to believe. When referring to this practice, the general assumption is that the confrontation will take place in an open courtroom. On the one hand, this is an advance because there are many witnesses to the confrontation: a judge, a jury, and often observers in the audience. On the other hand, the confrontation is extremely constrained by rites of courtroom procedure, and both parties are required to work under very confining circumstances. They are rarely allowed direct communication with one another; rather, communication is usually through their attorneys. These elements markedly compromise the benefits that are presumably obtained from the confrontation. In short, the principle of direct confrontation between accused and accuser is certainly a good one, but its implementation in the adversary system has reduced its efficacy enormously.

The central problem with the adversarial courtroom confrontration is that the two individuals are not permitted to speak directly to one another. The argument that in more volatile situations they might cause one another physical harm is no justification for the formidable constraints that are imposed upon both with regard to directly communicating with each other. In such cases the litigants could be provided with some kind of physical barrier such as a perforated steel screen (through which they could still converse). The argument that the accused and the accuser are still better off having representatives is, I believe, a residuum of the days of trial by champion. No matter how brilliant the lawyer and the judge, no matter how obsessive they are with regard to getting the details of the alleged incident, no matter how devoted they are to the collection of their data, the fact is that *they were not present as observers of the alleged incident*. Only the accused and the accuser were allegedly there. They know better than anyone else whether or not the events actually occurred. Similarly, they often know each other better than any of the other parties involved in the litigation. If the system were to allow the accused and the accuser to talk directly to each other, and confront each other with their opinions of one another's statements, much more "truth" would be obtained. Of course, less money would be made by the "middle men." In some cases their "services" could be dispensed with entirely. In other cases attorneys would still be necessary because of their knowledge of the law and other genuine services that they could provide their clients.

These factors are especially valid for custody litigation. The litigants know one another "inside out." Each knows better than anyone else when the other party is fabricating. Each knows the signs and symptoms of the other's lying: stuttering, the hesitations, the embarrasssed facial expressions, the "shit-eating grins," and the wide variety of other manifestations of duplicity. The adversary system does not give the individuals the opportunity for an "eyeball to eyeball" confrontation. I am convinced that this is one of the best ways of finding out who is telling the truth, and I am amazed that in all of its years of utilization, the system has strictly deprived itself of using this valuable source of information.

It is for this reason that I make joint sessions mandatory in custody evaluations I conduct (Addendum II). In fact, I will refuse to involve myself in such an evaluation if I do not have the opportunity to bring the involved parties together in the same room at the same time. I do the same thing when I am asked to conduct other kinds of evaluations, such as sex-abuse evaluations (Addendum I). Here, again, I am surprised that the tradition is for the courts to send a child to examiners such as myself and ask us to evaluate the child alone to find out whether or not there has been sex abuse. When I ask for the opportunity to bring the alleged abuser and the child into the same room at the same time (at my discretion), I am often met with an incredulous response. This too amazes me. Admittedly, there are extra complicating factors in such situations, such as the child's fear of the confrontation and the repercussions of the disclosures. However, these drawbacks notwithstanding (there is no situation in which there are no drawbacks), not including such joint interviews seriously compromises the evaluation.

The Issue of Conviction for the Client's Position

Most lawyers believe that they can be as successful helping a client whose cause they may not be particularly in sympathy with as they can with one whose position they strongly support. From their early days in law school, they are imbued with the idea that their obligations as lawyers is to serve the client and work as zealously as possible in support of his or her position. They are taught that they must do this even though they may not be in sympathy with the client's position and even though they might prefer to be on the opponent's side. This is another weakness of the adversary system. It assumes that attorneys can argue just as effectively when they have no commitment to the client's position as when they do.

In most law schools the students are required to involve themselves in "moot court" experiences in which they are assigned a position in a case. The assignment is generally made on a random basis and is independent of the student's own conviction on a particular issue. In fact, it is often considered preferable that the assignment be made in such a way that the student must argue in support of the position for which he or she has less conviction. On other occasions, the student may be asked to present arguments for both sides. Obviously, such experiences can be educationally beneficial. We can all learn from and become more flexible by being required to view a situation from the opposite vantage point. However, I believe that those attorneys who hold that one can argue just as effectively without conviction as one can if one has conviction are naive. Noncommitted attorneys are going to serve less effectively in most cases. Accordingly, before they enter the courtroom, their clients are in a weakened position. Most (but not all) attorneys are not likely to turn away a client whose position they secretly do not support. (One doesn't turn away a paying customer so quickly.) Accordingly, it would be very difficult for a client to find a lawyer who is going to admit openly that he or she basically doesn't have conviction for the client's position.

I recall a situation in which I had good reason to believe that an attorney was basically not supporting his client, the father in a custody case, and that his lack of conviction contributed to his poor performance in the courtroom. In this particular case I served as an impartial examiner and concluded that the mother's position warranted my support. However, once in the courtroom, I was treated as an advocate of the mother (the usual situation). Early in the trial the *guardian ad litem* suggested that I, as the impartial examiner, be invited into the courtroom to observe the testimony of a psychiatrist who had been brought in as an advocate for the father's side. The father's attorney agreed to this. I was a little surprised when I learned of this, because I did not see what he had to gain by my having direct opportunity to observe (and potentially criticize) his client's expert. I thought that there would be more to lose than gain for this attorney because his own expert's testimony would be likely to provide me with more "ammunition" for the mother.

While the advocate expert testified, I took notes and, as was expected, the father's attorney provided him ample time to elaborate on his various points. (This is standard procedure when questioning an expert who supports one's position.) When I took the stand, I was first questioned by the mother's attorney, the attorney whose position I supported. He, in turn, gave me great flexibility with regard to my opportunities for answering his questions. Then the father's attorney began to question me. To my amazement, he allowed me to elaborate on points on which I disagreed with him. At no point did he confine me to the traditional yes-no questions that are designed to weaken and distort my testimony. He persistently gave me the opportunity for elaboration and naturally, I took advantage of it.

During a break in the proceedings, when the judge and attorneys were conferring at the bench, I heard the judge ask him, "Why are you letting Gardner talk so much?" I believe this was an inappropriate statement for the judge to make, but it confirms how atypical and seemingly inexplicable was the father's attorney's examination of me. The lawyer shrugged his shoulders, said nothing, and on my return to the stand continued to allow me great flexibility in my answers. I had every reason to believe that he was a bright man and "knew better." I had no doubt that he did not routinely proceed in this way. To me, this attorney's apparently inexplicable behavior was most likely motivated by the desire (either conscious or unconscious) that his own client, the father, lose custody because of his recognition that the mother was the preferable parent for these children at the time. He "went through the motions" of supporting his client, but did so in such a way that he basically helped the other side win the case.

Therapists, in contrast, generally work in accordance with the principle that if they have no conviction for what they are doing with their patients, the chances of success in the treatment are likely to be reduced significantly—even to the point of there being no chance of success at all. If, for example, the therapist's feelings for a patient are not strong, if he or she does not have basic sympathy for the patient's situation, if the relationship is not a good one, or if the therapist is not convinced that the patient's goals in therapy are valid, the likelihood of the patient being helped is small. Without such conviction the therapy becomes boring and sterile—with little chance of any constructive results.

A.S. Watson (1969), an attorney, encourages lawyers to refuse to support a client's attempts to gain custody when the attorney does not consider the client to be the preferable parent. He considers such support to be basically unethical because one is likely to be less successful with a client for whose position one does not have conviction. This is a noble attitude on this attorney's part. Unfortunately, far too few lawyers subscribe to this advice, and most succumb to the more practical consideration that if they do not support their client's position, they will lose him or her and the attendant fee (which in divorce cases may be considerable).

The Issue of Emotions and Objectivity

Attorneys are taught in law school that emotions compromise objectivity. They use the word *objectivity* to refer to the ability to "stay cool," think clearly, and thereby handle a situation in the most judicious and "clear-headed" way. Emotions are viewed as contaminants to such clear thinking i.e., are *subjective*. Objectivity is equated with the ability to deal with a situation in the most judicious way. And this is the concept of the word that I will utilize here. Accordingly, they are taught that if one gets emotional in a legal situation, one's clients may suffer. This polarization between emotions and objectivity is an oversimplification and compromises thereby many attorneys' capacity to optimally represent their clients. I believe there is a continuum between objectivity and emotions. To set up a dichotomy between emotions and objectivity is unrealistic and not consistent with the realities of the world. An emotion is a fact that exists. That one cannot measure it or weigh it does not negate its existence. To say that a thought is objective and a feeling is not objective is to make an artificial distinction between two types of mental processes. Emotions have many more concomitant physiological responses outside the brain than do thoughts, but this does not mean that emotions are thereby "not real" (the implication of the word *subjective*). With regard to the aforementioned continuum, at one end are thoughts with little if any emotional concomitants. At the other end are emotions with little if any associated thoughts. As one moves along the continuum from the cognitive (thoughts) end toward the affective (emotional) end, the percentage of thoughts decreases and the percentage of emotions increases. At some point along this continuum, closer to the affective end, are *mild* emotions. As I will discuss in detail below, I believe that extremely strong emotions generally will compromise objectivity, but mild ones are likely to *increase* objectivity—if used judiciously. Again, I use the word *objectivity* here to refer to the capacity to handle a situation in the most effective way.

Attorneys generally do not differentiate between strong and mild emotions and simply view all emotions as potentially contaminating attempts to learn the truth. Both mild and strong emotions are sources of information. When a psychotherapist, while working with a patient, exhibits emotions, he or she does well to determine whether or not they are in the mild or severe category. The therapist has to differentiate between emotions that will compromise objectivity and those that will enhance it. If a therapist experiences mild emotions—which are engendered by the patient's behavior and are similar to emotions that the vast majority of individuals are likely to have in that situation—then the expression of such emotions to the patient can prove therapeutic. For example, if a therapist finds him- or herself irritated because the patient is not fulfilling financial obligations, the therapist does well not only to confront the patient with the default but also to express the frustration and irritation that has been engendered by the patient's failure to live up to promises of payment. After all, if a psychotherapist is not going to be open and honest with the patient about his or her *own* emotional reactions, how can the therapist expect the patient to be so. Also, one of the services for which the patient is paying is the therapist's honest responses. Such expression of feelings by the therapist is a good example of the proper use of a mild emotion in the therapeutic process. It enhances the efficacy of the treatment. I am therefore in sharp disagreement with those who consider the presence of such emotions in the therapist to be necessarily inappropriate, injudicious, psychopathological, or a manifestation of a lack of objectivity.

Now to the issue of very strong emotions. These may be useful or not useful, therapeutic or antitherapeutic, in the treatment process. Because the therapeutic process is another "slice of life" in which the same general principles of living are applicable, my comments on the roles of emotions in treatment apply to their role in handling situations elsewhere. First, an example of a severe emotion in the therapeutic process. If a patient threatens to kill a psychotherapist, the therapist is likely to be frightened and/or extremely angry. And such feelings may be very powerful. If such feelings are used judiciously, the therapist may save his or her life and may even protect the lives of others. We see here how a strong emotion may be useful and not necessarily becloud objectivity. If the therapist, however, fears for his or her life when there is no actual threat, then he or she is likely to be delusional and is clearly compromised in the capacity to help the patient. Here inappropriate, strong, emotions are operative in reducing the therapist's objectivity. Now to a more common situation. If a therapist overreacts because of neurotic reactions to what the patient is saying, he or she becomes compromised as a therapist, e.g., getting angry at a patient for leaving treatment or having sex with a patient. Such overreaction results in injudicious, antitherapeutic, or even unethical handling of the matter—again reducing the therapist's objectivity. In short, emotions per se do not compromise objectivity; they may or they may not. When mild they are less likely to; when severe they are more likely to. Even severe emotions, used judiciously, can enhance one's efficacy (and thereby objectivity) in dealing with a situation.

Accordingly, lawyers have to be taught (preferably in law school) that the traditional advice that they should be unemotional is injudicious. They have to be taught to be sensitive to their emotions and to try to make the kinds of discriminations I have just described. They have to be taught (and some psychoanalysts have to be taught this as well) that emotional reactions are not necessarily neurotic and do not necessarily interfere with objectivity. Lawyers have to be taught to use their emotions to help their clients and not to deny their emotions and conclude that their expression will be a disservice to their clients. It is better for them to recognize that mild emotional reactions can often enhance their efficacy. We fight harder when we are angry to a reasonable degree. We lose our efficiency in fighting when our anger deranges us and we enter into states of rage and fury. We flee harder when we are frightened. However, if the fear becomes overwhelming, we may become paralyzed with our fear. And lawyers must be taught these functions of emotions in law school.

The failure of attorneys to appreciate these principles relating to emotions and objectivity has caused me difficulty on a number of occasions in the course of adversary litigation. As mentioned previously, I make every reasonable attempt to serve as an impartial examiner, rather than an advocate, in custody and sex-abuse litigation. By the time of litigation I generally feel deep conviction for a particular client's position. This is generally an outgrowth of my having committed myself strongly to the custody evaluation, worked assiduously at the task, and come to the point where I can firmly support one client's position over the other. In the course of the litigation I have expressed feelings— sympathy, irritation, frustration, and a variety of other emotions. Some lawyers have seized upon my admission of such feelings as a justification for discrediting me as being compromised in my objectivity. My attempts to explain that these emotions were engendered by the reality of the situation, and that I am reacting like any other human being, have often proved futile. My efforts to impress upon the attorneys that such emotions have an objectivity of their own and can enhance my understanding of the case are met with incredulity and distrust. And even presiding judges have usually agreed with the attorneys that it was inappropriate of me to have these emotions. Because of this prevailing notion among members of the legal profession, I have come to consider it injudicious to express my emotions and to be much more cautious about revealing them—so as not to compromise the position of the client whom I am supporting.

This is an unfortunate situation. On the one hand, I would like very much to state, with a reasonable degree of emotion, the position I hold and then explain that these attendant emotions do not necessarily compromise my objectivity. On the other hand, to do so just invites refutation. It gives an adversary attorney "ammunition." Although such utilization of my comments is completely unjustifiable, it is supported by a deep-seated misconception of the legal profession. At this point, I am following primarily the judicious course of not revealing the emotional factors that have played a role in the decision-making process. My hope is that attorneys will become more sophisticated regarding this issue, so that I might ultimately be able to provide more complete and honest testimony. My hope also is that the comments I have made here will play a role (admittedly small) in bringing about some elucidation of the legal profession on this point.

Many may conclude that I am being "too emotional" in my criticism of attorneys in this book. Such critics might even suggest that the aforementioned principles should then be applied to me. Accordingly, the questions might be asked: Is my "emotionalism" a normal, healthy reaction? Is it a reasonable emotional response of one who has observed terrible indignities being perpetrated on innocent parties by attorneys who have been trained to desensitize themselves to the psychological destruction they are perpetrating? Or am I just reacting neurotically? Obviously, I choose the former interpretation of my strong feelings on the subject. I leave it to the reader to decide whether or not my emotional reactions are warranted. Those who have personally observed the family traumas that I have already described will be in a better position to judge me.

Concluding Comments

L.L. Riskin, a law professor who is very critical of the adversary system and the educational system that emphasizes it inordinately, states (1982):

> Nearly all courses at most law schools are presented from the viewpoint of the practicing attorney who is working in an adversary system....There is, to be sure, scattered attention to the lawyer as planner, policy maker, and public servant, but 90 percent of what goes on in law school is based on a model of the lawyer working in or against a background of litigation of disputes that can be resolved by the application of a rule by a third party. The teachers were trained with this model in mind. The students get a rough image with them; it

gets sharpened quickly. This model defines and limits the likely career possibilities envisioned by most law students.

In further criticism of the narrowness of the adversary system he states:

> When one party wins, in this vision, usually the other party loses, and, most often, the victory is reduced to a money judgment. This "reduction" of nonmaterial values — such as honor, respect, dignity, security, and love—to amount of money, can have one of two effects. In some cases, these values are excluded from the decision makers' considerations, and thus the consciousness of the lawyers, as irrelevant. In others, they are present by transmutation into something else—a justification for money damages.

These "irrelevant" issues—"honor, respect, dignity, security, and love"—are the very ones that are central to this book. In custody litigation, when a lawyer focuses on the children, it does not insure that the humanity of the situation is being considered. Rather, the children are often the objects that are "won." Often there may be a trade-off of the children with monetary awards. Children become chattel, objects, or booty, with only lip service paid to the emotional consequences of the litigation. The adversary system and the legal education that promulgate the method program attorneys in their earliest phases of development to ignore these crucial elements in their work.

DEALING WITH
PARENTAL ALIENATION SYNDROME
CHILDREN AND THEIR PARENTS

Do ''Sex-Blind'' Custody Decisions Necessarily Serve the Best Interests of Children?

During the last few years, in association with my increasing involvement in child custody litigation, I have often had the thought that perhaps we should not have dispensed with the tender years presumption. If we are to consider the greatest good for the greatest numnber, I believe we probably would have done better to retain it. Of course, there would have been some children who would then have remained with the less preferable parent; however, many more children would have been spared the psychological traumas attendant to the implementation of the best interests of the child presumption and the widespread enthusiasm for the joint custodial concept. There is no question that custody litigation has increased dramatically since the mid-1970s and there is no question, as well, that this increase has been the direct result of these two recent developments.

What should we do then? Go back to the old system? I think not. I believe that there is a middle path that should prove useful. To elaborate: First, the displacement of the tender years presumption with the best interests of the child presumption was initiated primarily by men who claimed that the tender years presumption was intrinsically "sexist," because women, by virtue of the fact that they are female, are not necessarily preferable parents. State legislatures and the courts agreed. As a result, the best interests of the child presumption has been uniformly equated with the notion that custody determinations should be "sex blind." Considerable difficulty has been caused, I believe, by equating these two concepts. *It is extremely important that they be considered separately.* Everyone claims that he or she is in support of doing what is in the best interests of the children. Everyone waves that banner: each parent, each attorney, the mental health professionals who testify, and certainly the judge. No one claims that he or she is against their best interests. The situation is analagous to the position politicians take with regard to their support for widows, orphans, the handicapped, and the poor. All politicians wave that banner. Even the suggestion that a politician might not be in strong support of these unfortunates would be met with denial, professions of incredulity, and righteous indignation.

With regard to all those who claim that the best interests of the child is their paramount consideration, one could argue that a wide variety of possible custodial arrangements could serve children's best interests. One could argue that automatic placement with the father serves their best interests, and this was certainly the case up until the early 20th century. Or one could claim that automatic preference for the mother serves the children best, and this was the case from the mid-1920s to the mid-1970s. One could argue that placing them with grandparents, uncles, aunts, or in foster homes, adoption agencies, or residential cottages might serve children's best interests. Presently, the prevailing notion is that sex-blind custody evaluations automatically serve children's best interests. Although it may be an unpopular thing to say in the 1980s, I do not believe that sex-blind custody decisions necessarily serve the best interests of children, and the belief that they do is the fundamental assumption on which present custody decisions are being based. Somehow, the acceptance of the concept that fathers can be as paternal as mothers can be maternal was immediately linked with the concept that such egalitarianism serves the best interests of children. I do not accept this assumption of gender equality in child-rearing capacity and would go further and state that the younger the child, the less the likelihood that this assumption is valid. It follows then that I do not believe that sex-blind custody evaluations and decisions serve the best interests of children. I recognize that this is an unpopular position to take in the 1980s, that it might appear to be very undemocratic and even sexist of me (here with the prejudice being against men), but it is the opinion that I have. My hope is that the reader will read on with some degree of receptivity and will come to the same conclusion.

To elaborate: No one can deny that men and women are different biologically. No one can deny, either, that it is the woman who bears the child and has it within her power to feed it with her own body (although she may choose not to do so). I believe that this biological difference cannot be dissociated from certain psychological factors that result in mothers being more likely to be superior to fathers with regard to their capacity to involve themselves with the newborn infant at the time of its birth. After all, it is the mother who carries the baby in her body for nine months. It is she who is continually aware of its presence. It is she who feels its kicks and its movements. It is she who is ever reminded of the pregnancy by formidable changes in her body and by the various symptomatic reminders of the pregnancy: nausea, vomiting, fatigue, discomfort during sleep, etc. Even the most dedicated fathers cannot have these experiences and the attendant strong psychological ties that they engender. The mother, as well, must suffer the pains of the infant's delivery. Even though the father may be present at the time of birth and an active participant in the process, the experience is still very much the mother's. And, as mentioned, it is the mother who may very well have the breastfeeding experience, something the father is not capable of enjoying. All these factors create a much higher likelihood that the mother—at the time of birth—will have a stronger psychological tie with the infant than the father. This "up-front" programming places her in a superior position with regard to psychological bonding with the newborn infant at the time of birth. I believe that most individuals would agree that, if parents decided to separate at the time of birth and both were reasonably equal with regard to parenting capacity, the mother would be the preferable parent.

Some might argue that even if the aforementioned speculations are valid, the superiority stops at the time of birth and men are thereafter equal to women with regard to parenting capacity. Even here I am dubious. It is reasonable to assume that during the course of evolution there was a selective survival of women who were highly motivated child rearers on a genetic basis. Such women were more likely to seek men for the purposes of impregnation and more likely to be sought by men who desired progeny. Similarly, there was selective propagation of men who were skilled providers of food, clothing, shelter, and protection of women and children. Such men were more likely to be sought by women with high child-rearing drives. This assumption, of course, is based on the theory that there are genetic factors involved in such behavior. Women with weaker child-rearing drives were less likely to procreate, and men with less family provider and protective capacities were also at a disadvantage with regard to transmitting their genes to their progeny. They were less attractive to females as mates because they were less likely to fulfill these functions so vital to species survival. As weaker protectors they were less likely to survive in warfare and in fighting to protect their families from enemies.

Accordingly, although it may be the unpopular thing to say at the time of this writing (1987), I believe that the average woman today is more likely to be genetically programmed for child-rearing functions than the average man. Even if this speculation were true, one could argue that we are less beholden to our instincts than lower animals and that environmental influences enable us to modify these more primitive drives. I do not deny this, but up to a point. There are limitations to which environment can modify heredity, especially in the short period of approximtely 10–15 years since the tender years presumption was generally considered to be sexist. Environment modifies heredity primarily (and many would say exclusively) by the slow process of selective survival of those variants that are particularly capable of adapting to a specific environment. Accordingly, I believe that the strength of these genetic factors are still strong enough in today's parents to be given serious consideration when making custody decisions.

The Stronger, Healthy
Psychological Bond Presumption

It would appear from the aforementioned comments that I am on the verge of recommending that we go back to the tender years presumption. This is not completely the case. *What I am recommending is that we give preference in custody disputes to the parent (regardless of sex) who has provided the greatest degree of healthy, child-rearing input during the children's formative years.* Because mothers today are still more often the primary child-rearing parents, more mothers would be given parental preference in custody disputes. If, however, in spite of the mother's superiority at the time of birth, it was the father who was the primary caretaker — especially during the early years of life — such a father would be considered the preferable custodial parent. This presumption, too, is essentially sex blind (satisfying thereby present-day demands for sexual egalitarianism), because it allows for the possibility that a father's input may outweigh the mother's in the formative years, even though he starts at a disadvantage. It utilizes primarily the *psychological bond* with the child as the primary consideration in custody evaluations. I would add, however, the important consideration that the longer the time span between infancy and the time of the custody evaluation and decision, the greater the likelihood that environmental factors will modify (strengthen or weaken) the psychological bonds that the child had with each parent during the earliest years. I refer to this as the *stronger, healthy psychological bond presumption,* which, I believe, is the one that would serve the best interests of the child. It is important for the reader to appreciate that the parent who had the greater involvement with the child during infancy is the one more likely to have the stronger psychological bond. However, if the early parenting was not "good," then the bond that develops might be pathological. Accordingly, I am not referring here to any kind of psychological bond at all, but a *healthy* psychological bond. It is not a situation in which *any* psychological bond at all will do. It is for this reason that I refer to the presumption as the *stronger, healthy psychological bond presumption*. In order to clarify my position on these principles, I will first present a vignette that will serve as a basis for my subsequent comments.

Let us envision a situation in which a couple has one child, a boy. During the first four years of the child's life, the mother remains at home as the primary child rearer and the father is out of the home during the day as the breadwinner. When the child is four the mother takes a full-time job. During the day the child attends a nursery school and then stays with a woman in the neighborhood who cares for the children of working parents. At the end of the workday and over weekends both parents are involved equally in caring for the child. And the same situation prevails when the child enters elementary school. When the child is seven the parents decide to separate. Each parent wants primary custody. The father claims that during the three years prior to the separation, he was as involved as the mother in the child's upbringing. And the mother does not deny this. The father's position is that the court should make its decision solely on the basis of parenting capacity—especially as demonstrated in recent years—and claims that any custody decision taking his sex into consideration is "sexist" and is an abrogation of his civil rights.

In the course of the litigation the child develops typical symptoms of the parental alienation syndrome. He becomes obsessed with hatred of his father, denies any benevolent involvement with him at any point in his life, and creates absurd scenarios to justify his animosity. In contrast, his mother becomes viewed by him as faultless and all-loving. I believe that in this situation the child's psychological bond is strongest with the mother, and the symptoms of alienation are created by him in an attempt to maintain that bond. Because the child's earliest involvement was stronger with the mother, residua of that tie are expressing themselves at the age of seven. If the father had been the primary caretaker during the first four years of the boy's life, and if then both mother and father shared equally in child-rearing involvement, then I would consider it likely that the child would develop symptoms of alienation from the mother, the parent with whom the psychological tie is weaker. Under such circumstances, I would recommend the father be designated the primary custodial parent.

Recommendations for Mental Health PractionersDealing with Parents of Parental Alienation Syndrome Children

The vignette thus far has been used to demonstrate principles that could be utilized to prevent the development of a parental alienation syndrome. When, however, things have progressed to the point where such a syndrome has developed, the situation is generally more complex. I present in this section principles applicable to making recommendations under such circumstances. First, one does well to divide mothers of children with a parental alienation syndrome into two categories: 1) Those mothers who actively program the child against the father, who become obsessed with hatred of the former husband, and who actively foment, encourage, and aid the child's feelings of alienation. 2)

Those mothers who recognize that such alienation is not in the best interests of the child and are willing to take a more conciliatory approach to the father's requests. They either go along with a joint custodial compromise or even allow (albeit reluctantly) the father to have sole custody with their having a liberal visitation program. Although these mothers believe it would be in the best interests of the child to remain with them, they recognize that protracted litigation is going to cause all family members to suffer more grief than an injudicious custody arrangement, namely, one in which the father has more involvement (either sole or joint custody) than they consider warranted. I recognize that this division into two types of mothers is artificial and that in reality we have a continuum from those mothers who are in category one to those mothers who are in category two. To the degree that a particular mother falls into category one, my recommendations below for her category are applicable; in contrast, to the degree that the mother falls in category two, my recommendations below for her category are applicable.

With regard to mothers in category one, those who are fanatic in their animosity, I believe that the most important element in these children's therapy is immediate transfer by the court to the home of the so-called hated parent. Therapy alone, while living in the home of the so-called loved parent, is likely to prove futile. While still in that home the child is going to be exposed continually to the bombardment of denigration and other subtle influences contributing to the perpetuation of the syndrome. It is only via removal from the mother's home that there is any chance of interruption of this pathological process. Often I will recommend a month or so of absolutely no contact with the "loved parent," with the exception of short telephone calls a few times a week. And even here, I would recommend that the new custodial parent be permitted to monitor and even listen to telephone conversations in order to insure that the programming process is not continuing. In this period of decompression and debriefing, the child will have the opportunity to reestablish the relationship with the alienated parent, without significant contamination of the process by the brainwashing parent. Following this initial period, I generally recommend slow and judicious contact with the brainwashing parent, these being monitored so as to prevent a recurrence of the disorder. Of course, psychotherapy can be useful at that time as well, but it must involve both parents and the child in the same room together. Whether the child will ultimately go back to the mother depends upon how the treatment evolves and how successful the therapist is in helping the mother reduce her hostility. In some cases, the therapy may only be possible if ordered by the court, so hostile and uncooperative is the mother. However, the child will at least be residing in the home of the healthier parent and will derive the benefits from such placement, continuing hostile attitudes toward the father notwithstanding. My experience has been that in such cases the animosity gradually becomes reduced. In contrast, when such children are allowed to remain permanently in the home of the category one mother, the animosity continues unabated, can go on for years, and there is good reason to believe that it may become lifelong.

The treatment of the mother, however, is not likely to succeed unless she can work through her ongoing animosity toward the father. Often a central element in her rage is the fact that he is reestablished in a new relationship and she has not done so. Her jealousy here is a contributing factor to her program of wreaking vengeance on her former husband by attempting to deprive him of his children, his most treasured possessions. Another factor that contributes is the mother's desire to keep a relationship going with her former husband. The tumultuous activity guarantees ongoing involvement, accusation and counteraccusation, attack and counterattack, and so on. Most people, when confronted with a choice between total abandonment and hostile involvement, would choose the acrimonious relationship. And these mothers demonstrate this point well. To the degree that one can help her "pick up the pieces of her life" and form new involvements and interests, one is likely to reduce the rage. The most therapeutic experience such a woman can have is meeting a new man with whom she becomes deeply involved and forming a strong relationship. Ideally such a mother should have insight into the fact that she needs therapy and seek it voluntarily. My experience has been that most often this is not the case. Most often she is so blinded by her rage that she has little capacity for insight into what she is doing to herself, her former husband, and her children. Court-ordered therapy in such cases is not likely to work. Judges are often naive with regard to their belief that one can order a person into treatment. This is an extension of their general view of the world that ordering people around is the best way to accomplish something. Most judges are aware of the fact that they cannot order an impotent husband to have an erection or a frigid wife to have an orgasm. Yet, they somehow believe that one can order someone to have conviction and commitment to therapy. Accordingly, I generally discourage courts from ordering such treatment. However, on occasion I will recommend it in situations in which the person may be borderline for successful involvement in therapy. Under these circumstances the court order may be just what they need to get them involved.

Examiners involved in custody evaluations do well to make some assessment of the *nature* of the psychological bond that the child has with the parent who was primarily involved in the child's upbringing during the earliest years. One should try to ascertain whether the bond is primarily a healthy or an unhealthy one. Again, although I am dividing this bond into two types, I am well aware that there is a continuum from the healthiest to the sickest. Mothers in category one generally have had an unhealthy bond with the child prior to the litigation, and they are the ones who are more likely to be programming the child against the father. In extreme cases, as a result of the mother's indoctrination, the child may actually be brought to the point of having paranoid delusions about the father. A so-called *folie à deux* relationship may evolve in which the child acquires the mother's paranoid delusions about the father. In such cases, transfer is mandatory if there is to be any hope of salvaging the relationship with the father. In such cases, as well, treatment of the mother may be impossible. Then, at least the child will be with one healthy parent, rather than being brought up by a paranoid mother. Of course, this represents the most extreme form of the category one mother; less animosity is the usual case. To the degree that such mothers can be helped to work out their problems regarding their feelings about their former husbands and to the degree that they can be brought to appreciate the importance of the child's ongoing contact with him, rapprochement with her may be fostered. While the child is living with the father, contact with the mother is monitored by the therapist and father, with increased contact being given as her programming diminishes.

Mothers in category two have a healthy psychological bond with the child and therefore should be given preferential consideration in custody evaluations, and not be considered automatically to be actively programming their children. The therapeutic program recommended for category one mothers need not be instituted.

As mentioned, in the majority of the cases of parental alienation syndrome, it is the mother who is favored and the father who is denigrated. However, there are certainly situations in which the mother is deprecated and the father favored. For simplicity of presentation, and because mothers are more often the favored parent, I have used her as the example of the preferred parent—but recognize that in some cases it is the father who is the preferred parent and is the one who may be programming the child, whereas it is the mother who is the despised parent. In such cases the fathers should be divided into the aforementioned categories and given the same considerations as described for mothers. My purpose in this section has been to provide mental health practitioners with guidelines for advising courts on how to deal with parental alienation children and their families. Without proper placement of the child (for which a court order may be necessary), treatment may be futile. It has not been my purpose to present details for the treatment of such families. Rather, some guidelines have been provided.

Recommendations to Judges for Dealing with Parents of Children with Parental Alienation Syndrome

In Chapter Six I presented guidelines for judges for use in interviewing children with parental alienation syndrome. Here I present guidelines for the court when dealing with parents who contribute to their children's parental alienation syndromes. In many of these situations therapy may be impossible without the transfers described below. There are limits to what a court can ask of the therapist. If the child is seeing a therapist one to three sessions a week and is being exposed all the remaining hours to psychologically detrimental influences, it is not likely that the therapy is going to succeed. The courts have it in their power to bring about the transfers that can facilitate the therapeutic process. The courts in many of these situations can accomplish much more therapeutically than can therapists. In addition, the courts have the power to do preventive psychiatry via their transfers. The therapist often can do little but to try to pick up the pieces if the courts act injudiciously.

As discussed in Chapter Three, mothers are most often the ones who are the loved parents and fathers the hated parents. At least this has been the case for about 90 percent of the situations with which I have been involved. Accordingly, for simplicity of presentation I will usually refer to the mother as the "loved" parent and the father as the "hated" parent, but I recognize that in some situations the opposite is the case. I will be referring to the two categories of mothers described in the previous section, but recognize that we are dealing here with a continuum.

With regard to mothers in the aforementioned category one, those who are actively brainwashing their youngsters, children who are completely alienated from a parent and remain so over a year or two are not likely to become reconciliated during their formative years. A therapeutic approach conducted while the child is still living in the home of the brainwashing parent is not likely to prevent this outcome, because the programming parent is generally unreceptive to a therapeutic approach that aims at bringing a rapprochement between the alienated parent and the children. The only hope, therefore, is court intervention, with serious consideration given to mandatory transfer from the home of the allegedly loved parent to the home of the ostensibly hated one. Although this book repeatedly warns against the detrimental effects of custody litigation, the reader should not conclude that it has no place. It should be the last resort, rather than the first. And when more humane measures are not successful in bringing about a reconciliation between an alienated child and a parent, then the court remains the last hope. If the court does not successfully intervene, a total and permanent alienation may result. Such alienation may have profound effects on the children's personality development and can contribute to a number of psychopathological reactions. In the more common situation, where the children live with the mother and remain alienated from the father, there are detrimental effects on both boys and girls. Boys in this situation are deprived of a model for identification and emulation. They are deprived of all the benefits that can be derived from a father-son relationship. And girls are deprived of a heterosexual model upon whom their future heterosexual relationships will be based. And they will be deprived of the positive input that only a father can provide, especially with regard to the girl's sense of being a woman who is found attractive by a man. And both the children and the alienated parent may never reach a rapprochement; they may spend the rest of their lives deprived of the rich benefits that can be derived from a parent-child relationship.

One of the fringe benefits of the court-ordered transfer is that it provides the child with a face-saving alibi for the mother. Specifically, the child, when with the mother, can profess unswerving loyalty to her and need not admit that there is any affection for the father, even after the child has lived (sometimes even peacefully) with the father for a number of months following court transfer. The child can complain to the mother about all the indignities suffered at the father's home and the stupidity of the judge for having ordered the transfer. The child often professes innocence of any wish to live with the father: "The stupid judge makes me live with him. I hate every minute of it. Most judges don't know what they're doing. And that Dr. Gardner is a bigger idiot, because he told the judge that he thought it would be a good idea for me to live with my father. He's just a stupid ignoramus psychiatrist."

With regard to mothers in category two, i.e., those who do not brainwash their children, I believe that the children should remain with their mothers. In such cases the alienation is primarily of the child's origin. It stems from the threat of being required by the court to live with the father—the parent with whom the child has had the weaker psychological bond. It is not significantly the result of maternal programming. Once the litigation has been concluded and a final decision has been made by the court that the child shall be living primarily with the mother, then the child is likely to go back to its previous level of involvement with both parents—especially with regard to love and hate—and the hostility toward the father is likely to reduce significantly. Without the threat of placement with the father, the child can discontinue the utilization of the hostile maneuvers that were designed to insure its remaining with the mother.

My final position with regard to the principle that should be utilized by courts when ascertaining parental preference in custody disputes is this: Preference (but not automatic assignment) should be given to that parent (regardless of sex) with whom the child has established *over time* the strongest, *healthy* psychological bond. That parent (regardless of sex) who was the primary caretaker during the earliest years of the child's life is the one with whom the child is more likely to have established such a bond. Residua of that early bonding are likely to influence strongly subsequent bonding experiences with the parents. However, the longer the gap between the early bonding and the time of the dispute, the greater the likelihood other experiences will affect the strength of the bond. Whether or not these have resulted in the formation of an even stronger bond with the parent who was not the primary caretaker during the earliest years has to be assessed in the course of the evaluative process and the judicial proceedings.

I believe the courts have not been paying enough attention to the formidable influence of the early life influences on the child's subsequent psychological status. Early life influences play an important role in the formation of the child's psychological bond to the parent who was the primary caretaker during the earliest years. Courts have been giving too much weight to present-day involvement and ignoring the residual contributions of earlier bonding to present experiences. Mothers have been much more often the primary custodial parents during the child-rearing process. This produces a strong bond between the two that results in strong attachment cravings when there is a rupture (or threatened rupture) of the relationship. Accordingly, when there is a threatened disruption of this relationship by a "sex-blind" judge or joint-custodial mandate, mother and child fight it vigorously. Commonly, the mother brainwashes the child and uses him or her as a weapon to sabotage the father's attempts to gain primary custody. And the children develop their own scenarios, as well, in an attempt to preserve this bond. I believe that residua of the early influences play an important role in the attempts on the part of both parties to maintain the attachment bond.

The implementation of the presumption that children do best when placed with the parent who was most involved in child rearing, especially during the formative years, would reduce significantly the custody litigation that we are presently witnessing. It would result in many mothers automatically being awarded custody. It would not preclude, however, fathers obtaining custody, because there would be some fathers who would satisfy easily this important criterion for primary custodial assignment. The implementation of this presumption would still allow those parents who were only secondarily involved in the child's rearing (whether male or female) to still have the opportunity to seek and gain custody. They would, however, have to provide compelling evidence that the primary custodial parent's child-rearing input was significantly compromised and their own contributions so formidable that they should more justifiably be designated primary custodial parents.

Last, I would recommend that we replace the best interests of the child presumption with the *best interests of the family presumption*. The best interests of the child presumption is somewhat narrow. It does not take into consideration the psychological effects on the parents of the child's placement and the effects of the resultant feedback on the child's welfare. As mentioned, the strong bond that forms in early life between the child and the primary caretaker produces immensely strong cravings for one another when there is threatened disruption of the relationship. Just as the child suffers psychologically from removal from the parent, so is the adult traumatized by removal from the child. The psychological trauma to the adult caused by such disruption can be immense, so much so that parenting capacity may be compromised. And this negative feedback is not in the best interests of the child. But we are not dealing here simply with the question of placing the child with a parent in order to protect that parent from feeling upset about the child's being placed with the spouse. Rather, we are considering the ultimate negative impact on the child of the compromise of the bond with the primary caretaker. Accordingly, I am recommending that courts assign primary custody in accordance with the presumption that the *family's* best interests will be served by the child's being placed with that parent (regardless of sex) who was the primary caretaker during the formative years and is most likely to have developed the stronger, healthier bond with the child. Furthermore, the longer the parent continued to be primary caretaker, the greater the likelihood the *family's* interests will be served by placement with that parent. The implementation of this presumption will, I believe, also serve as a form of preventive psychiatry in that it will not only reduce significantly custody/visitation litigation but serve to obviate the terrible psychological problems attendant to such litigation.

THE EDUCATION AND TRAINING OF NONLEGAL PROFESSIONALS

On a few occasions I have been asked, when presenting my credentials to testify in court, what my formal training has been in custody litigation. My answer has been simply "none." The attorney here has generally been quite aware of the fact that I had no formal training in this area in that there was no such training in the late 1950s when I was in my residency. The attempt here was to compromise my credibility by attempting to demonstrate to the court that I am not qualified to testify on child custody matters. Asking me that question is the same as asking an internist, who like myself attended medical school in the mid-1950s, to state what education he had on the subject of AIDS during his or her training program. (Obviously, this question was not asked by the attorney whose position I supported.) Unfortunately, there are young people today who are asked the same question and must also provide the same answer. Considering the widespread epidemic of custody litigation that now prevails, the failure to provide training in this area at the present time represents a significant deficiency in the education and training of professionals doing such evaluations. Most people, like myself, have "learned from experience." Some have learned well and some have not. Accordingly, I would consider it mandatory that all child therapy programs in psychology, psychiatry, social work, and related disciplines require training and experience in child custody litigation. This should not only be at the theoretical level; actual clinical experience should be included as well.

I would emphasize in such programs the point that having professionals automatically serving as advocates ("hired guns") in child custody litigation is a reprehensible practice and a terrible disservice to the family, the legal profession, and the mental health professions as well. The attempt here would be to bring about a situation in which attorneys looking for hired guns would not be able to find any mental health professional who would allow him- or herself to be so utilized. Although I believe that this is an ideal that will never be reached (certainly not in an atmosphere where there are many hungry practitioners), it still cannot hurt to have the principle promulgated at the earliest levels of education and training. It is my hope that this principle would be incorporated into the ethical standards of the various professional societies. A strong statement that such advocacy is unethical would certainly help protect and discourage mental health professionals from prostitution of their talents and skills. Such refusal could be considered to be a kind of preventive psychiatry in that it would remove us from contributing to legal maneuvers that play a role in bringing about the parental alienation syndrome and other disorders that result from protracted divorce/custody litigation. Such training would also involve impressing upon the trainees the importance of their doing everything possible to discourage their patients from involving themselves in such litigation and to point out the variety of psychopathological reactions that can result from such involvement. Elsewhere (1986a), I have described many of these in detail. In addition, trainees should be advised to encourage their patients to involve themselves in mediation as a first step toward resolving their divorce/custody disputes. They should be helped to appreciate that adversary litigation should be the parents' very last resort, after all civilized attempts at resolving their difficulties have failed.

At the present time mediation is very much a "growth industry." Lawyers and mental health professionals are the primary individuals attracted to the field (O.J. Coogler, 1978; J.M. Haynes, 1981; R. Fisher and W. Ury, 1981; J. Folberg and A. Taylor, 1984). However, there are many others with little if any training or experience in these areas who are also being trained. At the present time there are no standards with regard to training requirements. These will inevitably have to be set up, and I believe that they should be set up soon. At the time of this writing (1987), mediation has been popular for seven to eight years. This might be considered too short a period to give us enough information to decide what the standards should be. Still, I think sufficient time has elapsed to enable us to propose guidelines as to what a training program should involve. My own view is that it should involve a program at the graduate level. I would consider two years of course work and a year of practical work under the supervision of experienced mediators to be optimum. During the first two years the program should provide courses in both law and psychology. There should be courses in basic law as well as marriage and divorce law. Courses in finance should cover the kinds of financial problems that divorcing people are likely to encounter. In the mental health area there should be basic courses in child development, child psychopathology, family psychodynamics, and interviewing techniques. Furthermore, there should be courses in mediation techniques and conflict resolution. This academic material would serve as a foundation for the clinical work in the third year. At the present time there are universities in the United States that are setting up such programs, and there is good reason to believe that they will be expanded. In addition, I believe that graduate programs in psychology, social work, and residency training programs would also do well to incorporate mediation training as part of their general curricula. However, I believe that training at these levels cannot provide the same kind of in-depth experience that one gets from a full two- or three-year program of the aforementioned type. Elsewhere (1986a), I have discussed the mediation process in detail and have described the ways in which it protects families from developing the kinds of psychological problems that adversary litigation brings about. The more one can do to lessen divorce/custody conflicts, the less the likelihood children will develop parental alienation syndromes and the less the likelihood they will have a need to fabricate sex abuse as a weapon in the context of such disputes.

CHILD ABUSE REPORTING LAWS

At this time, an increasing number of states are requiring all persons, professional and nonprofessional, to report immediately all cases of suspected sexual abuse. The most flimsy and preposterous suggestions of abuse are being reported. Many lives and careers have been destroyed as a result of such allegations. Innocent individuals have been wiped out financially in the attempt to prove themselves innocent. Careers have been ruined. One may never get back to the same level – even when completely innocent – because one's reputation may be marred permanently. Who would want to bring a child to a pediatrician charged with sexual molestation of a child? Who would bring his or her child to a psychotherapist who has been similarly accused? Who would want one's child to play at the home of a divorced father who is up on charges of having sexually molested his child? After months and even years of litigation the individual may be considered not guilty because "there wasn't enough evidence." This still leaves doubt in those who would have their children associate with the alleged abuser. A dramatic account of such a nightmare is described by L.D. Spiegel (1986). His is only one example of many such nightmares innocent individuals have suffered.

Mental health professionals are faced with a terrible dilemma regarding such reporting. If they do report the abuse, they will generally destroy the therapeutic relationship they have with the child and/or at least one of the parents. In addition, such reporting can easily be considered an illegal, immoral, and unconscionable divulgence of confidential material. Not to report the abuse may result in criminal action against the therapist. The courts and the law appear to be oblivious to the implications of such divulgence to therapy. They give the therapist little option, little room to decide whether or not the allegation is indeed bona fide or fabricated. Laws requiring such automatic reporting are often based on the principle that if the child makes the allegation, the therapist should report it. The statutes appear to be based on the premise that children rarely if ever lie about sex abuse. They were formulated, I believe, at a time a few years ago when many sex-abuse workers were of that conviction. Unfortunately, at the time of this writing (1987) there are still some sex-abuse workers who still hold that children do not, under any circumstances, fabricate sex abuse. However, there is no question that sex-abuse investigators are becoming increasingly appreciative of the epidemic of fabricated allegations of sex abuse we are now witnessing.

Generally, the statutes take the position that the therapist *must* report the allegation and leave it to community authorities to investigate and decide whether or not the allegation is true or false. The general presumption, however, is that the allegation is likely to be true, and the lawmakers appear to have been completely oblivious to the implications of such an allegation on the life of the alleged perpetrator, even if proven innocent. L. Denton (1987) reports the experience of a psychologist, Arne Gray, who was treating parents who were disciplining their two adopted children with "time outs" in the basement. The psychologist did not consider the disciplinary measures to be excessive enough to be considered reportable abuse or neglect. However, someone in the community reported the parents to the local Department of Social Services, because of the possibility that the parents were abusing the children. The psychologist testified in court that he saw no evidence for reportable abuse or neglect and considered the parents to be highly motivated for treatment, which he considered to be going well. Denton then states, "But the next day the judge issued two warrants for Gray's arrest on two charges of contributing to the delinquency of a minor. Three days later he issued two more warrants for Gray's arrest for failure to report suspected abuse and neglect."

As a result of these laws, we are now witnessing an avalanche of reports of sex abuse by therapists to child protection agencies. Many therapists are taking the position that it is better to report and "protect my ass" and to hell with confidentiality, the therapist-patient relationship, and professional ethics. Child protection agencies are being glutted with these cases and cannot possibly deal with them adequately. Another problem for therapists relates to the threat of malpractice suits for the grief and psychological trauma that may ensue when a family member is so reported. This is especially the case if the allegation proves to be fabricated. As a practitioner myself I am certainly not in support of widespread malpractice litigation. However, I am sympathetic with anyone who sues for malpractice after having been reported to a child protection agency when there has been a false allegation of sex abuse. To the best of my knowledge, reporting laws provide immunity from civil or criminal liability to those who report such abuse if they can demonstrate that they did so in good faith. Whether such protection will hold up in the future remains to be seen. It will certainly not prevent many from initiating malpractice litigation, which is psychologically traumatic even if one "wins." Another problem that results from such laws is that many families in which sex abuse has taken place now justifiably avoid therapy because they recognize that the therapist will be required to report the abuse, even at the time of the first session. Many therapists are now telling families at the beginning of the first interview that they will be required by law to report any abuse of the child. Obviously, many families are either turned away by such a statement or withhold any information that might even suggest the abuse. Under these circumstances the therapy for the abuse will be futile.

According to L. Denton (1987) most statutes require that the reporter have "reasonable suspicion" before being required to report the abuse. The word *reasonable* here is the point of difficulty. What may be reasonable to one therapist may be unreasonable to another. Therapists who believe that there is no such thing as fabricated sex abuse are likely to report every fantasy, no matter how absurd. And those who hold that fabrication is common, especially in the context of custody cases, will be less likely to report and will argue that there was no reasonable suspicion.

My own position on this issue is that therapists should not be required to report sex abuse, whether fabricated or genuine. In this way they will be allowed to work with these families and assist in the rectification of the problem. After all, families coming to therapists are already on the road to alleviation of their difficulties because they have recogized that there are problems for which they are seeking help. Requiring the therapist to report the sex abuse will destroy the treatment and will only increase the likelihood that the abuse will continue. However, if the therapist finds that the therapy is not successful and that there is no therapeutic relationship to be lost, because there was no relationship in the first place, then he or she should not only be permitted to report, but should be protected from prosecution or malpractice suits for having done so. Therapists should only report cases of sex abuse when they believe that they can no longer be of assistance and that outside agencies may be able to help where they cannot. Child protection agencies then can work closely with the family and have more power to interrupt the abuse.

With regard to those who make sex-abuse allegations, they should be required to stand up to their accusation and suffer some penalty if the accusation proves to be false, maliciously motivated, or frivolous. I recognize that laws requiring such potential repercussions are not without their difficulties. However, there is no question that the threat of such consequences will vastly reduce the number of false accusations. It may also reduce the number of bona fide accusations, but more will be gained than lost by such a policy. Such laws would certainly make many brainwashing parents think twice about initiating and/or promulgating a sex-abuse allegation in the context of a child custody dispute. At the present time there are no consequences for such maliciousness and perjury. If the allegation is proven false, the only thing the fabricating parent loses is one important bit of ammunition in the custody fight. There are no other consequences for the parents who fabricate the abuse, but parents who have been so charged may never live down the humiliation and public disgrace.

CONCLUDING COMMENTS

As mentioned, my experience with children who have genuinely been abused sexually is less than that with children who have fabricated sex abuse. This relates to my deep involvement in custody litigation in which the vast majority of children who profess sexual abuse are fabricators. Useful articles on the treatment of sexually abused children and their families have been written by J. Waterman (1986b), S. Long (1986), L. Damon and J. Waterman (1986), and K. MacFarlane (1986). Nor has it been the purpose of this book to discuss the psychological reactions of those who have been sexually abused, especially with regard to their prognosis and the effects of such abuse in adult life. I do not claim vast direct experience that has enabled me to observe and treat the subsequent psychological sequelae of bone fide sex abuse. J. Goodwin (1987) has written an excellent summary of the psychological sequelae of incest, the most common form of childhood sexual abuse. R. Lusk and J. Waterman (1986) have written a good summary of the literature on the effects of childhood sexual abuse. K. Fisher (1987) provides the findings of a group of panelists at the 1987 annual meeting of the American Orthopsychiatric Association, who discussed the adult sequelae of childhood sex abuse. She describes a wide variety of psychopathological disorders both in the sexual and nonsexual realms.

Although not a book on therapeutics, this is very much a book on preventive psychiatry. Criticisms of the adversary system are designed to contribute (admittedly in a small way) to changes in that system, changes that might very well bring about a reduction of the psychopathological processes that derive from its implementation. Here I have focused specifically on one such psychiatric disorder, namely, the parental alienation syndrome. Furthermore, implementation of the recommendations contained herein could result in a reduction of fabricated sex-abuse allegations, also a source of psychiatric disorder—especially in those children who are programmed to make the allegations and those parents who have been falsely accused. The *Sex Abuse Legitimacy Scale (SAL Scale)* has been introduced in the hope that it will prove useful for differentiating objectively between bona fide and fabricated sex abuse allegations. Here again, more precise differentiation cannot but be salutary for all parties. It is my hope also that the recommendations for judges will also result in more judicious decisions, and this too can prevent the development of psychopathology. Last , if the changes recommended in this chapter regarding the education of lawyers and mental health professionals are implemented, further psychopathology will be prevented.

REFERENCES

Alexander, G.J. (1984), Trial by champion. *Santa Clara Law Review*, 34(3):545–564.

Bazelon, D.L. (1974), The perils of wizardry. *The American Journal of Psychiatry*, 131:1317–1322.

Berger, S.J. (1985), Personal Communication.

Cahill, M.E. (1977), Sexually abused children: fact, not fiction. *Proceedings of the House of Representatives, Subcommittee on Crime, Serial #12, 95th Congress, 1st Session.* Washington, D.C.: U.S. Government Printing Office.

Conerly, S. (1986), Assessment of suspected child sexual abuse. In: *Sexual Abuse of Young Children*, ed. K. MacFarlane and J. Waterman, pp. 30–51. New York: The Guilford Press.

Coogler, O.J. (1978), *Structured Mediation in Divorce Settlement.* Lexington, MA: Lexington Books (D.C. Heath and Company).

Damon, L. and Waterman, J. (1986), Parallel group treatment of children and their mothers. In: *Sexual Abuse of Young Children*, ed. K. MacFarlane and J. Waterman, pp. 244–298. New York: The Guilford Press.

277

Denton, L. (1987), Child abuse reporting laws: are they a barrier to helping troubled families? *The American Psychological Association Monitor*, 18(6):1ff.

Derdeyn, A.P. (1976), Child custody contests in the historical perspective. *American Journal of Psychiatry*, 133:1369–1376.

_____(1978), Child custody: a reflection of cultural change. *Journal of Clinical Child Psychology*, 7(3):169–173.

Durfee, M., Heger, A.H., and Woodling, B. (1986), Medical evaluation. In: *Sexual Abuse of Young Children*, ed. K. MacFarlane and J. Waterman, pp. 52–66. New York: The Guilford Press.

Esquilin, S.C. (1987), Initial investigation of sexual abuse in young children. *New Jersey Psychologist*, 37(2):7–10.

Finkelhor, D. (1979), *Sexually Victimized Children*. New York: Free Press.

Fisher, K. (1987), Sexual abuse victims suffer into adulthood. *The American Psychological Association Monitor*, 18(6):25.

Fisher, R. and Ury, W. (1981), *Getting to Yes*. Boston: Houghton Mifflin Co.

Folberg, J. and Taylor, A. (1984), *Mediation: A Comprehensive Guide to Resolving Conflicts Without Litigation*. San Francisco: Jossey-Bass Publishers.

Forer, L.G. (1975), *The Death of the Law*. New York: David McKay Co., Inc.

Gardner, R.A. (1970), The use of guilt as a defense against anxiety. *The Psychoanalytic Review*, 57:124–136.

_____(1973a), *Understanding Children: A Parents Guide to Child Rearing*. Cresskill, NJ: Creative Therapeutics.

_____(1973b), *The Talking, Feeling, and Doing Game*. Cresskill, NJ: Creative Therapeutics.

_____(1979a), *The Parents Book About Divorce* (paperback edition). New York: Bantam Books, Inc.

_____(1979b), Death of a parent. In: *Basic Handbook of Child Psychiatry*, ed. J.D. Noshpitz, vol. IV, pp. 270–283. New York: Basic Books, Inc.

_____(1982), *Family Evaluation in Child Custody Litigation*. Cresskill, NJ: Creative Therapeutics.

_____(1985), Recent trends in divorce and custody litigation. *Academy Forum (A Publication of the American Academy of Psychoanalysis)*, 29(2):3–7.

_____(1986a), *Child Custody Litigation: A Guide for Parents and Mental Health Professionals*. Cresskill, NJ: Creative Therapeutics.

_____(1986b), *The Psychotherapeutic Techniques of Richard A. Gardner*. Cresskill, NJ: Creative Therapeutics.

Gettelman, S. and Markowitz, J. (1974), *The Courage to Divorce*. New York: Simon and Schuster.

Glieberman, H.A. (1975), *Confessions of a Divorce Lawyer*. Chicago: Henry Regnery Co.

Goodwin, J. (1987), Developmental impacts of incest. In: *Basic Handbook of Child Psychiatry*, ed. J.D. Noshpitz, vol. V, pp. 103–111. New York: Basic Books, Inc.

Groth, A.N. (1984), *Anatomical Drawings: For Use in the Investigation and Intervention of Child Sex Abuse*. Newton Centre, MA: Forensic Mental Health Associates.

Haynes, J.M. (1981), *Divorce Mediation: A Practical Guide for Therapists*. New York: Springer Publishing Co.

Kaufman, T.B. (1987), Where the legal process and the therapeutic process intersect. *New Jersey Psychologist*, 37(2):12-14.

Landsman, S. (1983), A brief survey of the adversary system. *Ohio State Law Journal*, 44(3):713–739.

Law of Evidence (1982), *Encyclopedia Britannica, Macropedia*, 7:1–6.

Legal Profession (1982), *Encyclopedia Britannica, Macropedia*, 10:779–784.

Lieberman, J.K. (1981), *The Litigious Society*. New York: Basic Books, Inc.

Lindsley, B.C. (1976), Custody proceedings: battlefield or peace conference. *Bulletin of the American Academy of Psychiatry and the Law*, 4(2):127–131.

_____(1980), Foreword to *Custody Cases and Expert Witnesses: A Manual for Attorneys*. M.G. Goldzband. New York: Harcourt Brace Jovanovich.

Long, S. (1986), Guidelines for treating small children. In: *Sexual Abuse of Young Children*, ed. K. MacFarlane and J. Waterman, pp. 220–243. New York: The Guilford Press.

Lourie, I.S. and Blick, L.C. (1987a), Child sex abuse. In: *Basic Handbook of Child Psychiatry*, ed. J.D. Noshpitz, vol. V, pp. 280–286. New York: Basic Books, Inc.

_____(1987b), Intervention in cases of sex abuse. In: *Basic Handbook of Child Psychiatry*, ed. J.D. Noshpitz, vol. V, pp. 431–439. New York: Basic Books, Inc.

Lusk, R. and Waterman, J. (1986), Effects of sexual abuse on children. In: *Sexual Abuse of Young Children*, ed. K. MacFarlane and J. Waterman, pp. 101–118. New York: The Guilford Press.

MacFarlane, K. (1986), Helping parents cope with extrafamilial molestation. In: *Sexual Abuse of Young Children*, ed. K. Macfarlane and J. Waterman, pp. 299–311. New York: The Guilford Press.

MacFarlane, K. and Krebs, S. (1986a), Videotaping of interviews and court testimony. In: *Sexual Abuse of Young Children*, ed. K. MacFarlane and J. Waterman, pp. 164–193. New York: The Guilford Press.

———(1986b), Techniques for interviewing and evidence gathering. In: *Sexual Abuse of Young Children*, ed. K. MacFarlane and J. Waterman, pp. 67–100. New York: The Guilford Press.

Neef, M. and Nagel, S. (1974), The adversary nature of the American legal system from a historical perspective. *New York Law Forum*, 20:123–164.

Nizer, L. (1968), *My Life in Court*. New York: Pyramid Publications.

Ramos, S. (1979), *The Complete Book of Child Custody*. New York: G.P. Putnam's Sons.

Riskin, L.L. (1982), Mediation and lawyers. *Ohio State Law Journal*, 43:29–60.

Russell, D. (1983), The incidence and prevalence of intra-familial and extra-familial sexual abuse of female children. *Child Abuse and Neglect*, 7:133–146.

Sopkin, C. (1974), The roughest divorce lawyers in town. *New York*, Nov. 4, 1974.

Spiegel, L.D. (1986), *The False Accusation Syndrome: A Question of Innocence: A True Story of False Accusations*. Parsippany, NJ: Unicorn Publishing House.

Thompson, C. (1959), The interpersonal approach to the clinical problems of masochism. In: *Individual and Family Dynamics*, ed. J. Masserman. New York: Grune & Stratton.

Waterman, J. (1986a), Family dynamics of incest with young children. In: *Sexual Abuse of Young Children*, ed. K. MacFarlane and J. Waterman, pp. 204–219. New York: The Guilford Press.

———(1986b), Overview of treatment issues. In: *Sexual Abuse of Young Children*, ed. K. MacFarlane and J. Waterman, pp. 197–203. New York: The Guilford Press.

Waterman, J. and Lusk, R. (1986), Scope of the problem. In: *Sexual Abuse of Young Children*, ed. K. MacFarlane and J. Waterman, pp. 3–12. New York: The Guilford Press.

Watson, A.S. (1969), The children of Armageddon: problems of custody following divorce. *Syracuse Law Review*, 21:55–86.

Weiss, P.S. (1975), *Marital Separation*. New York: Basic Books, Inc.

Yates, A. (1987), Should young children testify in cases of sexual abuse? *American Journal of Psychiatry*, 144(4):476–480.

Addendum I

PROVISIONS FOR ACCEPTING AN INVITATION TO SERVE AS AN IMPARTIAL EXAMINER IN SEX-ABUSE LITIGATION

Whenever possible, I make every reasonable attempt to serve as a court-appointed impartial examiner, rather than as an advocate, in sex-abuse litigation. In order to serve optimally in this capacity I must be free to avail myself of any and all information, from any source, that I consider pertinent and reasonable to have. In this way, I believe I can serve best the interests of children, parents, and other parties who may be involved in such litigation. Accordingly, before agreeing to serve in this capacity, the following conditions must be agreed upon by both parents and both attorneys:

1) The presiding judge will agree to appoint me impartial examiner to conduct an evaluation of the concerned parties.

2) I will have available to interview *all* concerned parties for as many interviews (individual and in any combination)

as I consider warranted. Generally, these would include such persons as the allegedly abused child, the alleged abuser, and any other members of the child's family who are potential sources of information for me. In addition, I will have the freedom to invite any and all other parties whom I would consider possible sources of useful information.

3) Information will be gathered primarily from the aforementioned clinical interviews. Although I do not routinely use formal psychological tests, in some evaluations I have found certain psychological tests to be useful. Accordingly, the involved parties shall agree to take any and all psychological tests that I would consider helpful. In addition, they will agree to have the child take such tests if I consider them warranted. Some of these tests will be administered by me, but others by a psychologist of my choosing if I do not consider myself qualified to administer a particular psychological test.

4) In order to allow me the freedom of inquiry necessary for serving optimally parties involved in sex-abuse litigation, the parties shall agree to a modification of the traditional rules of confidentiality. Specifically, I must be given the freedom to reveal to one party what has been told to me by the other (at my discretion) so that I will have full opportunity to explore all pertinent points with both parties. This does not mean that I will not respect certain privacies or that I will automatically reveal all information provided me—only that I reserve the right to make such revelations if I consider them warranted for the purpose of collecting the most meaningful data.

5) The parties shall agree to sign any and all releases necessary for me to obtain reports from others, e.g. psychiatrists, psychologists, social workers, teachers, school officials, pediatricians, hospitals (general and psychiatric), etc. This includes past records as well as reports from professionals who may be involved with any of the parties at the time

of the litigation. Although I may choose not to request a particular report, I must have the freedom to request any and all such reports if I consider them useful sources of information.

6) My fee for conducting a sex-abuse evaluation is $150 per full hour of my time. Time spent in interviewing as well as time expended in report preparation, dictation, pertinent telephone conversations, court preparation, and any other time invested in association with the evaluation will also be billed at the $150 per hour fee. My fee for court appearances is $200 per hour while in court and $120 per hour travel time to and from my office. During the course of the evaluation, payment shall be expected at the time services are rendered. In order to insure that the evaluation is neither interrupted nor delayed because of nonpayment, payment must be made no later than one week from the date of service.

Prior to the initial interview the payer(s) will deposit with me a check (in my name) for $2,000. This shall be deposited in the Northern Valley-Englewood Savings and Loan Association branch in Cresskill, New Jersey, in my name, in a day-to-day interest bearing account. This money, with accrued interest (taxable to the payer), shall be returned *after* a final decision has been made by the court and after I have received a letter from *both* of the attorneys that my services are no longer being enlisted.

This payment is a security deposit. It will not serve as an advance retainer, in that the aforementioned fees will not be drawn against it, unless there has been a failure to pay my fee. It also serves to reassure the nonpayer that my objectivity will not be compromised by the fear that if I do not support the paying party, my fee will not be paid.

The average total cost for an evaluation is generally in the $1,000-$2,000 range. Although this figure may initially appear high, it is generally far less costly than protracted litigation. If as a result of the evaluation the litigation is shortened (often the case) or the parties decide not to litigate further over the sex-abuse allegation, then the net savings may be significant. It is very difficult, if not impossible, to predict the cost of a particular evaluation because I cannot know beforehand how many interviews will be warranted and whether or not I will be asked to testify in court.

On occasion, I am invited to conduct evaluations in cities at varying distances from Cresskill, New Jersey. This generally entails situations in which there is a choice between my travelling to the distant location and all interviewees travelling to New Jersey and acquiring temporary accomodations in the area of my office. Although I prefer that the evaluation take place in my office, I have on occasion agreed to conduct the evaluation elsewhere. However, my fees for such evaluations are higher than for those conducted in my office and is determined by the distance I have to travel and the time I am being asked to be away from my office. My fee schedule for such distant evaluations is available on request.

7) Both attorneys are invited to send to me any material that they consider useful to me.

After receiving 1) the court order signed by the presiding judge, 2) the signed statements (this document) from both parties signifying agreement to the conditions of the evaluation, and 3) the $2,000 deposit, I will notify both parties that I am available to proceed with the evaluation as rapidly as is feasible. I generally cannot promise to meet a specific deadline because I cannot know in advance how many interviews will be required, nor can I predict how flexible the parties will be regarding availability for appointments I offer.

9) Upon completion of my evaluation—and prior to the preparation of my final report—I generally meet with the parties and present them my findings and recommendations. This gives them the opportunity to correct any distor-

tions they believe I may have and/or alter my opinion before it becomes finalized in my report. In addition, it saves the parties from the unnecessary and prolonged tension associated with wondering what my findings are.

Both attorneys are invited to attend this conference. However, this invitation should be considered withdrawn if only one attorney wishes to attend because the presence of only one attorney would obviously place the nonrepresented parent in a compromised position. When a guardian ad litem has been appointed by the court, he or she will also be invited to attend this conference— regardless of the number of attorneys present. Before accepting this invitation attorneys should appreciate that the discussion will be completely free and open. Accordingly, during this conference it would be improper for an attorney in any way whatsoever to restrict or otherwise discourage a client from answering questions or participating in the discussion. After this conference the final report is prepared and sent simultaneously to the court, the attorneys, and the parents.

10) After this conference I strictly refrain from any further communication with any party involved in the evaluation. However, I am willing to discuss any aspect of the case with *both* attorneys at the same time, either personally or by conference telephone call. Such communication may occur at any time from the end of the aforementioned conference to the end of the trial. This practice enables me to continue to provide input to the attorneys regarding what I consider to be in the child's best interests. And this may be especially important during the trial. However, in order to preserve my status as impartial, any information I provide either attorney is only given under circumstances in which the other is invited to participate.

11) When there is a significant passage of time between the submission of my report and the trial date, I will on occasion invite the primary participating parties for an inter-

view update prior to my court appearance. This enables me to acquaint myself with developments that succeeded my report and insures that my presentation in court will include the most recent information. All significant adult participants will be invited to this meeting and, if appropriate, the allegedly abused child (especially if a teenager). This conference will be held as long as at least one party wishes to attend.

My experience has been that conducting the evaluation in the manner described above provides me with the optimum conditions for providing the court with a thorough and objective recommendation.

12) Often one party will invite my services as an impartial examiner and the other will refuse to participate voluntarily. On occasion, the inviting party has then requested that the court appoint me impartial examiner and order the reluctant side to participate. Generally, there are three ways in which courts respond to this request:

A. The court responds affirmatively and appoints me the impartial examiner. In such cases I then proceed in accordance with the above provisions (1-11).

B. The court is not willing to formally designate me its appointed impartial examiner, but rather orders the reluctant side to cooperate in interviews with me as if I were the advocate of the initiator. (This usually occurs when the presiding judge orders both parents to be evaluated by each one's selected adversary examiner.) In such cases, I still do not view myself to be serving automatically as the advocate of the initiating party. Rather, I make it understood to all concerned that I will proceed as closely as possible with the type of evaluation I conduct when serving as impartial examiner, *even to the point of testifying in court as an advocate of the initially reluctant party.* In that eventuality, if the initially reluctant party requests a court appearance, that party will be responsible for my fees (item 6) beyond the point at which my final report has been sent to the court, attorneys, and the clients. The party who initially invited me, however, will still have the obligation to pay for my report, whether or not it supports that party's position. I believe that this plan insures my input to the court regarding what I consider to be in the child's best interests and precludes my serving merely as a hired advocate.

C. The court refuses to order my participation, but recognizes the right of the inviting party to enlist my involvement as an advocate. In such cases I proceed in accordance with provision 13.

13) On occasion, I am willing to *consider* serving as an advocate in sex-abuse litigation. However, such participation will only be considered after evidence has been submitted to me that: 1) the non-participating side has been invited to participate and has refused and 2) the court has refused to order such involvement. If I do then suspect that the participating party's position merits my consideration, I would be willing to interview that party with no promise beforehand that I will support his or her position. On occasion I have seen fit to support the participating party in this manner, because it was obvious to me that the party's needs would be served best by my advocacy and/or not to do so would have deprived that party of sorely needed assistance. On other occasions I have concluded that I could not

serve with conviction as an advocate of the requesting party and so have refused further services to the client.

Richard A. Gardner, M.D.

I have read the above, discussed the provisions with my attorney, and agree to proceed with the evaluation. I agree to pay _____% of the $2,000 advance security deposit and _____% of the fees in accordance with the aforementioned payment schedule. I recognize the possibility that Dr. Gardner may *not* ultimately support my position in the litigation. Nevertheless, I will still fulfill my obligation to pay _____% of his fees. I appreciate that this may entail the payment of fees associated with his preparing reports that do not support my position and even testifying in court in support of my adversary (with the exception of the situation in which item 12B is operative).

Date:_____   _____
                                        Parent's Signature

Revision No. 4

Addendum II

PROVISIONS FOR ACCEPTING AN
INVITATION TO SERVE AS AN IMPARTIAL
EXAMINER IN CUSTODY/VISITATION
LITIGATION

Whenever possible, I make every reasonable attempt to serve as a court-appointed impartial examiner, rather than as an advocate, in custody/visitation litigation. In order to serve optimally in this capacity I must be free to avail myself of any and all information, from any source, that I consider pertinent and reasonable to have. In this way, I believe I can serve best the interests of children and parents involved in such conflicts. Accordingly, before agreeing to serve in this capacity, the following conditions must be agreed upon by both parents and both attorneys:

1) The presiding judge will agree to appoint me impartial examiner to conduct an evaluation of the concerned parties.

2) I will have available to interview all members of the immediate family—that is, the mother, father, and children—

for as many interviews (individual and in any combination) as I consider warranted. In addition, I will have the freedom to invite any and all other parties whom I would consider possible sources of useful information. Generally, these would include such persons as present or prospective parental surrogates with whom either parent may be involved and the housekeeper. Usually, I do not interview a series of friends and relatives each of whom, from the outset, is particularly partial to one of the parents (but I reserve the right to invite such parties if I consider it warranted).

3) Information will be gathered primarily from the aforementioned clinical interviews. Although I do not routinely use formal psychological tests, in some evaluations I have found certain psychological tests to be useful. Accordingly, the parents shall agree to take any and all psychological tests that I would consider helpful. In addition, they will agree to have one or more of the children take such tests if I consider them warranted. Some of these tests will be administered by me, but others by a psychologist of my choosing if I do not consider myself qualified to administer a particular psychological test.

4) In order to allow me the freedom of inquiry necessary for serving optimally families involved in custody/visitation litigation, the parents shall agree to a modification of the traditional rules of confidentiality. Specifically, I must be given the freedom to reveal to one party what has been told to me by the other (at my discretion) so that I will have full opportunity to explore all pertinent points with both parties. This does not mean that I will not respect certain privacies or that I will automatically reveal all information provided me — only that I reserve the right to make such revelations if I consider them warranted for the purpose of collecting the most meaningful data.

5) The parties shall agree to sign any and all releases necessary for me to obtain reports from others, e.g. psychi-

atrists, psychologists, social workers, teachers, school officials, pediatricians, hospitals (general and psychiatric), etc. This includes past records as well as reports from professionals who may be involved with any of the parties at the time of the litigation. Although I may choose not to request a particular report, I must have the freedom to request any and all such reports if I consider them useful sources of information.

6) My fee for conducting a custody evaluation is $150 per hour of my time. Time spent in interviewing as well as time expended in report preparation, dictation, pertinent telephone conversations, court preparation, and any other time invested in association with the evaluation will also be billed at the $150 per hour fee. My fee for court and deposition appearances is $200 per hour while in court and $120 per hour travel time to and from my office. During the course of the evaluation, payment shall be expected at the time services are rendered. In order to insure that the evaluation is neither interrupted nor delayed because of nonpayment, payment must be made no later than one week from the date of service.

Prior to the initial interview (with both parents together) the payer(s) will deposit with me a check (in my name) for $2,000. This shall be deposited in the Northern Valley-Englewood Savings and Loan Association branch in Cresskill, New Jersey, in my name, in a day-to-day interest bearing account. This money, with accrued interest (taxable to the payer), shall be returned *after* a final decision has been made regarding custody/visitation and after I have received a letter from *both* of the attorneys that my services are no longer being enlisted.

This payment is a security deposit. It will not serve as an advance retainer, in that the aforementioned fees will not be drawn against it, unless there has been a failure to pay my fee. It also serves to reassure the nonpayer that my objectivity will not be compromised by the fear that if I do not support the paying party, my fee will not be paid.

The average total cost for an evaluation is generally in the $2,000-$4,500 range. Although this figure may initially appear high, it is generally far less costly than protracted litigation. If as a result of the evaluation the litigation is shortened (often the case) or the parties decide not to litigate further over custody/visitation (also a common occurrence), then the net savings may be significant. It is very difficult, if not impossible, to predict the cost of a particular evaluation because I cannot know beforehand how many interviews will be warranted and whether or not I will be asked to testify in court.

On occasion, I am invited to conduct evaluations in cities at varying distances from Cresskill, New Jersey. This generally entails situations in which there is a choice between my travelling to the family's location and all interviewees travelling to New Jersey and acquiring temporary accomodations in the area of my office. Although I prefer that the evaluation take place in my office, I have on occasion agreed to conduct the evaluation elsewhere. However, my fees for such evaluations are higher than for those conducted in my office and is determined by the distance I have to travel and the time I am being asked to be away from my office. My fee schedule for such distant evaluations is available on request.

7) Both attorneys are invited to send to me any material that they consider useful to me.

8) After receiving 1) the court order signed by the presiding judge, 2) the signed statements (this document) from both parties signifying agreement to the conditions of the evaluation, and 3) the $2,000 deposit, I will notify both parties that I am available to proceed with the evaluation as rapidly as is feasible. I generally cannot promise to meet a specific deadline because I cannot know in advance how

many interviews will be required, nor can I predict how flexible the parties will be regarding availability for appointments I offer.

9) Upon completion of my evaluation—and prior to the preparation of my final report—I generally meet with both parents together and present them my findings and recommendations. This gives them the opportunity to correct any distortions they believe I may have and/or alter my opinion before it becomes finalized in my report. In addition, it saves the parents from the unnecessary and prolonged tension associated with wondering what my findings are.

Both attorneys are invited to attend this conference. However, this invitation should be considered withdrawn if only one attorney wishes to attend because the presence of only one attorney would obviously place the nonrepresented parent in a compromised position. When a guardian ad litem has been appointed by the court, he or she will also be invited to attend this conference—regardless of the number of attorneys present. Before accepting this invitation attorneys should appreciate that the discussion will be completely free and open. Accordingly, during this conference it would be improper for an attorney in any way whatsoever to restrict or otherwise discourage the client from answering questions or participating in the discussion. After this conference the final report is prepared and sent simultaneously to the court, the attorneys, and the parents.

10) After this conference I strictly refrain from any further communication with either parent or any other party involved in the evaluation. However, I am willing to discuss any aspect of the case with *both* attorneys at the same time, either personally or by conference telephone call. Such communication may occur at any time from the end of the aforementioned conference to the end of the trial. This practice enables me to continue to provide input to the attorneys regarding what I consider to be in the children's

best interests. And this may be especially important during the trial. However, in order to preserve my status as impartial, any information I provide either attorney is only given under circumstances in which the other is invited to participate.

11) When there is a significant passage of time between the submission of my report and the trial date, I will on occasion invite the primary participating parties for an interview update prior to my court appearance. This enables me to acquaint myself with developments that succeeded my report and insures that my presentation in court will include the most recent information. All significant adult participants will be invited to this meeting and on occasion one or more of the children (especially teenagers). This conference will be held as long as at least one party wishes to attend.

My experience has been that conducting the evaluation in the manner described above provides me with the optimum conditions for providing the court with a thorough and objective recommendation.

12) Often one party will invite my services as an impartial examiner and the other will refuse to participate voluntarily. On occasion, the inviting party has then requested that the court appoint me impartial examiner and order the reluctant side to participate. Generally, there are three ways in which courts respond to this request:

A. The court responds affirmatively and appoints me the impartial examiner. In such cases I then proceed in accordance with the above provisions (1-11).

B. The court is not willing to formally designate me its appointed impartial examiner, but rather orders the reluctant side to cooperate in interviews with me as if I were the advocate of the initiator. (This usually occurs when the presiding judge orders both parents to be evaluated by each one's selected adversary examiner.) In such cases, I still do not view myself to be serving automatically as the advocate of the initiating party. Rather, I make it understood to all concerned that I will proceed as closely as possible with the type of evaluation I conduct when serving as impartial examiner, *even to the point of testifying in court as an advocate of the initially reluctant party.* In that eventuality, if the initially reluctant party requests a court appearance, that party will be responsible for my fees (item 6) beyond the point at which my final report has been sent to the court, attorneys, and the clients. The party who initially invited me, however, will still have the obligation to pay for my report, whether or not it supports that party's position. I believe that this plan insures my input to the court regarding what I consider to be in the children's best interests and precludes my serving merely as a hired advocate.

C. The court refuses to order my participation, but recognizes the right of the inviting party to enlist my involvement as an advocate. In such cases I proceed in accordance with provision 13.

13) On occasion, I am willing to *consider* serving as an advocate in custody/visitation litigation. However, such participation will only be considered after evidence has been submitted to me that: 1) the non-participating side has been invited to participate and has refused and 2) the court has refused to order such involvement. If I do then suspect that the participating party's position merits my consideration, I would be willing to interview that party with no promise beforehand that I will support his or her position. On occasion I have seen fit to support the participating party in this manner, because it was obvious to me that the children's

needs would be served best by my advocacy and/or not to do so would have deprived them of sorely needed assistance. On other occasions I have concluded that I could not serve with conviction as an advocate of the requesting party and so have refused further services to the client.

Richard A. Gardner, M.D.

I have read the above, discussed the provisions with my attorney, and agree to proceed with the evaluation. I agree to pay _____% of the $2,000 advance security deposit and _____% of the fees in accordance with the aforementioned payment schedule. I recognize the possibility that Dr. Gardner may *not* ultimately support my position in the litigation. Nevertheless, I will still fulfill my obligation to pay _____% of his fees. I appreciate that this may entail the payment of fees associated with his preparing reports that do not support my position and even testifying in court in support of my adversary (with the exception of the situation in which item 12B is operative).

Date:_____   _____

                                              Parent's Signature

Revision No. 32

Addendum III

SEX ABUSE LEGITIMACY SCALE
(SAL SCALE)

An Instrument for Differentiating Between
Bona Fide and Fabricated Sex-Abuse Allegations of Children

Richard A. Gardner, M.D.

Clinical Professor of Child Psychiatry
Columbia University
College of Physicians & Surgeons

WARNING: In order to be used in a meaningful way, this instrument *must* be used in association with the information provided by Dr. Richard A. Gardner in chapters 3, 4, and 5 of his book, *The Parental Alienation Syndrome and the Differentiation Between Fabricated and Genuine Child Sex Abuse* (Cresskill, New Jersey: Creative Therapeutics, 1987). The book explains how best to evaluate and score each of the items in the scale. Failure to use these guidelines may result in misleading or erroneous conclusions.

Creative Therapeutics, PO Box R, Cresskill, NJ 07626-0317

ISBN: 0-933812-19-1

Packets of 25 copies of the SEX ABUSE LEGITIMACY SCALE may be obtained at $12.50 per packet + $2.50 postage and handling from Creative Therapeutics, P.O. Box R, Cresskill, N.J. 07626-0317.

INSTRUCTIONS

The differentiating criteria in this scale are most applicable when the sex abuse has taken place in a family situation in which the father (or stepfather) is the alleged offender and the mother is the accuser. It is also applicable when the alleged offender is known to the family and can be identified. This would include relatives, frequent visitors to the home, and babysitters. The scale is most valid if all three parties (child, accuser, and accused) are interviewed, individually and in various combinations, as warranted. The scale is less valuable (but may still be useful) when the alleged offender is unknown or inaccessible for interview. It is applicable to both boys and girls as the victims of the alleged incest.

Medical evidence may provide the most compelling confirmation that the child has been sexually abused. Medical evidence includes findings such as damage to the genital or rectal tissues; general body trauma; foreign objects in the genital, rectal, or urethral openings; the presence of a sexually transmitted disease; and pregnancy (obviously, applicable only to teenagers). When such evidence is present, the SAL Scores can provide additional data—generally confirmatory, but in rare situations nonconfirmatory. When medical evidence is not present, the SAL Scores may be the primary sources of information about whether or not the sex-abuse allegation is valid.

The items are worded so that the greater the number of *Yes* answers, the greater the likelihood that the sex abuse is genuine. In contrast, the smaller the number of *Yes* answers, the greater the likelihood the sex abuse has been fabricated. The differentiating criteria are divided into three categories, from the most to the least valuable. In order to give greater weight to the more valuable criteria, the following point scores are to be given for *Yes* answers in each of the three categories.

Part A. Very Valuable Differentiating Criteria—3 points for each *Yes* answer.
Part B. Moderately Valuable Differentiating Criteria—2 points for each *Yes* answer.
Part C. Differentiating Criteria of Low But Potentially Higher Value—1 point for each *Yes* answer.

Checks are placed in the *Yes*, *No*, or *Not Clear or Not Applicable* columns to the right of each item, in whichever column is appropriate. The total number of *Yes* responses in each category is multiplied by the appropriate factor for that category to obtain a weighted score for that part. The sum of the weighted part scores (Part A + Part B + Part C) is referred to as the *Sex Abuse Legitimacy Score (SAL Score)*. Separate SAL Scores are calculated for the child (maximum 60 points), the accuser (maximum 27 points), and the accused (maximum 27 points). A cumulative SAL Score of all three parties is not computed.

Because of the large number of criteria and because no individual can be expected to satisfy all or even most of them—even in cases of proven sexual abuse—SAL Scores in the range of 50% of the maximum or more are highly suggestive of bona fide sexual abuse. In contrast, when the abuse is fabricated, the SAL Scores are usually quite low (below 10% of the maximum) and may even be close to or at the zero level in many cases. Accordingly, when using this scale, the best way to interpret the findings is to consider very low SAL Scores (below 10% of the maximum) to be strongly indicative of fabrication. From that low point, the higher the SAL Score above the 10% level, the greater the likelihood the abuse is genuine. This is especially the case when the SAL Score exceeds 50% of the maximum.

The SAL Scale was developed by Dr. Richard A. Gardner from studies conducted between 1982 and 1987 of children who made allegations of sex abuse. As a result of these studies, Dr. Gardner concluded in some cases that the children were indeed sexually abused and in other cases that they were not. The criteria he used for making this differentiation are embodied in this scale. The items that were selected for inclusion in this scale appeared to be clinically useful indicators for differentiating between bona fide and fabricated sex-abuse allegations. Face validity only is claimed for these items. These clinical studies indicated into which of the part categories (A, B, or C) the item should reasonably be placed. Clinical experience also suggested the cutoff levels for differentiating between the two classes of sex abuse. Accordingly, the cutoff levels and their significance should be viewed as preliminary and tentative. They may be modified after more extensive studies (by Dr. Gardner and possibly others) and will be revised, if necessary, in future editions of this scale.

The examiner does well to give serious consideration to conclusions derived from the SAL Scale, but not to make the complete decision on the basis of its findings. Rather, it is crucial that other data be considered

3

before coming to a final conclusion. These other sources of information would include medical reports, reports from other examiners, and interviews with other parties (especially those who claim to have been witnesses to the alleged abuse).

The SAL Scale is not designed to be used as a questionnaire, wherein the examiner asks the interviewee his or her opinion regarding whether or not a criterion is present. If direct input from the interviewee is elicited, it is very likely that the conclusions will be contaminated by the bias of the respondent. Rather, the scale should be used *after* the interviews with the child, accuser, and accused have been completed. Both individual and joint interviews *must* be conducted in order to properly assess conflicting data that is often provided. This is especially the case for the child's items, because parental input may be crucial if one is to assess adequately each item, and properly score it. It is only after all of these interviews have been completed that the examiner is in a position to properly utilize the scale. Before completing the evaluation, the examiner should review the SAL Scale (not in the interviewee's presence), in order to be sure that *all* items have been considered. Not to do so will compromise significantly the value of the findings.

The Child Who
Alleges Sex Abuse

Name _____ DOB: _____
Address _____
Date(s) of interview(s) _____

Part A Very Valuable Differentiating Criteria (3 points for each *Yes* response)	Yes	No	Not Clear or Not Applicable
1. Very hesitant to divulge the sexual abuse			
2. Fear of retaliation by the accused			
3. Guilt over the consequences to the accused of the divulgences			
4. Guilt over participation in the sexual acts			
5. Provides specific details of the sexual abuse			
6. Description of the sex abuse credible			
7. If the description of the sex abuse does *not* vary over repeated interviews, check *Yes*. If the description *does* vary, check *No*.			
8. Frequent episodes of sexual excitation, apart from the abuse encounters.			
9. Considers genitals to have been damaged			
10. Desensitization play engaged in at home or during the interview			
11. Threatened or bribed by the accused to discourage divulgence of abuse			
12. If a parental alienation syndrome is *not* present, check *Yes*. If a parental alienation syndrome *is* present, check *No*.			
13. If the *complaint* was *not* made in the context of a child custody dispute or litigation, check *Yes*. If there *is* such a dispute, check *No*.			
Total *number* of checks in the *Yes* column for Part A (items 1–13) _____ (maximum 13)			

Part B *Moderately Valuable* *Differentiating Criteria* (2 points for each *Yes* response)	*Yes*	*No*	*Not Clear or Not Applicable*
14. If the description does *not* have the quality of a well-rehearsed litany, check *Yes*. If it *does* have a litany quality, check *No*.			
15. If there is *no* evidence of a "borrowed scenario" (description taken from other persons or sources), check *Yes*. If the description appears to have been taken from external sources, check *No*.			
16. Depression			
17. Withdrawal			
18. Compliant personality			
19. Psychosomatic disorders			
20. Regressive behavior			
21. Deep sense of betrayal, especially regarding the sex abuse			
Total *number* of checks in the Yes column for Part B (items 14–21) _____ (maximum 8)			

Part C *Differentiating Criteria of Low* *But Potentially Higher Value* (1 point for each *Yes* response)	*Yes*	*No*	*Not Clear or Not Applicable*
22. Sleep disturbances			
23. Abuse took place over extended period			
24. Retraction with *fear* of reprisals by the accused, rather than retraction with *guilt* over the consequences to the accused of the divulgences			
25. Pseudomaturity (girls only)			
26. Seductive behavior with the accused (girls only)			
Total *number* of checks in the Yes column for Part C (items 22–26) _____ (maximum 5)			

Computation of the Child's *Sex Abuse Legitimacy Score*	*Number of* *Yes Checks*	*Multiply* *by Factor*	*Weighted Score*
Score Part A (items 1–13)		x3	(maximum 39)
Score Part B (items 14–21)		x2	(maximum 16)
Score Part C (items 22–26)		x1	(maximum 5)
SAL Score (sum of scores A+B+C) _____ (maximum 60)			

A SAL Score of 6 or below indicates that the sex-abuse allegation is extremely likely to have been fabricated.

SAL Scores from 7 through 29 are inconclusive. However, the closer the SAL Score is to 7, the more likely the allegation was fabricated; the closer it is to 29, the more likely the abuse took place.

SAL Scores of 30 and above are strongly suggestive of bona fide sex abuse.

5

The Accuser
(Especially when the
accuser is the mother)

Name _____DOB: _____

Address _____

Date(s) of interview(s) _____

Part A *Very Valuable* *Differentiating Criteria* (3 points for each *Yes* response)	*Yes*	*No*	*Not Clear or Not Applicable*
1. Initially denies and/or downplays the abuse			
2. If the complaint was *not* made in the context of a child custody dispute or litigation, check *Yes*. If there *is* such a dispute, check *No*.			
3. Shame over revelation of the abuse			
4. If she does *not* want to destory, humiliate, or wreak vengeance on the accused, check *Yes*. If such attitudes are present, check *No*.			
5. If she has *not* sought a "hired gun" attorney or mental health professional, check *Yes*. If such professionals have been or are being sought, check *No*.			
6. If she does *not* attempt to corroborate the child's sex-abuse description in joint interview(s), check *Yes*. If she *does* exhibit such behavior, check *No*.			

Total *number* of checks in the *Yes* column for Part A (items 1–6) _____ (maximum 6)

Part B *Moderately Valuable* *Differentiating Criteria* (2 points for each *Yes* response)	*Yes*	*No*	*Not Clear or Not Applicable*
7. Appreciates the psychological trauma to the child of repeated interrogations			
8. Appreciates the importance of maintenance of the child's relationship with the accused			
9. Childhood history of having been sexually abused herself			
10. Passivity and/or inadequacy			

Total *number* of checks in the *Yes* column for Part B (items 7–10) _____ (maximum 4)

Part C *Differentiating Criterion of Low* *But Potentially Higher Value* (1 point for each *Yes* response)	*Yes*	*No*	*Not Clear or Not Applicable*
11. Social isolate			

Total *number* of checks in the *Yes* column for Part C (item 11) _____ (maximum 1)

Computation of the Accuser's *Sex Abuse Legitimacy Score*	*Number of* *Yes Checks*	*Multiply* *by Factor*	*Weighted Score*
Score Part A (items 1–6)		x3	(maximum 18)
Score Part B (items 7–10)		x2	(maximum 8)
Score Part C (item 11)		x1	(maximum 1)
SAL Score (sum of scores A+B+C) _____ (maximum 27)			

A SAL Score of 3 or below indicates that the sex-abuse allegation is extremely likely to have been fabricated.

SAL Scores from 4 through 13 are inconclusive. However, the closer the SAL Score is to 4, the more likely the allegation was fabricated; the closer it is to 13, the more likely the sex abuse took place.

SAL Scores of 14 and above are strongly suggestive of bona fide sex abuse.

The Accused
(Especially when the accused is the father)

Name _____ DOB: _____
Address _____
Date(s) of interview(s) _____

Part A *Very Valuable* *Differentiating Criteria* (3 points for each *Yes* response)	*Yes*	*No*	*Not Clear or Not Applicable*
1. Bribed and/or threatened the child to keep the "secret"			
2. Weak and/or feigned denial			
3. If the complaint was *not* made in the context of a child custody dispute or litigation, check *Yes*. If there *is* such a dispute, check *No*.			
4. Presence of other sexual deviations			
Total *number* of checks in the *Yes* column for Part A (items 1–4) _____ (maximum 4).			

Part B *Moderately Valuable* *Differentiating Criteria* (2 points for each *Yes* response)	*Yes*	*No*	*Not Clear or Not Applicable*
5. Childhood history of having been sexually abused himself			
6. Reluctance or refusal to take a lie detector test			
7. History of drug and/or alcohol abuse			
8. Low self-esteem			
9. Tendency to regress in periods of stress			
10. Career choice which brings him in close contact with children			
Total *number* of checks in the *Yes* column for Part B (items 5–10) _____ (maximum 6)			

Part C *Differentiating Criteria of Low* *But Potentially Higher Value* (1 point for each *Yes* response)	*Yes*	*No*	*Not Clear or Not Applicable*
11. Moralistic			
12. Controlling			
13. Stepfather or other person with frequent access to the child			
Total *number* of checks in the *Yes* column for Part C (itemse 11–13) _____ (maximum 3)			

Computation of the Accused's *Sex Abuse Legitimacy Score*	*Number of* *Yes Checks*	*Multiply* *by Factor*	*Weighted Score*
Score Part A (items 1–4)		x3	(maximum 12)
Score Part B (items 5–10)		x2	(maximum 12)
Score Part C (item 11–13)		x1	(maximum 3)
SAL Score (sum of scores A+B+C) _____ (maximum 27)			

A SAL Score of 3 or below indicates that the sex-abuse allegation is extremely likely to have been fabricated.

SAL Scores from 4 through 13 are inconclusive. However, the closer the rating is to 4, the more likely the allegation was fabricated; the closer it is to 13, the more likely the sex abuse took place.

SAL Scores of 14 and above are strongly suggestive of bona fide sex abuse.

Author Index

Subject Index